MUSIC IN IRISH CULTURE

Chapter 1 was first published as 'Listening to the Future: Music and Irish Studies', in Liam Harte and Yvonne Whelan (eds), *Ireland Beyond Boundaries: Mapping Irish Studies in the Twenty-First Century* (London: Pluto, 2006), pp.198–215.

Chapter 4 was first published as 'Paddy Sad and Paddy Mad: Music and the Condition of Irishness', in Marie-Claire Considère-Charon, Philippe Laplace and Michel Savaric (eds), *The Irish Celebrating: Festive and Tragic Overtones* (Newcastle-upon-Tyne: Cambridge Scholars Press, 2008), pp.58–70.

Chapter 5 was originally published as 'Bringing It All Back Home? The Dynamics of Local Music-Making in *The Commitments*', *An Sionnach*, 1, 2 (Fall 2005), pp.21–40.

Chapter 7 was originally published as *Representations of Irish Traditional Music in Contemporary Fiction* (Cork: The Traditional Music Archive and The Irish Traditional Music Society, January 2008), Ó Riada Memorial Lecture No. 19, pp.1–18.

Chapter 9 was first published as '"The same sound but with a different meaning": Music, Politics and Identity in Bernard Mac Laverty's *Grace Notes*', *Éire-Ireland: An Interdisciplinary Journal of Irish Studies*, 37, 3 & 4 (Fall/Winter 2002), pp.5–24.

MUSIC IN IRISH CULTURAL HISTORY

GERRY SMYTH
Liverpool John Moores University

IRISH ACADEMIC PRESS
DUBLIN • PORTLAND, OR

To my brother George,
my sisters Sheila and Joan,
and my cousin Kevin

First published in 2009 by Irish Academic Press

2 Brookside,
Dundrum Road,
Dublin 14,
Ireland

920 NE 58th Avenue, Suite 300
Portland, Oregon,
97213-3786
USA

www.iap.ie

© 2009 Gerry Smyth

British Library Cataloguing in Publication Data
An entry can be found on request

ISBN 978 0 7165 2984 2 (cloth)
ISBN 978 0 7165 2985 9 (paper)

Library of Congress Cataloging-in-Publication Data
An entry can be found on request

All rights reserved. Without limiting the rights under copyright reserved alone, no part of this publication may be reproduced, stored in or introduced into a retrieval system, or transmitted, in any form or by any means (electronic, mechanical, photocopying, recording or otherwise) without the prior written permission of both the copyright owner and the above publisher of this book.

Printed in Great Britain by the MPG Books Group, Bodmin and King's Lynn

Contents

Acknowledgements		xi
Introduction: In Search of Irish Music		xv
1.	Listening to the Future: Music and Irish Studies	1
2.	Betrayal as Theme and Influence in Thomas Moore's 'On Music'	15
3.	Music in James Joyce's 'The Dead': Sources, Contexts, Meanings	32
4.	Paddy Sad and Paddy Mad: Music and the Condition of Irishness	51
5.	Bringing It All Back Home? The Dynamics of Local Music-Making in *The Commitments*	65
6.	Celtic Music: From the Margins to the Centre (And Back Again?)	84
7.	Listening to the Novel: The Role and Representation of Traditional Music in Contemporary Irish Fiction	102
8.	No Country for Young Women: Celtic Music, Dissent and the Irish Female Body	124
9.	'The same sound but with a different meaning': Music, Politics and Identity in Bernard Mac Laverty's *Grace Notes*	141
10.	'Sing your melody, I'll sing along': Mimetic and Diegetic Uses of Music in *Once*	158

Notes	172
References	181
Index	190

Acknowledgements

I am not usually big on printed thanks – I prefer to look people in the eye, or at least to be in the same room, when I talk about them. I break from my normal practice, however, in order to acknowledge a number of individuals who have contributed to my engagement with and enjoyment of Irish music during the past twenty years.

My first debt is as always to the administrative and academic staff of the School of Media, Critical and Creative Arts at Liverpool John Moores University (LJMU). An English lecturer whose chief research interest is Irish music may seem a little odd, and perhaps more than a little indulgent, especially during the era of the Research Assessment Exercise (RAE) and the well-nigh obsessive drive for 'windows'. I feel immensely fortunate, therefore, to be a member of the Department of English at LJMU, and to have had such a stimulating and supportive environment in which to work. I also salute Ron Moy, Stuart Borthwick and Simone Kruger who run the Popular Music unit at LJMU, and who have offered support at various points during my 'lost' decade. I am grateful also to the many gifted students upon whom I have imposed my musical prejudices over the past twenty years, especially Alice Bennett, Jenny Black, Simon Bottom, Matt Fenwick, Gemma Fry, Moira Hutton, Jasbir Kaur, Bob Kettle, Toby Lynch, Caroline McDonnell, Janine Melvin and Nic Orton. Bill Sweeney remained an industrious research student through difficult times; his work on the history of Irish media was truly illuminating and has informed my thinking about modern Irish cultural history in countless unacknowledged ways.

There are a number of colleagues working in the general field of Irish Studies whose ideas and opinions on various aspects of Irish music I have benefited from over the years. Of these I would especially like to thank Aidan Arrowsmith, Seán Campbell, John McDonagh, Noel

McLaughlin, Martin McLoone, Meabh Ní Fhuarthain, Eugene O'Brien, John O'Flynn, Michael Parker, Lance Pettitt, Helen O'Shea and Bruce Stewart. Jonathan Moore was extremely helpful when I was external examiner for the Irish Studies course at the University of North London; his colleague Tony Murray told me fascinating tales about punk-era London. Willy Maley and Matt Campbell will recall a memorable night in Bath in July 1996 when Van the Man turned up, and I backed Terry Eagleton on guitar. Roddy Doyle answered my questions on Irish fiction patiently, when all we really wanted to talk about was the previous evening's Steely Dan concert. I enjoyed arguing with Gerald Dawe about the relative merits of Belfast and Dublin in the history of Irish rock. Bernard Mac Laverty accepted my gushing enthusiasm for *Grace Notes* with humour and modesty. I would like to thank Shaun Richards for allowing me to talk about Clannad and The Pogues to his students at the University of Stafford when I was supposed to be discussing twentieth-century European drama.

Over the past decade I have inflicted my interest in Irish music (sometimes by invitation) on people from various academic institutions around the world. Deirdre O'Brien was a hospitable host at Nottingham Trent University, as was Ondrej Pilny when I visited Charles University, Prague. I exchanged ideas with Mícheál Ó Súilleabháin at the EFACIS Annual Conference (2001) in Aarhus, Denmark, organised by Michael Böss. Dave Clark invited me to speak at the University of La Caruña in Galicia, and led an excellent pub crawl through that fascinating city. It was during that trip that I met Ciarán Carson, with whom I talked long into the night about musical matters. Judith Gantley and Géraldine Lance looked after me in Monaco during my tenure (September–October 2006) as Academic-in-Residence at the Princess Grace Irish Library, during which time I worked on my book about music and contemporary British fiction. I watched a lot of football in Monaco with the artist Jack Murray, and I also had the pleasure of meeting (and performing for) the family of Mark Armstrong. At an Irish poetry symposium which coincided with my visit, I met a number of people with whom I enjoyed talking about music and related matters, including Fran Brearton, Catríona Clutterbuck, Lucy Collins, Selina Guinness, Peter McDonald, Justin Quinn and Moynagh Sullivan.

Mel Mercier afforded me the incredible honour of delivering the Seán Ó Riada Memorial Lecture at University College Cork in February

2007; Mary Mitchell-Ingoldsby was a helpful source for all my queries relating to that trip. Ken Monteith invited me to speak at La Guardia Community College, Queens, NY, during which trip I enjoyed conversations with Claire Bracken and Mary McGlynn.

I am grateful to all the editors and convenors with whom I have worked on projects relating to Irish music, especially Marie-Claire Considère-Charon, Colin Coulter, Liam Harte, Matthew Low, Ian Peddie and Michel Savaric. Neil Sammells commissioned a guest edition of the *Irish Studies Review* on music, and was supportive throughout a pretty fraught process. Besides those mentioned elsewhere, I would also like to thank in relation to that project Emma Hart, Paul Hyland, Marion Leonard, Marie McCarthy, Caroline Netherton, Rob Strachan and Patrick Zuk.

My former student Stephen Langstaff is playing a venue near you soon! Check out his brilliant music on MySpace. I would also like to thank the various musicians and producers with whom I have collaborated in recent years, especially Jon Thorpe, Ian Lewis of Whitby Studios, Ellesmere Port, and the Wallasey folk band Reckless Elbow. Martin O'Neill, Ray Tierney and Paul Webster shared the trials and the rewards of amateur music-making in Dublin in the late 1970s. Dave Courtney and Seán Murray were co-members of Puking Spiders, the only punk band in Tenerife in the early 1980s. John Braine and DJ Françoise were extremely helpful regarding the Dublin clubbing scene when I spoke to them as part of the research for *Noisy Island*. Máire Ní Chathasaigh answered my inquiries politely after I saw her performing at the Shrewsbury Folk Festival in August 2008. My thanks to Chas Smash (Carl Smyth) of Madness who contacted me out of the blue and invited me to comment on the band's new album, and who got me backstage passes for the band's Aintree gig in April 2007.

Sam Thompson is the kind of technological whiz kid to which every ageing academic should have access.

My brother George Smyth tutored me during my undergraduate years at the University of Popular Music (where I majored in Beatles and US West Coast rock 1965–1969), aided by my sisters Sheila and Joan, and my cousin Kevin.

I am extremely grateful to Lisa Hyde of Irish Academic Press for listening to my ideas for this book, and for the energy, enthusiasm and integrity she has brought to the project.

Thanks to my wife Stacey, my children Lizzie and Esther, my stepchildren Holly and Duncan, and to all my extended family for their love and support.

Finally, I should like to thank the owners and staff of the Elahee Indian restaurant in Crouch End, where the serendipitous discovery of my book *Beautiful Day* (deposited there by the restaurant's chief patron) primed Lisa to be well disposed towards a proposal for the present volume.

Introduction

IN SEARCH OF IRISH MUSIC

In April 2009 I dined with my family in a small restaurant in the town of Katoomba in the Blue Mountains, about 100 kilometres west of Sydney. The layout of this establishment was somewhat odd, with random tables, alcoves and bar stools dispersed throughout the room. The dark wooden furniture was set off by subdued lighting, and the overall ambience was one I would describe as new-age with shades of hippy and frontier chic. The excellent food was served by a polite but rather aloof young woman wearing a long skirt and patterned cotton blouse. The meal was accompanied by soft background music which I learned was either called, or by a band called, Magical Strings. I recognised some O'Carolan tunes and some other Irish melodies played by a string ensemble of indeterminate constitution.[1] On requesting to examine the CD, however, I was informed by the waitress that the music was relayed via an MP3 player (an Apple iPod, to be precise) which had been hooked up to the restaurant's speaker system.

As this book was in the final stages of preparation, I was at this time particularly sensitised to the sound of 'Irish music' wherever and whenever I encountered it. A number of things about this particular episode struck me as interesting, however. For one thing, hearing what sounded like Irish music in a place about as far away from Ireland as one can get on the planet reminded me of the geographical scope of the culture associated with that small island in the North Atlantic. Whether considered in terms of the great diaspora through which it has been disseminated throughout the modern era, or in terms of the time–space compression which has emerged as a key component of postmodern critical theory, Irish music may be regarded as a truly global phenomenon. Then again, the absence of the CD itself raised the issue of the ways in which cultural experience is mediated by technology, and the manner in which changes in technology impact upon the aesthetic and emotional relationship we have (or are encouraged to have) with cultural texts.

The most resonant point for me, however, concerned a homology that I perceived to obtain between the music and the context. There appeared to exist, in other words, an intentional analogue between the space – in terms of its décor, its staff and its general atmosphere – and a specific kind of music which someone believed suited or complemented the place. In old-fashioned terms, we might say that the patrons were being 'interpellated' as a specific kind of subject – one who would be *au fait* with the music and all that it connoted. Of course, this may have been nothing more than an effect of my heightened sensitivity, or it could have been just plain coincidence; perhaps the new album by Guns 'n' Roses or Coldplay or Lily Allen was blasting out of the restaurant speakers by the time I got to the end of the road, but I doubt it. It just wasn't that kind of place.

I think there are two obvious yet nonetheless fundamental points to be gleaned from this anecdote. Firstly, 'Irish music' represents a contested concept, an idea under erasure. Its meaning, its value, indeed its very possibility are all context-dependent: *who* is performing *what* kind of music using *what* kind of technology to *what* standard for *which* audience? Discrepancies in any one of these clauses can disrupt the 'Irishness' of any musical experience. The fact is that the sounds that some people hear, identify and respond to as Irish simply do not, for whatever reason, register in that way for other people. Part of what this book is about is attempting to account for both the process of identification and the discrepancies between identifications.

Secondly, despite its problematical status, the idea of an Irish music has proved to be a remarkably successful global phenomenon throughout the modern era. We know that the fate of small-scale local cultures in the global age is an extremely vexed issue. We may suspect that the current case is exacerbated by the question marks that hang over the very possibility of 'Irish music', regardless of whether the practices which contribute to such an idea qualify (or ever did qualify) to be described as small-scale or local. We may not be able to agree what it is. Nevertheless, variations, approximations and invocations of 'Irish music' are available everywhere and all the time: in bars, clubs and restaurants, in specialised venues and in arterial spaces, in terraced streets and in official buildings, in stadia and in bedrooms.

This book represents an attempt to engage with these two related issues: the contentious ways in which the idea of Irish music has evolved during the modern era, and the specific cultural acts wherein that idea has been activated. Certainly, such an engagement involves thinking about a variety of musical phenomena – that is, the specific sounds produced by particular agents at certain times, in so far as it is my ability to describe and/or analyse them. Also, and more significantly from my perspective, it requires thinking about the ways in which music has been and continues to be represented in a great variety of cultural contexts. I am less concerned with attempting to define an Irish music, in other words, than to consider what various people *say* or *feel* or *think* or *believe* Irish music is, what it means, and how it can modify the individual subject's emotional engagement with the world.

It should be clear from the outset that such an approach could not be described as musicology, nor as ethnomusicology, nor even as cultural musicology; it is, rather, an expression of the various theoretical, methodological and archival discourses with which I have engaged over the course of a twenty-year career in Irish Studies. If this array of assumptions, approaches and techniques needs a name, then it's probably best to refer to it as 'cultural history'.

Like many of my contemporaries, I lived through music during my adolescence. Thinking, talking and reading about it, listening to, composing and performing it constituted the principal forms of creative culture in which I was involved into my twenties. Thereafter, as a professional musician, my relationship with music altered although I continued to engage with it in various modes of greater or lesser sophistication. As a result of this saturation, and despite the lack of any formal training, I was well disposed towards a scholarly response to music when such a possibility first occurred to me. My first published essay as a job-seeking postgraduate (1992) was about the competing models of Irish music informing audience response at the Irish bar in Liverpool where I regularly performed. Although the rest of the decade was dominated by theory wars, especially the energetic controversies attending postcolonialism and revisionism, my engagement with Irish music never ceased, and my sense of it as a vital element of Irish cultural history never wavered. I returned to the subject with a long chapter on the negotiation of space and place in the music of U2 which was included in my book *Space and the Irish Cultural Imagination* (2001).

One of the reasons why I maintained an interest in music, even as my research tended in other directions, was the observation of music's emergence as an increasingly important subject in the general area of the humanities. Thus, the sociologist Pierre Bourdieu:

> [Art] and cultural consumption [including quite centrally music] are predisposed, consciously and deliberately or not, to fulfil a social function of legitimating social differences (1984: 7);

the cultural musicologist Simon Frith:

> There is such a thing as society and it is through music more than any other cultural activity that people become part of it (1992: 177);

the ethnomusicologist Martin Stokes:

> Music is not just a thing that happens 'in' society. A society ... might also be usefully conceived as something which happens 'in' music (1994: 2);

the novelist/journalist Hanif Kureishi:

> [the] alternative history of our time [may be] told from the standpoint of popular music, which is as good a position as any to look from, since pop, intersecting with issues of class, race and particularly gender, has been at the centre of post-war culture (1995: xix);

and the music historian Marie McCarthy:

> What is common across all time and cultures is the fact that the transmission of music is an integral part of the generational transmission of culture, occurring primarily during childhood and adolescence (1999: 2).

Such assertions resonated clearly with my understanding of what modern cultural criticism was supposed to encompass: the construction of social difference, the role of cultural activity in the formation of society, the intersection of art with discourses of class, race and gender, the impact of tradition on contemporary aesthetic practices. During the

1990s, under the auspices of interdisciplinarity, cultural studies and postmodern critical theory, music escaped the restrictive academic ghettoes into which it had been consigned and moved to the centre of the critical agenda. And it was in response to that development, and under the influence of writers such as those quoted above, that I set myself the task of thinking seriously about the role of music in Irish cultural history.

The ensuing programme of research resulted in the publication of *Noisy Island: A Short History of Irish Popular Music* (2005) and its companion volume (co-written with Seán Campbell) *Beautiful Day: Forty Years of Irish Rock* (2005). While preparing those texts I also began to accumulate a number of pieces – published and unpublished essays, reviews, conference papers, encyclopaedia entries, and the like – all focused to some extent on the role and representation of music in Irish cultural history. The current volume represents an attempt to bring some of those pieces together in a single text which, taken as a whole, constitutes a coherent response to Irish music as an historical, political, social, economic and cultural phenomenon. The chapters are informed by an array of theoretical, methodological and archival discourses which I have gathered across two decades of study. My hope is that the approach to music pursued here accords with American cultural musicologist Lawrence Kramer's description of 'a full, open engagement with music as lived experience, experience rendered vivid and vivified by a host of overlapping cultural associations' (2003: 134). Only then can Irish music begin to assume a significance within the academy comparable to the significance it holds for the people who engage with it everywhere and every day as part of the process of discovering who they are and what they want.

Listening to the Future: Music and Irish Studies

For twenty-five centuries, Western knowledge has tried to look upon the world. It has failed to understand that the world is not for the beholding. It is for hearing. It is not legible, but audible.

Our science has always desired to monitor, measure, abstract, and castrate meaning, forgetting that life is full of noise and that death alone is silent: work noise, noise of man, and noise of beast. Noise bought, sold, or prohibited. Nothing essential happens in the absence of noise. Today, our sight has dimmed; it no longer sees our future, having constructed a present made of abstraction, nonsense, and silence. Now we must learn to judge a society more by its sounds, by its art, and by its festivals, than by its statistics. By listening to noise, we can better understand where the folly of men and their calculations is leading us, and what hopes it is still possible to have (Attali 1985: 1).

MUSIC AND IRISH STUDIES

I think it is fair to say that music has not loomed particularly large in the legend of Irish Studies. When I say 'Irish Studies', I do not mean the widely dispersed engagement with diverse Irish cultural produce – the analysis of Irish cultural activity that has been part of the fabric of national political debate since at least the late eighteenth century. I mean the specialised academic field that began to emerge as a discrete intellectual/institutional formation during the 1970s. This particular idea of Irish Studies was still in the process of evolving when I first encountered it as an undergraduate during the late 1980s. Since that time it has consolidated into a recognisable – and highly successful – academic field, with all the hallmarks that one might expect: national and international federations, university departments with undergraduate and postgraduate degrees, research scholarships, chairs, conferences, journals, publisher lists, monograph series, etc.

This latter-day Irish Studies has tended to be dominated by a range of literary-critical and historical discourses, which have in turn mediated a number of issues with which those working in the field will be more or less familiar. These issues include the representation of women within Irish history; the legitimacy of colonialism and postcolonialism as paradigms for the analysis of Irish culture; the political provenance of revisionism; and the scope of post-national (some might even claim post-political or post-historical) Ireland.

Music, to restate, has not fared particularly well under this dispensation.[1] Of course, the same is true of a good many other areas: issues such as disability, sexuality, inward migration, repatriation, institutional crime (to name just a few) all await fuller development. But the inattention suffered by music in contemporary Irish Studies is particularly surprising when one considers the island's age-old reputation as home to a highly musical race.

Music was an immensely important aspect of first-millennium, medieval and early modern Irish culture, and was indeed recognised as such by commentators of various persuasion. The Welsh-Norman cleric Giraldus Cambrensis, for example, famously (although reluctantly) acknowledged the prowess of the natives, writing: 'It is only in the case of musical instruments that I find any commendable diligence in the people. They seem to me to be incomparably more skilled in these than any other people that I have seen' (1982: 103). The systematic association of Irishness with musicality, however, began in earnest during the First Celtic Revival of the eighteenth century when figures such as Joseph Cooper Walker and Charlotte Brooke became concerned to vindicate an ancient Irish culture in support of a politically valid modern nation (Smyth 1998: 64–71). Music was fully politicised shortly thereafter with the debates that emerged around the antiquarian practices of Edward Bunting and the romantic adaptations of Thomas Moore (Smith 2000; White 1998; see Chapter 2).

During the eighteenth and nineteenth centuries, all sides in the colonial debate made tactical use of some supposed special Irish feeling for music. For sympathetic English ideologues such as Matthew Arnold, it was a cultural concession: Arnold granted the Celts an advanced cultural sensibility (relative to the Saxons and Latinate Normans with whom they shared the Atlantic archipelago), but at the cost of an ability to function effectively in 'the real world' (Smyth 1996; see Chapters 4 and 6). Moreover, Arnold's racism (for such it was) was underpinned by the scholarly and scientific discourses in which he couched his analysis; the stereotypes in which he trafficked – poetic but flighty Celts, practical but dull Saxons, strenuous but insolent Latins – are still the currency with which significant numbers of people (some of whom are worryingly powerful) trade. One of the most enduring ideas underpinned in Arnold's influential analysis was that of 'the musical Irish' with their wistful, feckless attitude towards the mystery of life (or at least the mystery of life under British rule). This idea has in turn given rise to the remarkably long-lived, Janus-faced stereotype which pits elegiac Paddy Sad (think misty mountains, low whistles and slow airs) against festive Paddy Mad (think smoky pubs and diddley-eye tunes) in a constant battle for the 'meaning' of Irishness (see Chapters 4 and 10).

For the Anglo-Irish, music offered a respectable means of *being* Irish which did not threaten the 'Anglo' part of their composite identity. A classic example of the schizophrenic Anglo-Irish condition may be observed in Samuel Ferguson's review (from 1834) of a book entitled *Irish Minstrelsy*, which had been published by James Hardiman in 1831. Although proceeding from an extremely partial understanding of what music is, 'music' nonetheless became the platform upon which Ferguson attempted to construct a viable Anglo-Irish role within the narrative of Irish cultural (and political) history. In a move which curiously anticipates certain developments in late twentieth-century critical theory, Ferguson opted for a kind of ironic maturity with regard to contemporary colonial relations. He could not countenance an innate 'essential' identity in the cultural produce (including the music) of Gaelic civilisation – that would exclude himself and the Anglo-Irish fraction he represented; but he was willing to make strategic use of such a concept in order to resist any totalising imperial narrative which might attempt to integrate all forms of regional otherness into a single corporate 'Britishness'. All this made for an extremely complex critical politics in which the Anglo-Irish subject is never precisely sure who are his allies and who his enemies. A collateral effect in this instance was that music became a vital clue as to the wider cultural and political fate of the various colonial communities vying for control of the national nomenclature. Thus it has remained down to the present.

As for the Irish themselves, music was a compensation for being born into a politically vanquished race – a comfort when they wished to remember, and a distraction when they wished to forget. It was during the nineteenth century that music began to perform the important socio-political functions in Irish life, both at home and among the diaspora, with which we are still coming to terms today. Music was both a private, affective action and a public, social ritual whereby the subject could 'perform' their Irish identity, fired by the belief that each individual musical act – be it a composition or a performance or simply listening to a piece of music – was in some way part of an ancient, ongoing tradition which confirmed (and, with each new act, reconfirmed) the validity of both the individual and the nation. Irishness and musicality remained locked together following the political revolution of the early twentieth century. With the growth in recording and playback technology in the years after 1922, 'Irish music' was capable of being disseminated to great numbers of people in a variety of new media, although with the proliferation of performance contexts came an increase in the uncertainty regarding the precise nature of the phenomenon. The controversy rages on; nevertheless, by the late twentieth century the twin concepts of a more or less identifiable musical style and an apparently innate musical proclivity infused Irish music-making at every level, offering itself to both domestic and international audiences as one of the most palpable signs of a modern Irish identity, whether located in Boston or Boyle, Kerry or Katoomba.

The question of how a range of alternative musical practices – such as art music and various 'foreign' popular genres – fare in this narrative is fraught with the many difficulties born of belief, conviction and downright prejudice. If music became an important measure of Irish identity at some point during the nineteenth century, then, by a reciprocal manoeuvre (and as part of the much wider project of cultural nationalism), Irishness soon became a measure of music. The effect was to bring a socio-political agenda to bear upon musicological discourse: what exactly were the criteria according to which musical Irishness was to be considered? How 'Irish' is that tune, that instrument, that arrangement, that performance, that sound? What systems – institutional and otherwise – exist for demarcating the gradations of musical identity (*non-Irish, Irish, Irisher, Irishest*), and, when these gradations have been established, to reward the worthy and sanction the undeserving?[2]

The main points to be noted at this stage is that music and Irishness have been locked together for almost as long as we can reckon; that this relationship has become more and more self-consciously politicised as time has passed; and that the modern field of Irish Studies has by and large failed to engage with either of these facts. As I shall go on to suggest towards the end of this chapter, the concept of Irish musicality may be *much* more significant than we imagine; but even an initial glance exposes the untenability of a modern scholarly field that has marginalised one of the most important and powerful cultural manifestations of its object.

MUSIC AND CRITICISM

Of course, people continue to analyse and criticise and understand Irish music in a wide range of institutional contexts and discursive languages. Most of the higher educational institutions across the island possess dedicated music departments, for example, offering students the opportunity to study various aspects of the art tradition – performance, composition, education, history and theory, and so on. The *Encyclopaedia of Music in Ireland* has been in preparation for a number of years under the general editorship of Barra Boydell and Harry White. Then there is the Irish World Music Centre, founded in 1994 under the direction of Professor Micheál Ó Súilleabháin who, as a charismatic (and controversial) composer, performer and facilitator, constitutes one of the most visible public faces of modern Irish traditional music. There are besides a multitude of official and semi-official societies, associations and boards dedicated to various aspects of Irish musical practice. Such institutions are energetic and committed, providing spaces in which scholars, performers and interested amateurs can explore various aspects of the country's rich musical heritage. While some are engaged in recovering a 'lost' Irish art repertoire, others conduct in-depth analyses of traditional melodic structure or the geo-social development of folk composition.[3]

Such work is useful and necessary. Disciplinary 'hard yards' are always made by scholars working closely with relatively minor aspects of their field: classifying, categorising, counting. At the same time, it seemed to me when I first became interested in this subject that none of the principal music traditions in Ireland (art, folk or popular) had managed to develop a coherent theoretical response to the Irish cultural condition as defined and engaged by the new Irish Studies. By 2000, Irish rock music had produced two general book-length studies (Prendergast 1987; Clayton-Lea and Taylor 1992), both characterised by a high degree of journalistic speculation and a more or less complete absence of any wider critical engagement. In 1988 and 1994, two journalists (Éamon Dunphy and John Waters) produced books which attempted to place U2 against the background of developing Ireland; whereas the first was hampered by a limited knowledge of the rock tradition, the second was compromised by a fast-and-loose attitude towards highly sensitive critical and cultural theories. The country's premier popular music magazine, *Hot Press*, continued to carry the flag for intelligent rock journalism; under the percipient editorship of Niall Stokes, music coverage has always been integrated into a wider socio-political analysis. Apart from a few speculative essays (Keohane 1997: McLaughlin and McLoone 2000: Rolston 2001), however, at the outset of the millennium the world still awaited the first extended response from the contemporary Irish Studies community to the phenomenon of Irish popular music.

This was the gap that I attempted to plug with the publication of my book *Noisy Island: A Short History of Irish Popular Music* (2005). Whatever its merits or shortcomings *qua* study, this text at least had the virtue of acknowledging popular music as a serious element within the evolving Irish cultural imagination, and thereby helping to establish it as a legitimate field of study for subsequent scholarship. If it achieved nothing else, *Noisy Island* broached a methodology, a series of theoretical concepts, and an archive of primary sources, all of which are now available for re-visitation and (more importantly) for revision within the Irish critical imagination.

The other two traditions making up the Irish musical triumvirate have likewise been poorly served until relatively recently. This is not to deny that commentary and analysis proliferate with regard to these traditions, much of it of a high scholarly standard. By and large, however, such responses tend to be couched in the specific disciplinary languages under whose auspices they operate. Some scholars attempted to bring new theoretical methods to bear upon both the art tradition and traditional music (Ó Súilleabháin 1998; White 1998); but the fact was that even five years ago the gulf between musicology, ethnomusicology and mainstream Irish Studies remained unbridged, and appeared likely to remain so for the foreseeable future.

Even as the current volume was in preparation, however, a number of titles appeared which betokened an understanding of music's role in Irish cultural history that was both more active and more ambitious. One such text is John O'Flynn's *The Irishness of Irish Music* (2009), which, as its title suggests, tackles a key question head-on: what is the nature of the connection between a range of different music traditions and the abstract notion of national identity referenced by those people who live on, or who are in some manner or to some degree affiliated to, the island of Ireland? It will surprise no-one to discover that the answer to that question is ... contested; in formulating it in such a way, however, and in seeking out associations across discrete cultural/critical lines, O'Flynn opens up areas of inquiry which necessarily impact upon any wider engagement with questions of Irish identity.

In *The Making of Irish Traditional Music* (2008), Helen O'Shea undertakes a thorough deconstruction of the myths surrounding Irish traditional music. The paradox she discovers at the heart of that style is the idea of 'a national tradition that absorbs outside influences without being changed by them' (3). That particular national tradition, she avers, trails a legacy of chauvinism, sexism and unexamined prejudice – tendencies which have only been exacerbated in recent years under the impact of rapid socio-economic change. O'Shea's pejorative estimation of contemporary practices is all the more striking when considered in relation to the love she clearly bears for the music; at the same time, such a judgement is at odds with the generally positive associations that traditional music tends to attract.

Seán Crosson examines the relationship between two national obsessions in *'The Given Note': Traditional Music and Modern Irish Poetry* (2008). The former, he claims, resides at the heart of the latter, whether as metaphor, as formal example or as a desired model of communication between the creative artist and the receiving audience. Different poets have emphasised different elements of that relationship at various times. Throughout their careers, for example, both Séamus Heaney and Ciarán Carson have evinced a strong relationship with traditional music. Whereas the former's poetry is impelled by a lyrical imperative – 'an almost mythologized "I"' (255), as Crosson says – that is at odds with the precepts of traditional music, Carson's work aspires to a more performative aesthetic, one in which 'the communities that inhabit landscape, and create, perform and listen to traditional music' (255) are central.

In *The Keeper's Recital* (1998), Harry White claimed that '[in] Irish poetry, drama and fiction, the very trace of music as a dislocated presence in Irish affairs is unmistakable' (159). This tentative thesis becomes the central subject of White's *Music and the Irish Literary Imagination* (2008), in which he claims

> that the quest for the Irish Omphalos entails a consideration of music not simply as a striking absence but as a vital presence in the Literary Revival and in contemporary Irish literature. It rests on the premise that music is the 'sovereign ghost' of the Irish literary imagination. Wallace Stevens's tantalizing formula for the imagination itself seems particularly expressive of that ambiguous but enduring relationship between music and literature which has been formative in Irish writing at least since the beginning of the nineteenth century, and which strongly inheres in the poetry and drama of Irish writers for two centuries afterwards (3–4).

This invocation, of what is undoubtedly a glamorous and rightly celebrated literary tradition, by a representative of a somewhat neglected discipline might be regarded as born out of frustration. White's thesis is nonetheless compelling: literature's domination has distorted the modern Irish critical imagination, making it difficult to 'hear' (by which I mean identify and understand) the crucial ways in which Irish identity has been negotiated (and modified) in a range of sonic registers. The energy of Irish music has been displaced into a literary tradition which as a result benefited from, even as it helped to marginalise, Irish musical discourse during the twentieth century.

White's suspicions regarding the relations between music and literature in Irish cultural history is something to which I shall turn in the next section (and return to in various chapters throughout this book). In the meantime, my hope is that his study, along with the others here mentioned, signals the arrival of music as an essential element within the landscape of modern Irish Studies. After decades of *looking* at the ways in which issues of tradition and identity have been broached, in other words, it might be time to begin seriously to *listen* to the sound of Irishness as it has been made and remade throughout Irish cultural history.

MUSIC AND LITERATURE

What would a fully calibrated discourse of Irish music criticism look like? As I have indicated, one crucial element with which it would have to come to terms was broached in *Music and the Irish Literary Imagination*: the degree to which Irish creative energy has been siphoned off, so to speak, by artists working in written media. The roll call of 'great Irish writers' is well known: while the likes of Wilde, Yeats, Synge, Joyce, Shaw, Beckett, Kavanagh, Heaney, Friel and so on are now part of the fabric of modern Irish culture, most non-specialists would be hard pressed to name half a dozen Irish composers from the last two centuries. The same is also true of the fine arts. In some senses, it would appear, Irish cultural history has been warped by its literary riches; the price of an unrivalled pantheon of writers may have been the lack of a more balanced artistic tradition in which each of the arts – with their peculiar ways of articulating human experience – is allowed to develop.

One curious aspect of the way in which Irish artistic activity has evolved during the modern era is the propensity of imaginative writers to write *about* music. Music continues to crop up from time to time as a consideration in the analysis of literary figures such as Joyce and Beckett. Indeed, 'musical Joyce' is now a recognised sub-specialist field, especially in the United States of America where academic territorialisation can be a pretty brutal business (Bauerle 1993; Weaver 1998). One of the things that has emerged from the study of music in Joyce and Beckett, however, is the realisation that these writers were far from unique in their concern with music, and that the modern western literary tradition has in fact been obsessed with music – or more precisely, with calculating the essential properties of music in relation to literature, and with the question of what occurs when the former is represented through the medium of the latter (Aronson 1980; Benson 2006; Wolf 1999). Generally speaking, literature since the time of Rousseau has suffered something of an inferiority complex in relation to music; because their chosen medium represents a double alienation from reality (firstly through verbalisation, secondly through writing), many writers have coveted (and attempted to reproduce) the properties of a cultural practice they perceived to be both beautiful and truthful in a way that mere writing never could be (Smyth 2008: 16–29).

Literature's concern with music has proved something of an embarrassment for its attendant critical discourses, which after all have both an intellectual and a material investment in the institution of literature. Since its inception in the eighteenth century, modern literary criticism has been anxious enough about its object of study (writing), *and* about its own relationship with that object, without having to worry about incursions from alien disciplines. Some Joyce critics, as indicated above, are aspirationally interdisciplinary, attempting to explore the ways in which writing and music interrogate each other in the great man's work. Irish Studies, however, by and large continues to operate within established disciplinary boundaries. In this context, we may observe that the dearth of musical analysis in the field reflects a long-established trend within cultural criticism, in which music has tended to be marginalised in favour of 'properly' literary or 'properly' historical analysis (however these are defined, and the routes have been mapped many times).

Everywhere we look in Irish writing, however, we find music and musical imagery – and not only in the high modernist work of writers such as Joyce and Beckett, but throughout the canon. Consider, as a more or less random example, Joseph O'Connor's *Star of the Sea* (2002). Now, we know from his earlier writings that O'Connor is interested in music. The novel *Cowboys and Indians* (1991) featured an Irish exile in London trying to make it big with a rock band; and the journalism collected in *The Secret World of the Irish Male* (1994) is inundated with musical references. *Star of the Sea* (which became something of a 'reading group' classic in the UK after its endorsement by day-time chat hosts Richard and Judy) is set on a famine ship sailing from Ireland to New York in 1847. One of the principal characters composes an anti-recruiting ballad based upon an incident described at an early point in the story. The narrative details the creative process in great depth, describing first of all the 'real' events behind the song and the immediate circumstances leading to its composition. We are shown how the song evolves in response to aesthetic and institutional circumstances, how it relates to the 'real' incident, and how certain images and locutions are invoked, rejected and improved.

O'Connor's introduction of the dynamics of folk composition is in keeping with the carnivalesque nature of the text as a whole, which incorporates a variety of narrative discourses (including visual imagery) during its course. (This technique is repeated in *Redemption Falls* (2007), another novel in which music features as a key narrative element.) There is another level on which this particular instance functions, however.

Although anti-recruiting ballads abound within the Irish folk tradition, the variation described in *Star of the Sea* is clearly based on a well-known version entitled 'Arthur McBride' which was definitively covered by Andy Irvine and Paul Brady on a recording made in 1976 – a recording which remains in many ways a benchmark for the fusion of a number of different Irish musical sensibilities (traditional, folk, pop and rock). Indeed, *The Purple Album* (as it is sometimes referred to) marks the culmination of a decade of agonising over the relations between 'real' Irish music and the great variety of styles and genres with which it was – sometimes happily, sometimes kicking and screaming – linked (Smyth 2005: 18–24; 66–77). O'Connor's invocation of 'Arthur McBride' in the context of his novel sets in motion a process of intertextual resonance concerning (among other things) the relations between writing and music, between past and present, and between authenticity and adaptability – issues which go to the heart of the Irish cultural condition.

Critics such as Seán Crosson and Harry White have begun the process of gauging the relationship between music and literature in Irish cultural history. As a contribution to the same process, I have attempted to engage with this relationship in various chapters of the present volume. Although my emphasis has been by and large on fiction rather than on poetry or drama, I share these critics' commitment to a re-orientation of contemporary Irish Studies in the light of music's vital role in Irish cultural history. While Irish Studies provides the immediate context for such a re-orientation, the wider context concerns the role of noise in the history of human experience – or, more precisely, in the history of thinking about human experience.

MUSIC AND NOISE

Thus far I have commented on: a) the ubiquity of musical discourse throughout Irish cultural history; b) the relative failure of modern Irish Studies and modern music studies in Ireland to achieve a meaningful interface; and c) the basis of a criticism which would be alert both to the presence and to the function of music within Irish literary texts. All these issues come into focus in the work of the French theorist and philosopher Jacques Attali who, as the quote which prefaces this essay shows, wished to place 'noise' at the centre of human history, and more radically, *at the centre of human thought about human history*. The goal of his celebrated study, *Noise: The Political Economy of Music*, is 'not only to theorize *about* music, but to theorize *through* music' (1985: 4). Noise is everywhere, he avers, the most fundamental sign of human activity and – when it is organised into the formal practices we are disposed to call 'music' – of the attempt to order the natural world in response to our fears and desires. 'Listening to music is listening to all noise,' Attali claims, 'realizing that its appropriation and control is a reflection of power, that it is essentially political' (6).

Attali tracks the history of the 'appropriation and control' of noise over three phases or 'zones':

> In one of these zones, it seems that music is used and produced in the ritual in an attempt to make people *forget* the general violence; in another, it is employed to make people *believe* in the harmony of the world, that there is order in exchange and legitimacy in commercial power; and finally, there is one in which it serves to *silence*, by mass-producing a deafening, syncretic kind of music, and censoring all other human noises.
>
> Make people Forget, make them Believe, Silence them. In all three cases, music is a tool of power ... (19).

These zones are examined at length in chapters on 'Sacrificing', 'Representation' and 'Repetition' – the latter being the dominant form of noise organisation during the era of capitalism (see Chapter 9). The suggestiveness of this model for a re-oriented history of Ireland cannot be overestimated. An Attalian analysis of Ireland during the modern era encourages us to acknowledge the many and various ways in which 'noise' has been organised in relation to Irish identity, whether on the island or elsewhere: noise industrial, technological, sectarian, sporting, and so on *ad infinitum*. At a more fundamental level, however, such an analysis could help us to trace how a state-sponsored quest for a 'representational' noise was gradually overcome in the latter half of the twentieth century by systems (both aesthetic and institutional) of 'repetition' which represent the logic of the community at this particular stage of its economico-political development. 'Janis Joplin, Bob Dylan, and Jimi Hendrix say more about the liberatory dream of the 1960s than any theory of crisis', writes Attali (6); in which case I would suggest that the likes of Kíla, U2 and Gerald Barry say as much as any political or economic theory ever could about the state of Ireland in the noughties – a time and place, it is worth remembering, in which Irish music attained successful brand status, to the great satisfaction of the government and the institutions it sponsors.[4]

Attali also theorises 'the seeds of a new noise' (133), however, a different way of making music in which 'in embryonic form, beyond repetition, lies freedom: more than a new music, a fourth kind of musical practice. It heralds the arrival of new social relations. Music is becoming *composition*' (20). By this term Attali means a form of music that 'calls into question the distinction between worker and consumer, between doing and destroying ... to compose is to take pleasure in the instruments, the tools of communication, in use-time and exchange-time as lived and no longer as stockpiled' (135). 'Composition' is associated with any form of music used – however temporarily, in however fragmented or unstable a context – beyond the confining power of sacrifice, representation or repetition. Attali's theory of 'composition' (formulated during the early 1970s) anticipated the advent of the digital revolution in music-making which, based on technological (cheaper hardware, file-sharing, MP3, and so on) and other socio-cultural developments, has changed forever not only the ways in which 'music' can be made, but also the ways in which it functions to create meaning in a variety of social, political and cultural contexts. 'Composition' is no doubt a utopian notion, but I would suggest that it is precisely such a form of noise that modern Ireland – with its relentless 'stockpiling' of just about everything material and immaterial – could benefit from at this particular stage in its history.

Above all, what the attempt to 'theorize through music' leads Attali to is a recognition of music's predictive power – the fact that '[music] is prophesy. Its styles and economic organization are ahead of the rest of society because it explores, much faster than material reality can, the entire range of possibilities in a given code' (12). Which is to say: music – defined now as the political organisation of noise – has throughout history constituted a clear exercise of power and at the same time a highly sensitive form of resistance to, and subversion of, established discourses of power. Therein lies the source of its political importance: 'Music, the quintessential mass activity, like the crowd, is simultaneously a threat and a necessary source of legitimacy; trying to channel it is a risk that every system of power must run' (14). We ignore music at our peril, in other words, for at the same time as it affords us an insight into *how things are*, it offers us an enabling impression of *how things might be*.

MUSIC AND ...

In an historical formation in which it figures so prominently as an index of identity, it becomes imperative to understand music's role in the formation of discourses of power and dissent. By *listening* to Irish cultural history – rather than just looking at it or reducing it to one or another series of theoretical abstractions – we shall come not only to a stronger sense of where we have come from and where we are, but also, in the political struggles that are conducted over the relations between music, noise and silence, of where we might be going. If some noises can tell us a lot about the former, others – predictably less well known and more difficult to discern – can alert us to the latter, providing us with echoes of our future and of the struggles that lie in wait.

Of course I am not suggesting that we all become music specialists overnight. But Irish Studies cannot afford to remain ignorant of the role and function of music within its object practices. For those with ears to hear, the isle is indeed full of noises – as is the global diasporic culture that claims affiliation with the homeland; but while we are encouraged to consider some of these as 'sweet airs, that give delight and hurt not' – in other words, as music – many others carry all the pejorative weight of the word ('STOP THAT *NOISE!*'), and are as a consequence marginalised or condemned in a variety of aesthetic, moral, legal and/or political discourses. Trying to discover the difference between these two concepts – the processes whereby the one is formally or institutionally separated from the other, and the means by which such processes are resisted – presents the Irish Studies community with one of its most pressing, as well as potentially rewarding, tasks.

I began this chapter with Attali's indictment of traditional forms of knowledge and his repositioning of noise at the centre of human experience. I end with his bold call for us to begin listening seriously to the world:

> Can we make the connections? Can we hear the crisis of society in the crisis of music? Can we understand music through its relations with money? ... The noises of society are in advance of its images and material conflicts. Our music foretells our future. Let us lend it an ear (11).

Betrayal as Theme and Influence in Thomas Moore's 'On Music'

Thomas Moore's 'On Music' was published in the third number of his *Irish Melodies* series in 1810. Here is the lyric:

When thro' life unblest we rove,
Losing all that made life dear,
Should some notes we used to love
In days of boyhood, meet our ear;
Oh! how welcome breathes the strain,
Wak'ning thoughts that long have slept
Kindling former smiles again
In faded eyes, that long have wept!

Like the *gale* that sighs along
Beds of oriental flowers,
Is the grateful breath of song
That once was heard in happier hours;
Filled with balm, the *gale* sighs on,
Though the flowers have sunk in death;
So, when pleasure's dream is gone,
Its memory lives in Music's breath.

Music! oh, how faint, how weak,
Language fades before thy spell!
Why should feeling ever speak,
When thou canst breathe her soul so well?
Friendship's balmy words may feign,
Love's are even more false than they;
Oh! 'tis only Music's strain
Can sweetly soothe, and not betray (1910: 194).

Like all the melodies adapted by Moore, 'On Music' has a complex genealogy. Veronica Ní Chinnéide identified the tune as 'The Banks of Banna', which Moore would have sourced from the first volume of a series entitled *Scotish Airs* edited and published in Edinburgh by George Thomson in 1793 (1959: 121). 'The Banks of Banna' was a song written around 1774 by the Anglo-Irish politician George Ogle (1742–1814) – MP for Wexford and Dublin, opponent of Catholic Emancipation, one-time suitor to Mary Wollstonecroft, and (towards the end of his life) Grand Master of the Orange Order (Kelly 2008).[1] 'The Banks of Banna' should not be confused with Ogle's rather more famous song 'Molly Asthore' which begins with the line 'As down by Banna's banks I strayed'. Both songs relate tales of disappointed love as narrated by a deceived young man, although with its macaronic title and refrain ('Ah! gramachree, my colleen oge, my Molly, asthore') one is clearly more 'Irish' than the other.[2]

'On Music' is not one of the better known songs from *Irish Melodies*. It retains an interest, however, in so far as it functions in part as an example of *meta-art* – which is to say, it is a text in which the medium (in this case, music) is explicitly invoked at a thematic level. The 'meta' turn in art is always interesting. For one thing, it offers the artist an opportunity to reflect upon the function and limitations of their work and, by extension, the function and limitations of the human subjects who create, feature in and consume such works. In this sense, 'On Music' may be observed to be in critical dialogue with the process of its own making. The writer has composed a song about music, deploying a dense, highly stylised use of language to warn about (among other things) the dangers of language. Moore's lyric is a particularly interesting instance, moreover, in as much as it incorporates a number of themes that resonate strongly throughout the revolutionary context in which it was composed. As it turns out, Moore's short (and somewhat bland) lyric may be regarded as a highly motivated intervention in contemporary cultural politics.

The first two numbers of *Irish Melodies* drew extensively on Edward Bunting's famous *General Collection of the Ancient Irish Music*, first published in 1796.[3] Bunting had been commissioned at the precocious age of 21 to transcribe the airs he heard played by the musicians who gathered at the famous Belfast Harp Festival of 1792. He augmented his collection with tunes picked up on field trips in Ulster and

Connaught during 1793. Moore was a student at Trinity, along with his friend Robert Emmet, when Bunting's collection appeared a few years later. We also know that this early foray into musical antiquarianism took place within the general context of the rise of Irish republicanism, which was to precipitate the Rebellion of 1798 and Emmet's own abortive insurrection of 1803.

Moore (aided by his collaborator, the composer Sir John Stevenson) reset some of the melodies from Bunting's collection (as well as from many other sources), gave them keys, added grace and passing notes, and lyrics which he believed to be in sympathy with the spirit of the 'original' melodies. He was criticised at the time, however, for betraying the spirit of the music; he did so, apparently, by 'translating' supposedly pristine Irish melodies into the romantic idiom of the drawing room – worse still, the *English* drawing room, wherein a modicum of wild Irish romance went a long way. Such indeed formed the basis for much of the subsequent suspicion of this aspect of Moore's career. The controversy thus ignited remains with us still: as Harry White comments, 'the *Melodies* inaugurated a bitter quarrel between tradition and innovation which would long thrive in Irish musical discourse' (1998: 47).

The relationship between the Irish 'originals' and Moore's 'translations', and the recurring idea that such a relationship constitutes the 'betrayal' of the former by the latter, forms the basis of this chapter. Such an analysis obliges us to pay particular attention to the idea of betrayal as represented in a range of contemporary political, poetic and philosophical discourses. Before that, however, it is necessary to look at the relationship between Bunting and Moore a little more closely, and to consider what precisely might be at stake in their quarrel.

BUNTING AND MOORE

We observe immediately that Moore's lyric turns on a key opposition between music (which is positive and deserving, a cause for good) and language (which is treacherous) – an opposition most clearly expressed in the final verse. Conceptually, sonically and etymologically, 'friendship' is haunted by the possibility of 'feigning' – by the possibility (and this counts for 'love' also) that the treacherous subject is secretly committed to a reality other than that to which they apparently subscribe.

Crucially, language is impugned as the means by which disloyalty is enabled to disguise itself.

This is something Moore brilliantly instantiates by revealing the diverse connotations of one particular word within his own text. In the second stanza, the noun 'balm' carries the traditional associations which it had been accruing throughout the evolution of the English language. This particular instance combines a literal reference to an 'aromatic fragrance, agreeable perfume' (derived in this instance from the 'beds of oriental flowers') with a figurative use in which the word signifies 'a healing, soothing, or softly restorative agency or influence' (Simpson and Weiner, *OED*, I: 913). This latter definition implies a certain narrative in which the subject, exposed to a world that is both hostile and treacherous, seeks relief for the pain, unhappiness and/or depletion they have suffered. Just so in the textual world of 'On Music', which is characterised by loss, sorrow and the absence of pleasure. The lyric suggests that music is a balm that can enable us to endure the inimical environment that is the common fate of our species.

By the time it recurs in the third stanza, however, the word has changed both in form and meaning. The *OED* definition of the adjective 'balmy' as 'deliciously soft and soothing' (I, 914) carries remote, yet nonetheless sinister, overtones of wheedling, flattery and deception. The 'balming' agent or influence can overwhelm the subject's physical and mental resources; wallowing in the comfort of the present, they are unable to detect any hostile agenda threatening their future.[4] This latter usage, moreover, necessarily modifies an understanding of the first. The noun 'balm' pretends to be one thing (*on* the side of music, *against* 'life' and its negative associations); another reality was always lying dormant within the word, however, secretly waiting an opportunity to speak its truth and to turn its back on previous associations. In this way, the treachery of language is implicitly linked with the language of treachery.

Moore is implicated here in a seemingly contradictory aesthetic; even as he deploys language to extol music's superiority over language, he cannot help revealing the inherently treacherous nature of language itself. This dilemma, moreover, has a direct resonance within his own career: the whiff of 'betrayal' hovers around many responses to *Irish Melodies*, not least that of Edward Bunting himself who, in the 'Preface' to his *Ancient Music of Ireland* published in 1840

> [deplored] the fact, that in these new Irish melodies the work of the poet was accounted of so paramount an interest, that the proper order of song-writing was in many instances inverted, and, instead of the words being adapted to the tune, the tune was too often adapted to the words, a solecism which could never have happened had the reputation of the writer not been so great as at once to carry the tunes he deigned to make use of altogether out of their old sphere among the simple and tradition-loving people of the country – with whom, in truth, many of the new melodies, to this day, are hardly suspected to be themselves (1840: 5).

Bunting has a problem with Moore's lyrics, then, the inference being that there was a discrepancy (amounting to a betrayal of sorts) between Moore's undoubted gifts as a poet and the 'proper' context within which the original musical works (whether 'airs' or songs) belong. The real issue, however, lies in the poet's decision to expose the fragile beauty of the original airs to a radically inappropriate harmonic system (in which context it was Sir John Stevenson who was the chief culprit). Throughout his long collecting and publishing career, Bunting's allegiance remained always with what in the preface to his first collection he described as 'the old melodies … [which] have been preserved pure and handed down unalloyed, through a long succession of ages' (1796: unpaginated). It was specifically in the melody – the single line of musical notes progressing through time – that the essential beauty of Irish music resided. Harmony was a decadent European perversion – a betrayal, in fact – of Irish melody.

Moore was sensitive to such charges, and attempted to refute them on a number of occasions and in a number of ways throughout his career. In a preface to the same edition in which 'On Music' appeared, he describes his intention to retrieve 'the *pure* gold of the melody [that] shines through the ungraceful foliage which surrounds it',[5] and this may be regarded as an intertextual rejoinder to Bunting's notion of *pure* melody preserved in an ancient 'unalloyed' tradition. 'Purity' remains, but it is a question of emphasis and strategy: Bunting asserts the existence of a pristine, inalienable melody which it is his job to transcribe, whereas for Moore, the value of the melody must be excavated from where it lies (like so much of Irish cultural history) hidden beneath the accretions of the ages.

Thirty years later, in a journal entry from July 1840, Moore defended the 'very allowable liberties' he took with the melodies by suggesting that had he not done so, 'many of the airs now most known and popular would have been still sleeping, with all their authentic dross about them, in Mr Bunting's first volume' (Dowden 1988: 2141). The irony here is that to some ways of thinking, Bunting himself had already played extremely fast and loose with the musical material he transcribed at the Belfast Harp Festival, and he was therefore guilty to some degree of the charges he levelled at Stevenson and Moore. The Irish harp music encountered by Bunting in Belfast in 1792 was modal in structure – which is to say, it was composed in terms of an ancient system of musical modes that was alien to the tonal system which had been developing in European art music since the Middle Ages. Bunting's engagement with these alien forms necessitated an act of translation into a contemporary idiom – the tonal structures characteristic of European art music in which he had been trained.

Despite his 'translation' of modal harp airs (complete with bass accompaniment[6]) into the idiom of the even-tempered pianoforte, however, Bunting was adamant that he had preserved the original melodies intact, not only in spirit but also in form. This was to form the basis of his critique of Moore's adaptations. It was his ostensible subscription to the guiding criteria of 'accuracy … impartiality [and] integrity' (1840: 2) – both in terms of the original melody and his transcription of it – that underpinned his resentment (albeit of a polite kind) towards Moore.

However, many have regarded Bunting's own practice to be an act of cultural violence perpetrated upon the music. In the introduction to *The Complete Collection of Irish Music* (1855), George Petrie expressed his disappointment with Bunting's disregard for the authenticity of the tunes he collected, and exposed what he considered to be 'the irrationality and untruthfulness … [and] unsoundness' of Bunting's antiquarian practice (1902: ix–x). Petrie believed Bunting to be mistaken in his conviction (expressed in the preface to the 1797 volume) that there was only one true version of each discrete melody – an error compounded by his deference to injudicious sources:

> It is, in fact, to this careless or mistaken usage of Mr Bunting and other collectors of our melodies, of noting them from rude musical interpreters, instead of resorting to the native singers – their proper despositories – that we may ascribe the great inaccuracies – often destructive of their beauty, and always of their true ex-

pression – which may be found in the published settings of so many of our airs (1902: xi).

Perhaps more damningly, Petrie also attacked Bunting's musicological skills, accusing him of 'falsifying the accents, and marring the true expression of the melody through it entirely, and rendering it incapable of being correctly sung to the original song' (xi). The latter point picked up on something Petrie had noted in a review published nearly forty years earlier, in which he described Bunting's attempts to render the music of O'Carolan in standard notation as '[bordering] on barbarism' (quoted in White 1998: 39).

Although he does not use the term, Petrie clearly feels that Bunting has *betrayed* the 'true expression' of Irish music in a number of key respects. According to Mary Trachsel, however, Petrie himself was implicated to some degree in the same act of betrayal:

> When Bunting and his successors employed music literacy to preserve 'authentic' Irish music, they introduced into the discourse of this music a text-based concept of 'authenticity' alien to a strictly oral tradition. The inescapable irony of their position is that in attempting to wrest from the past 'pure' Irish music, free from the contaminations and distortions of 'outside' influences, their own practice or oral-to-literate translation was itself a transformative event (1995: 38).

The fact is that Bunting brought the values of European art music to bear upon a kind of music – modal in structure and non-textual in nature – that was resistant to those values. As Mícheál Ó Súilleabháin delicately puts it: 'While preparing the tunes for publication, [Bunting] obviously found himself presented with a musical idiom, even in his own notebooks, not wholly in keeping with his musical understanding' (O'Sullivan 1983: xvi). That was his job, however. Bunting's response to Irish music was as contingent – as in dialogue with contemporary discourses – as those of Moore, Petrie and the other great collectors would be in their time. In the fevered political climate of the 1790s, the antiquarianism which served as the pretext for the Belfast Festival was mitigated by a more interventionist agenda in which the past was recruited as an active agent within the present. As White points out, this necessitated an act of translation – in effect, the interpretation of historical forms in the light of contemporary concerns and, more importantly, by the use of contemporary forms.[7] The 1797 collection is, as a result, 'circumscribed ... by Bunting's practical concessions to contemporary musical sensibility' (White 1998: 39).

Bunting's melodies were already 'betrayals', then, already removed from a mythical originary trace by the time Moore encountered them. Every act of salvation on his part was also an act of betrayal to some degree. Bunting's entire career may in fact be traced in terms of a tension, a growing realisation on the one hand and a constant disavowal on the other, of the fact that harmony always existed *in potentia* in relation to Irish melody, even in the modal forms in which he first encountered the melodies at the Belfast Harp Festival in 1792.

Moore, meanwhile, continued to ply his trade copiously and without compunction. His lyrics provided an outlet for the resentment he felt towards England generally, and specifically towards those who had betrayed the efforts of noble men. White suggests that '[the] essence of Moore's understanding was an association which [he] repeatedly drew between the inherent nature of Irish melody as he apprehended it and the historical condition of oppression, lament and betrayal which he believed to be its source' (1998: 45). The conjoining of the words 'melody', 'oppression' and 'betrayal' is key here: the complex musical interrelations between Bunting, Moore and Petrie are haunted by the spectres of fidelity and its other: betrayal. This in turn may be regarded as an effect of a contemporary political climate in which issues of betrayal and friendship (both practical and conceptual) were very much to the fore.

'THE HEARTS THAT TREASON CANNOT TAINT'

Treason and betrayal were fundamental terms within the Irish political vocabulary in the 1790s and 1800s. These two concepts are related in their connotations of deception and disloyalty, although the first emerges in the main from a political/legal discourse and refers to the relationship between a nominal ruler (crown or government, for example) and the people over whom that ruler claims jurisdiction, while the second carries connotations of an interpersonal discourse of friendship and trust between individuals.[8] The crime of treason may be regarded as the institutional embodiment of a sentiment – the feeling of being betrayed by someone who stands to you in a relation of trust – that is both extremely powerful and more or less universal across the historical and geographical experience of the species.

Moore would have been exposed to both the political and interpersonal variations during the 1790s and 1800s – a period which saw two revolutionary actions (1798, 1803) as well as an Act of political Union (1801). The United Irishmen was considered a treasonous organisation, membership of which during those dangerous times carried a nominal death sentence. Moore's close friendship with, and subsequent championing of, a number of high-profile revolutionaries (including Lord Edward Fitzgerald and Robert Emmet) rendered him vulnerable to establishment panic, although a charge of sedition appears never to have been seriously levelled at him.[9] His aspirations for Ireland, and for the kind of relationship he favoured between Ireland and Britain, were typically complex, but it seems clear that he did not consider himself (or indeed those who took arms) to be traitors in so far as it was precisely the legitimacy of Britain's rule (and its right to identify and punish 'traitors') that was at issue.

While Moore may have managed to avoid the charge of 'treason' in his own mind as well as for the contemporary authorities, he was at the same time much exercised by the associated notion of 'betrayal'. Despite its attempt to develop a secret cell system, the United Irishmen organisation was in fact prey from the outset to an *ad hoc*, although nevertheless extensive, system of government informers which succeeded in hindering (and eventually thwarting) the revolution at every turn.[10] Both Fitzgerald and Emmet were apprehended on the information of informers. Their fate is testament to the near impossibility of a popular front rebellion. Treachery from within looms large throughout world history, although it should be said that perfidy on the part of friends and/or allies was particularly reprehensible to the Irish republicans of the 1790s, given the ostensible anti-sectarian basis of their movement.

'Betrayal' of one form or another is a ubiquitous presence within the popular balladry associated with the Rebellion. While 'traitors' and 'informers' are maligned, the qualities of loyalty, faithfulness and truth (in the sense of 'remaining true' to a cause or to a person) are emphasised. An extreme case is provided by a 'patriot mother' who tells her prisoner son that she would rather see him dead than live on as an informer (Moylan 2000: 40). Sometimes, specific acts of betrayal are described during the course of the narrative (as in 'The Song Of Prosperous' [42] or 'In Collon I Was Taken' [52]), while on other occasions ('The Memory of the Dead' [102–3] or 'The Shamrock Cockade' [2]) abstract ideas of betrayal and faithfulness are invoked. Typically, each side in the conflict claims an inalienable right to recognise, condemn and punish treachery. In one of the most famous anti-rebel ballads of the period, loyalist soldiers vow to 'make all the traitors and croppies lie down' (61), while the yeoman captain who captures the croppy boy (in the version written by Carroll Malone and first published in *The Nation* in 1845) utters the curse: 'may all traitors swing' (75).

In some ballads, the contextual status of political treason is revealed. Shortly after 'The Banished Defender' indicts 'those traitors who forced me from my native soil', he denies that he himself is a traitor because he was 'fighting in defence of my God, my country and my creed' (56). The eponymous narrator of 'Bold Robert Emmet' likewise forswears the name of 'traitor': 'My crime is the love of the land I was born in' (115). The connection between political treason and personal betrayal also forms a recurring theme: 'Was it treason?' asks the narrator of 'The Bothers John and Henry Sheares', before going on to condemn 'The base informer ... / Who, Judas-like, could sell the blood of true men, / While he clasped their hands as friends' (80).

Moore dealt circumspectly with the betrayal of Lord Edward Fitzgerald in his biography of 1831; 'treachery' (243) there most certainly was, but apart from one suspect (the staunch United Irishman Samuel Neilson, incidentally also one of the organisers of the Belfast Harp Festival of 1792) he is not forthcoming. In song-writing mode, however, he was unavoidably drawn in to the discourses of treason and friendship which attached to the theme of rebellion, and was influenced by many of the strategies whereby these concepts were accommodated within the wider revolutionary context. 'Let Erin Remember the Days of Old' turns on a distinction between an honourable past and a debased present in which 'her faithless sons betray'd her' (1910: 187) – a sentiment reprised in 'Oh For the Swords of Former Times' (216). The narrator of 'The Prince's Day' questions the invocation of loyalty in the context of Irish rebellion: 'Tho' fierce to your foe, to your friends you are true' (196). 'Come, Send Round the Wine' disdains sectarianism in favour of universal qualities – such as 'Truth, valour [and] love' (188) – available, apparently, to all men. Even non-political love songs, such as 'Believe Me, if all those Endearing Young Charms' (189), 'Tis the Last Rose of Summer' (202) and 'When First I Met Thee' (207) incorporate themes of fidelity and deception, and thus are implicated in the wider discourse of betrayal informing *Irish Melodies*.[11]

Music itself is a recurring theme throughout the series, invoked in famous songs such as 'The Harp that Once Through Tara's Halls' (182), 'She Is Far From the Land' (198), 'Dear Harp of My Country' (210) and 'Sing, Sing, Music Was Given' (227), as well as in numerous other pieces.[12] Of particular interest, however, are the instances in which (as in 'On Music') music and betrayal are conjoined. 'Oh! Blame Not the Bard' incorporates the dual sense of treachery (political treason and personal betrayal) introduced above:

> For 'tis treason to love her, and death to defend.
> Unpriz'd are her sons, till they've learned to betray (191)

At the same time the lyric insists upon music's role in formulating – and subsequently celebrating – an idea (an idea of Ireland and Irishness, in fact) worth fighting for. 'Avenging And Bright' (199) imagines a contemporary response to a famous act of betrayal from Irish history: the murder of the sons of Uisnech on the orders of King Conchobar Mac Nessa of Ulster. There is a contradiction at the heart of this lyric, however, and it resides in the demand for musical abrogation ('The harp shall be silent') in a musical form (the song itself). The same problem attends Moore's most explicit linkage of betrayal and music. In 'The Minstrel Boy', the 'warrior-bard' refers to his native country as a 'Land of song', proclaiming: 'Though all the world betrays thee, *One* sword, at least, thy rights shall guard, *One* faithful harp shall praise thee' (203, original emphases). The silence that is threatened by the destruction of the harp is belied, however, by the existence of Moore's song, and thus by the persistence of music in the context of Ireland's 'slavery'.

The lyric to 'On Music' maintains a complex economy of binary opposites: childhood and maturity; music and language; the ear and the eye; friendship/love and deception; pleasure and pain. The reference to 'betrayal' in the final verse appears to resonate in the first instance in relation to a 'non-political' discourse of love and friendship: despite face-to-face professions of commitment, it seems, the relationship between two individuals may be other than one of them suspects.

Whether music can in fact offer the unmediated access to truth claimed in the lyric is something we shall examine more closely below. In the meantime we should note that the interpersonal invocation of betrayal was closely linked (in contemporary revolutionary discourse as well as in Moore's own artistic practice) with a discourse of political betrayal in which the very meaning of 'treason' – the right to accuse someone of treason, as well as the right to feel betrayed – was itself at issue.

WORDSWORTHIAN ECHOES

There is yet another narrative of treason with which 'On Music' engages, in as much as Moore's short lyric displays the obvious influence of his contemporary, William Wordsworth. The effect is two-fold. The first element derives from the English poet's thesis on childhood, stated most forcefully in his 1807 'Ode: Intimations of Immortality from Recollections of Early Childhood'. This celebrated text (influenced no doubt by Rousseau) released powerful energies within modern culture which are still active today. Wordsworth proposed that the child bears traces of the 'glory' from which the soul has sprung, and that the wonder and joy (so different in kind and measure from adult pleasures) of which children are capable is evidence of their proximity to God. All too soon, however, 'Shades of the prison-house begin to close / Upon the growing boy' (1807a: 215). Adolescence and adulthood bring forgetting and immersion in the ways of the world; maturity is tinged with a constant sorrow, born from an intimation that 'there hath passed away a glory from the world' (214) and a vague desire for 'something that is gone' (215).

These intimations and desires manifest themselves in what the poet refers to as 'spots of time' (1799: 288), by which he appears to mean memories which are imprinted upon the mind with such power and clarity that they assume an emblematic presence within the consciousness of the subject. According to Wordsworth the most powerful 'spots of time' derive from Nature experienced during childhood; when re-experienced as memories, moreover, they exert a restorative influence upon the mature subject. Recollected 'spots of time' remind the adult, 'depressed / By trivial occupations and the round / Of ordinary intercourse', of the power of sensations experienced during childhood, and thus of the imminence of immortality. Two examples are cited in the original 'Two-Part Prelude' of 1799, although the most famous example is probably contained in the school classic 'I Wandered Lonely as a Cloud' (1807b), in which the pleasure of the dancing daffodils lies not only in their original apprehension but in each subsequent instance in which 'They flash upon that inward eye / Which is the bliss of solitude'. Although the language of treason is not deployed as such, there is a clear implication in Wordsworth's early poetry that adulthood constitutes a betrayal of the glories of childhood. Maturity represents a kind of 'fall' into knowledge; 'spots of time' offer the adult temporary relief from the sorrows of mortal life, but their true function is to keep alive the idea of pleasure untainted by knowledge of the phenomenal world. And just as the adult represents a betrayal of the child, so sensual reality represents a betrayal of Platonic 'reality' – 'that immortal sea' (1807a: 217) which surrounds the tiny island of consciousness we call life.

Moore was no worshipper at the shrine of 'the sublime Laker' (Dowden 1988: 1906), and indeed appeared to acquiesce with the opinion of many of his younger contemporaries in finding Wordsworth tedious and pompous.[13] Nevertheless, 'On Music' displays a clear Worthsworthian influence relatable to both of the elements described above. The first verse describes a classic 'spot of time', as the jaded adult hears a strain of music first encountered 'In days of boyhood'. The sound brings relief to a mature subject damaged by the exigencies of life, disappointed by feigned friendship, and cynical about false love. In the second verse, Moore's deployment of natural imagery – the 'oriental flowers' which retain a physical and emotional impact even after the flowers have died – recalls Wordsworth's daffodils. And as with the latter, the sound of 'notes we used to love' liberates the memory of past pleasures, while also providing pleasure for the remembering subject in the present. What Nature is for Wordsworth, in other words, music is for Moore.

Wordsworth employed strategic musical imagery in the 'Two-Part Prelude' as, for example, when he declares that 'The mind of man is fashioned and built up / Even as a strain of music', or when he describes 'the bleak music of that old stone wall' (1799: 234, 241). In the penultimate stanza of the 'Ode' he bids the birds 'sing, sing a joyous song! ... We in thought will join your throng' (1807a: 217). The latter is a particularly interesting image, given the debates regarding the derivation of language which were so actively engaged during the later eighteenth century – debates in which, once again, the concept of betrayal featured strongly.

LANGUAGE, MUSIC AND BETRAYAL IN ROUSSEAU

If Moore was influenced by Wordsworth on a range of conceptual and formal matters, then it seems clear that both men were influenced (directly or otherwise) by one of the most productive and most prominent thinkers of the age. The wide-ranging thought of Jean-Jacques Rousseau reverberates throughout the fifty-year period on either side of the century, and may be observed throughout 'On Music' in the representation of childhood, maturity, language, music and the relationships between all these. It is present most forcefully in Moore's short lyric in the representation of pleasure and betrayal.

'Everything is good coming from the hands of the Author of things, everything degenerates in the hands of man' (1979: 183) – thus Rousseau begins *Emile*, his narrative of a fictional experiment with childhood education. The sense of betrayal implied in this sentence is present throughout Rousseau's voluminous output, and it structures his thinking with regard to the many diverse subjects with which he engaged. It so happens that one of the most important of those subjects was music. In common with many of the late eighteenth century's greatest thinkers, Rousseau was obsessed with music. His interest extended to composition and performance, but it was as a 'philosopher' of music that he was most influential. In his *Letter on French Music* (1752), in two chapters of *The New Heloïse* (1761), in eight chapters of the *Essay on the Origin of Languages* (1763), and in a *Dictionary of Music* (1767) Rousseau wrote extensively on what he thought music was, how it worked, what sort of pleasure it afforded, and how these matters connected with his theories on other matters of human experience (for example, education and social organisation).

Music was especially important to Rousseau because he linked it directly to the origins of speech, and discovered in it the same symptoms of latter-day cultural decline which elsewhere he detected in speech itself.[14] 'Good' or 'proper' music was derived from melody; melody derived from human language, which itself first emerged when the species evolved to the point at which it needed to express complex emotions.

Rousseau was concerned to track the gradual overtaking of melody – which he understood to be the pure, spontaneous element of song – by harmony – which he characterised as the skilful arrangement of multiple musical voices in consort. He thought of harmony, in Jacques Derrida's terms, as a 'dangerous supplement' (1974: 141ff) with which culture diluted and perverted the natural energy of music. In fact, as Derrida demonstrates at length in Part II of *Of Grammatology*, Rousseau's *Essay* opposes speech to writing, as presence to absence, and liberty to servitude. For Rousseau, just as writing represented a perversion of some pre-historical moment of face-to-face speech in which language and subjectivity, individual and community, were wholly commensurate, so the process by which harmony overtook melody represented a perversion of nature by culture, a falling away from pristine interpersonal encounters in which melody and meaning were entirely commensurate, before the need for a musical score and before the abstract conventions and sophistries of harmony, or its even more insidious fellow, counterpoint.

If Wordsworthian echoes pervade the opening verse of 'On Music', the final one – consisting of an elaborate structure based on the relations between emotion (feeling), music, abstract thought and language – is redolent of Rousseau. In the latter's model, emotion precedes intellectual perception and would (in the infancy of the species) have been articulated in pre-linguistic interjections – a kind of super-sensitive music locked in to the emotions as they struck the present-oriented subject.[15] This system was compromised with the evolution of language, however, and its provision of abstract thought removed in space and time from the face-to-face encounter. Nevertheless, something of the power of that primordial system survives in modern music, and this accounts for its continuing attraction in 'civilised' society. Music, it appears, offers a fast-track to the emotions, without the need for the brittle medium of language which so readily facilitates falsity and feigning. In a civilisation crippled by the duplicities of abstract thought, music soothes the subject with the offer of emotional certainty.

Rousseau's theory of music links to his wider socio-political vision, in which various positive values (childhood, simplicity, speech, Nature) are betrayed by their binary opposites: adulthood, complexity, writing, culture. As Derrida demonstrates with such exhaustive detail in *On Grammatology*, however, Rousseau's own work cannot support such a division. In fact, the writings on music reveal his concept of Nature to be the product of cultural representation; and just as writing is ontologically wedded to the possibility of speech, so harmony is ontologically wedded to the possibility of melody. As Christopher Norris puts it: 'There is always a harmony *within* melody, no matter how carefully Rousseau attempts to keep the two principles apart' (1987: 108). To put it in the figurative terms which I have pursued throughout this chapter: harmony and melody remain 'friends' (with all the opportunities and complexities that such a relationship entails), despite the recurring instinct which characterises their relationship as that of betrayer and betrayed.

Bunting's championing of melody clearly allies him with Rousseau. The former, we recall, insisted on the integrity of the pure, ancient Irish melody over and against 'versions' of the same air; equally, he objected to modern adaptations which exposed the pristine melodic line to the alien concept of harmony. Just as it proved impossible for Rousseau to conceptualise the nature of music without revealing that harmony has been present from the outset as a fundamental element of music's natural resources, so Bunting could only preserve the notion of an Irish melody uncorrupted by harmony by acts of discursive violence. All Rousseau's key oppositions, in fact, disintegrate in the light of melody's inherent 'friendship' with harmony. This, in turn, brings us back to the question of the relationship between friendship and betrayal in the *Irish Melodies* in general, and in 'On Music' in particular.

CONCLUSION

The fear of interpersonal betrayal would appear to be a universal emotion among our species, and one that has as a consequence assumed a ubiquitous presence in cultural production. Such a fear haunts all those texts in which the subject invests their trust in some kind of emotional commitment – family, friendship, and love are probably the most common, although the 'team' narrative (sporting or adventurous, for example) in which diverse individuals come together to expedite a particular desire is also popular. This latter example broaches the realm of 'treason' – that is, when a group's (or team's) desire for change brings them into conflict with the established political dispensation. Besides fear of betrayal from within the group, each member is constituted as a traitor vis-à-vis the standing political power, which, among other things, persecutes opposition groups in order to maintain its monopoly on decisions regarding trust and treachery.

This was the situation facing the United Irishmen during the 1790s as they experienced treachery from within their organisation as well as (literal) condemnation from the political power they opposed. A modified variation of the same situation confronted Thomas Moore when, in the years shortly after the abortive military actions, he began to set words to the 'original' melodies collected by Bunting and others. Each element of the process was fraught with the possibility of treason and betrayal: the content of the lyrics, the series' unexpected success in England, the commercial exploitation of the 'pure gold' of the melodies, and the exposure of the latter to an 'alien' musical system. Among all these difficulties, Moore clung to the one thing which, he believed, was above suspicion: music. As we have observed in relation to Bunting, Wordsworth and Rousseau, however, this was a misguided conviction. The appeal to music's reputed location outwith discourse – outwith history, in fact – was vain, for nothing, it so happens, is more discursive, more historicised, than music. This should not be a cause for impeachment, however; Moore was not the only figure, before or since, to struggle with this realisation.

Music in James Joyce's 'The Dead': Sources, Contexts, Meanings

One of the most famous passages in the canon of Irish literature occurs in 'The Dead', the long short story by James Joyce which concludes *Dubliners*. A middle-aged, middle-class man named Gabriel Conroy is preparing to leave the city-centre home of three female relatives after an evening of Christmas festivities. He is arrested by the sight of his wife Gretta standing at the turn of the stairs, apparently enraptured by the sound of music drifting down from the next floor. The song to which she is listening is a folk ballad entitled 'The Lass of Aughrim', sung on this occasion by a professional tenor named Bartell D'Arcy. Later, we discover that Gretta has been profoundly affected by the song, apparently because it reminds her of a boy named Michael Furey with whom she was romantically (although innocently) involved during her youth in Galway. As his wife drifts off to sleep, Gabriel stares wistfully out of the window of their Gresham Hotel room, reflecting upon the nature of time, love and death. Even as he does so, he becomes (like Stephen Dedalus, Leopold Bloom, Richard Rowan and Humphrey Chimpden Earwicker) a symbol of a peculiarly Irish response to modernity, and thus an alternative to the subject-hero of the hegemonic nationalism with which Joyce's career was coterminous.

If Joyce had never written another word, his reputation as an exceptional artist would have been secured by *Dubliners* in general, and by 'The Dead' in particular. The latter is a masterpiece of control and insight – 'a lynchpin in Joyce's work' as his biographer Richard Ellmann put it (1983: 252) – in which the experiences of a group of unremarkable people in a Dublin house at a particular point in time come to resonate throughout the history of the island, as well as outwards to the experience of the species as a whole.

Such commentary as the text has attracted has tended to be

'disciplined' – by which I mean that analyses, naturally enough, tend to be dominated by the training and the purview of the analyst. Thus we have not only the biographical text of the biographer Richard Ellmann, but the literary critical text of the literary critic Terence Brown (1998); the folkloric text of the folklorist Hugh Shields (1990, 1993); and the historical text of the music historian Harry White (1999). All these 'productions' offer excellent and compelling readings of 'The Dead' in their own terms. In this chapter I wish to attempt a more integrated approach, however, in the hope of an understanding which would itself be the synthesised product of a variety of insights derived from biographical, folkloric, historical, musicological and philosophical discourses. For present purposes, such an understanding necessitates engagement with three interrelated elements: a) the ballad text which stands at the centre of Joyce's celebrated story; b) the musical context within which the narrative is set, including an appreciation of the author's relationship with music; and c) the potential philosophical bases of the text's key scene, in which a man looks at a woman listening to music.

'THE LASS OF AUGHRIM'

Ballads constitute an intriguing form of cultural textuality. Historically speaking, the ballad is one of the most successful of musical forms, and one of the reasons for this must be the 'universal' themes with which it typically deals: love, belief, crime, humour, etc. At the same time, ballads are notoriously protean when considered in historical and geographical terms. The 'same' text may exist in multiple forms, with variant lyrics, melodies and narrative structures dispersed over numerous 'versions'. A suggestive analogy for this process might be the biological variation that occurs in natural species when considered from a range of geographical and historical perspectives. Like species, ballads constantly mutate in relation to the environment through which they move, adapting again and again in response to the host of factors (including quite centrally indigenous musical traditions) which bear upon their existence. The task of tracking these variations is the work of professional folklorists and musicologists, some of whose work I shall allude to in the following observations.[1]

The first recorded version of the song upon which 'The Lass of

Aughrim' is based is from an early eighteenth-century Scottish MS source (ca. 1730) entitled 'Fair Isabell of Rochroyall' (Child 1905: 161). Already present at this stage are a number of elements which, with different emphases and significance, recur throughout the subsequent variants. A noble woman rides to the castle of her lover, Lord Gregory, having dreamt about him. When she asks for admittance, Lord Gregory's mother pretends to be her own son, and questions the woman on the intimate details of the relationship. When the mother lies about Lord Gregory's whereabouts, the woman bemoans the prospects for herself and her child (of whom Gregory is presumably the father), at which point – inconsistent with her otherwise treacherous intentions – the mother pledges support. Lord Gregory wakens from a dream of his lover, only to be told by his mother that Isabell has recently departed from the castle. He curses his mother for her interference, and sets off at once to follow Isabell. He soon finds her dead body, however (there is no mention of the child), at which point he too succumbs.[2]

The roots of 'Fair Isabell of Rochroyall' lie beyond historical scrutiny, although its form and language led Child to suggest that it emerged from the oral ballad tradition of the late medieval period (1885: 215). The Irish folklorist Hugh Shields points to a parallel 'in European ballads, to the scene in which the admission of a visitor is made conditional on a test by love tokens' (1990: 59). Another authority claims, however, that '[no] continental version exists, and only a few in America' (Leach 1955: 253); unlike the majority of the Scottish ballads that began to be systematically noted during the eighteenth century, therefore, the narrative may be indigenous to that part of the world.[3] Do we dare to speculate on the relationship between text and reality – that is, the possibility of an Ur-text which is based, as many occasional ballads are, on actual historical events? The answer must be: no. No doubt every culture has produced historical variations on the basic story, in which the fate of young lovers is manipulated by third parties motivated by jealousy or vested interests. It is the archetypal nature of the text which has contributed to its success, however, and indeed which drew Joyce to it as a source of the energies he wished to activate within his own work.

The ballad's modern Scottish credentials were cemented by the influential version entitled 'The Bonny Lass of Lochroyan' included in his two-volume *Ancient and Modern Scottish Songs* by the collector David

Herd in 1776.⁴ It was around this period, moreover, that the ballad made its way to Ulster and from there to the rest of Ireland. Shields (1993: 47) has constructed a conjectural cartography of the process:

'Lass of Roch Royal'	S. Scotland
'Lass of Loch Ryan'	do.
'Annie O'Loughran'	N. Co. Down
'Lass of Aughrim'	Midlands, Cos. Galway, Waterford, Cork
('Lass of Ocram'	England)
'Lass of Arrams'	Cos. Cork, Clare
'Lass of Ormond'	Co. Clare

Discussing the same subject in a different context, Shields further suggests that 'the phonetic changes and the changes of toponym are so well in accord that the ballad seems very likely to have spread through Ireland – some two centuries or more ago – in a relatively simple movement from North to South' (1990: 60).

There is some debate as to whether Joyce was familiar with the ballad before he heard Nora Barnacle singing it some time after their first meeting on 10 June 1904 and his commencement of 'The Dead' about two years later (Curran 1968: 41–2; Geckle 1974: 86–7). The thirty-five verses which, according to his sisters, Joyce purported to know while still living at home, points to 'Fair Isabell of Rochroyall', although how and why he would have encountered that fairly arcane text at that time is not easily understandable. (He is more likely to have encountered a thirty-six stanza version, entitled 'Fair Annie of Lochroyan', included in *The Ballad Book* (115–21) by the Irish writer William Allingham in 1864.) In any event, Nora's version – learned from the singing of her mother, and heard in its entirety by Joyce when he visited Mrs Barnacle at her Galway home in August 1909 – was in all likelihood derived from the version listed as 'H' in Child (1885: 224–5), entitled 'The Lass of Aughrim', and based on a version sung by an agricultural labourer in Tyrrelspass, County Westmeath around 1820. This version includes a stanza (#3) which closely resembles the one quoted by Joyce in 'The Dead':

> The dew wets my yellow locks,
> The rain wets my skin,
> The babe's cold in my arms,
> Oh Gregory, let me in!

'The Lass of Aughrim' differs significantly from 'Fair Isabell of Rochroyall' and many of its Scottish variants in so far as the mother's role as saboteur of the liaison is excised; it is Lord Gregory himself who questions the lass and who turns her (and their child) from his door.[5] From the caring, betrayed lover of the earlier version, in other words, he becomes a classic folk demon – the callous aristocrat who exploits and abandons a poor 'lass' of the people. (This is also the pattern in the version by Robert Burns from 1793.) An apt example in this instance would be 'The Lord of the Valley' who, in *Moore's Melody*, 'with false vows came' across the dark moor, leaving an indelible 'stain upon the snow of fair Eveleen's fame' (1910: 187).

Another key moment in the generally southwards migration of the ballad was the celebrated version entitled 'The Lass of Arrams', performed by Mrs Elizabeth ('Bess') Cronin and recorded at her Macroom home (in County Cork) in 1952 by the folklorist Alan Lomax (Kennedy and Lomax, 1961). This version retains many features inherited from 'Fair Isabell of Rochroyall', including the reference to the class equality between the protagonists; the confrontation between the lass and her lover's mother; the latter's feigning and unexpected offer of assistance with the baby; reference to the exchange of love tokens; Lord Gregory's awakening and censure of his mother; his search for the lass and the implication of their bond in death. Mrs Cronin's version also retains a variation on the lines quoted in 'The Dead':

> The rain beats at my yellow locks and the dew wets me still,
> My babe is cold in my arms, Lord Gregory let me in.

It is difficult to understand how Mrs Cronin's version might have co-existed alongside the one known by Mrs Barnacle, or how the former could have been *re-integrated* into the folk tradition (from an earlier Scottish version) once Irish versions such as 'The Lass of Aughrim' had gained currency. Nevertheless, it is clear that Mrs Cronin's mid-twentieth-century version retains links with the early eighteenth-century, thirty-five-verse version referenced as 'Child 76A'; it is likewise clear that the differences between Mrs Barnacle's 'Lass of Aughrim' and Mrs Cronin's 'Lass of Arrams' present a number of problems which bear significantly upon an interpretation of 'The Dead'.

Because of the central role afforded the ballad in Joyce's story, the relationships between Gabriel and Gretta on the one hand, and between

Joyce himself and Nora on the other, seem to invite comparison with the one between Lord Gregory and 'the lass'. In 'The Lass of Aughrim' (the version derived – via Nora and her mother – from Child H), that relationship may be regarded as a tragedy of betrayal and exploitation.[6] Gabriel's culpability is thus implicit: with his privileged access to metropolitan culture, he is (like Lord Gregory) guilty in some manner and to some degree of the moral exploitation of a simple country girl. His narcissism, materialism and inability to empathise are exposed by her capacity for 'love'; and this was an inference which fitted well with Joyce's impugnation of the central male character, and of the patriarchal culture which that character in some senses embodied.

If we retain the figure of the intervening mother, as in the versions derived from 'Fair Isabell of Rochroyall' (including 'The Lass of Arrams'), however, a different reading becomes available. This is the understanding pursued by Donagh MacDonagh (1969) and George L. Geckle (1974), both of whom assume a straightforward analogy between Gabriel, Lord Gregory and James Joyce himself. Such a reading points to the fact that Gabriel's mother plays a role not unlike Lord Gregory's, in as much as both women oppose (for equally selfish reasons) what they consider to be ill-fated attachments for their sons. One could add that Gabriel's vision of Gretta on the stairs might also be considered to echo the point at which Gregory awakens from a dream, while their journey back to the Gresham Hotel – including periods in which Gretta walks 'before him' – (Joyce 2000: 168) – recalls the lord's pursuit of the dismissed lass. Once there, as Geckle points out, 'Gabriel has in one sense a "comely corps" in the bed next to him since Gretta "had locked in her heart for so many years that image of her lover's eyes"' (1974: 94). The imagery with which 'The Dead' concludes is likewise an echo of the death of the ballad lovers: Gabriel '*stretched* himself cautiously along under the *sheets* and lay down beside his wife' who 'was *fast asleep*' (175–6, added emphases) – a description which rehearses the double death at the end of 'Fair Isabell of Rochroyall' and 'The Lass of Arrams'. The inference is that Gabriel and Gretta are now romantically 'dead' to each other, their fate sealed by the inimical intervention of a third party (the dead Michael Furey).[7]

The image of Gabriel as a 'good' Lord Gregory is attractive and interesting, and all the more so if one extrapolates (as MacDonagh and Ellmann do) from the Gabriel/Gretta relationship to the Joyce/Nora one that underpins it. A question mark must remain over the extent to which Gabriel can assume the role of the betrayed lover, however. To my mind, it is more likely that the lord/lass relationship pertains to the aborted liaison between Gretta and Michael Furey, with Gabriel figured (alongside his own mother) as one of those implicated in the separation of the young lovers. Such, at any rate, is what Gabriel begins to suspect as he ruminates in the dark hotel room on his relationship with his emotionally estranged wife. In such an analysis, in fact, Gabriel may be regarded as neither a 'good' nor a 'bad' Gregory, but someone, like many of the protagonists in *Dubliners*, cut off from passion entirely, neither hero nor anti-hero but a 'non-hero' located outwith life itself. That, to Joyce's mind, was the real betrayal and the real tragedy: the denial, through a combination of political, historical and social circumstances, of contemporary Irish people's right to an emotional life. This raises the issue of Irish history, and the way in which music functioned within that society.

THE MUSICAL CONTEXTS OF 'THE DEAD'

Much research in recent years has been undertaken to try to understand the breadth of musical activity taking place in Ireland during the nineteenth century. In his book *The Keeper's Recital*, Harry White offered a detailed overview of the field, focusing in particular on the development of art, folk (or traditional) and religious music throughout the period. White describes a situation in which the possibility of a valid Irish art music is gradually, but decisively, eclipsed by the emergence of a 'folk' sensibility rooted in the notion of an authentic Irish identity which is itself preserved within the island's vernacular music.

This situation is reflected to a great extent in 'The Dead', a text which (like the rest of *Dubliners*) is inundated with musical references, and in which (as so many commentators have reminded us) comprehension of such references is key to understanding the emotional dynamics of the story. Reference is made throughout the narrative to various styles with which those in attendance would have been more or less familiar. Mary Jane has 'the organ in Haddington Road' (138) and Aunt Julia 'was still the leading soprano in Adam and Eve's'; later, Aunt Kate expostulates the decision (decreed in 1903 by Pope Pius X) of the Catholic Church to expel women from church choirs. Through such details we learn of music's central role in contemporary religious discourse, and the extent to which it was implicated in the development of a form of Irish identity which was itself moving into a position of discursive hegemony during this period.

'Popular' music is also represented with the story. The word 'goloshes' reminds Gretta of 'Christy Minstrels' (142), a generic name for the blackface troupes which were popular throughout Britain and Ireland in the latter part of the nineteenth century. Later, Freddy Malins makes reference to the Gaiety pantomime, another form of popular entertainment. Freddy has been particularly impressed with a 'negro chieftain' who has, he maintains, 'one of the finest tenor voices he had ever heard'.[8] Bartell D'Arcy's 'careless' response is indicative of the gulf in taste (at least so far as he feels it) between such vulgar fare and the music to which he, as a professional, trained singer, subscribes.

Such a model contains its own gradations and levels, however. 'Proper' art music is invoked within the text in the pedagogical practice associated with Aunt Kate and Mary Jane, and also with the latter's performance of her 'Academy' piece (referring to the Royal Irish Academy of Music). Although he likes music, Gabriel cannot listen to his cousin's performance; distracted by the task in front of him, he has no intellectual space to give over to the consideration of such 'pure' – that is, non-programmatic (and apparently non-functional) – music.

Dance music represented an area in which popular and art traditions overlapped to a certain degree during the nineteenth century. As the vernacular form became infused with the values of art music (single-authored composition, large-scale ensemble performance, the use of devices and techniques borrowed from sonata form), so the meaning and function of dancing as a social practice evolved. The institutionalisation of bodily movement in public space, and in particular the intermingling of the sexes, rendered dancing an immensely popular, and at the same time potentially dangerous, social practice (Clark and Crisp 1981). Some of these values and developments are active within 'The Dead', the occasion for which, after all, is described as 'the Misses Morkan's annual dance' (138). During the evening various characters either participate in, or perform accompanying music for, waltzes (143), quadrilles (144) and lancers (147), and such music occupies a strategic position in relation to all the other genres introduced during the course of the story.

Another 'grey' area, musically speaking, was opera, one of the most popular forms among the Irish middle class during the nineteenth century (Allen 1998). This is a fact borne out by the ubiquity of its presence within the work of that class's great chronicler. In 'The Dead', opera forms a central topic of conversation during dinner, with Bartell D'Arcy – a tenor about whom '[all] Dublin is raving' (145) – taking a prominent role.[9] The discussion, with its references to particular works, singers and styles, communicates important information about the cultural values of this class at this moment in Irish history. More than that, however, the discourse of opera introduces themes – particularly themes of love and death – which interact in a highly subtle manner with the main concerns of the story. To take one obvious example, Aunt Julia's rendition of 'Arrayed for the Bridal' from Bellini's *I Puritani di Scozia* (1835) demonstrates her familiarity with a certain strand of popular European opera, and associates her (and her class) with the cultural capital located therein. At the same time, the song itself figures ironically in relation to Julia's status as a spinster approaching the end of her own life, and more poignantly still on the opportunity for consummated love missed by Gretta and Michael Furey.

Signally absent from all this musical activity is the indigenous folk tradition itself – until, that is, Bartell D'Arcy's unexpected performance of (a part of) 'The Lass of Aughrim'. As White and others have revealed, a variety of figures (collectors, composers, ideologues) had gradually emerged to insist over the course of the nineteenth century that this tradition was fundamental to any corporate notion of national identity. Gradually the conviction arose that, because of its antiquity, its roots among the cultural practices of the population, its geographical specificity – because of these and numerous other factors which could be strategically introduced into any debate, the 'folk' music of the peasantry articulated the truth of Irishness in a way that no popular or art (or variation thereof) tradition ever could. Such a conviction ensured, as White puts it, that 'the ethnic repertory ... would predominate in all considerations of music as a modern art form in Ireland' (1998: 52).

It is just such a conviction, seemingly, that Joyce invoked in 'The Dead' with the introduction of a supposedly authentic native ballad characterised by 'the old Irish tonality' (165). The extra-textual status of 'The Lass of Aughrim' alludes to the growing strength of a nationalist movement (and that movement's convictions vis-à-vis its cultural identity) with which the protagonists of his fiction are obliged to come to terms. At the same time, and as we have seen at length in the preceding section, the song itself tells a story which – with its dramatic portrayal of powerful emotions such as desire and jealousy – reflects on the fate of the characters within 'The Dead' (Furey, Gretta and Gabriel) and on that of the writer himself (Joyce's complex attitude towards Nora Barnacle and her early attachments).

Generations of critics have by and large acquiesced with the contention, most elegantly formulated by Terence Brown, that Joyce invoked 'The Lass of Aughrim' towards the end of his story in order '[to set] in opposition the music with which an Irish Catholic middle class at the turn of the century could feel comfortable and a music which speaks for a more vital, dangerous territory of the national consciousness' (1998: 39). However, such critical orthodoxy begs the question: wherein does such 'vitality' and such 'danger' reside?

Not, I think we may reasonably assume, in B'Artell Darcy's performance which, coming as it does from a singer trained in *bel canto* style, would have been possessed of a vocal 'grain' fundamentally at odds with that required by a vernacular ballad. The discrepancy between the art tradition (to which he subscribes) and the vernacular tradition (from which, in principle at least, 'The Lass of Aughrim' is drawn) may be clearly heard in a comparison of the version performed by the Irish tenor Frank Patterson in John Huston's film version of *The Dead* (1987) with the version performed by Mrs Elizabeth Cronin referenced above. Leaving aside for a moment the 'authenticity' of the song-text itself, Patterson gives a good impression of what D'Arcy's performance of the fragment would have sounded like, in so far as his voice (like that of the fictional character he plays) has been trained in the *bel canto* techniques of the western art tradition. A more apposite example is provided, perhaps, on a recording made less than a decade after the time at which 'The Dead' is set: John McCormack's performance of Moore's 'The Harp that Once Through Tara's Halls' (Hast and Scott 2004). I say 'apposite' because it seems clear that D'Arcy's voice (like that of McCormack and Patterson) would have been much more 'at home' with *Moore's Melody* than with a song such as 'The Lass of Aughrim'. When a trained tenor performs one of Moore's songs, voice and song 'converge' in terms of both their conceptual (what the songs are about) and formal (how they are sung) discourses. D'Arcy's attempt at a traditional ballad represents an excursion into very uncertain territory indeed, however. The hesitation Gabriel discerns in his performance stems from more than just uncertainty about the words of the song, or hoarseness brought on by a cold: it derives in the main, I would suggest, from the fact that this particular performance instantiates a clash of fundamental cultural assumptions.[10]

Mrs Cronin 'inhabits' 'The Lass of Arrams' in an extremely comfortable and confident manner – in a very different manner, that is to say, to Bartell D'Arcy's halting, truncated rendition (as described by Joyce). This must be put down to the fact that, unlike the fictional character, she was 'at home' in an ongoing tradition in which cultural artefacts such as the ballad are long-established, familiar currency. If we accept that the power Joyce attempted to invoke with his introduction of 'The Lass of Aughrim' at this juncture in the narrative may be heard encoded in Mrs Cronin's rendition of 'The Lass of Arrams', we must also accept that a voice further removed (in terms of breathing, dynamics, phrasing, resonance and so on) from that of McCormack or Patterson (or, by inference, Bartell D'Arcy) is difficult to imagine. To this list of inauspicious ballad interpreters, moreover, must be added one more name: Michael Furey, who, as Gretta says, 'was going to study singing only for his health' (174). No doubt the version Furey sang for Gretta before his untimely death would have been the one known to his fellow Galwegian Mrs Barnacle – a version (similar to Child H) which had become established in the area over the course of the nineteenth century. Furey's aspirations take him away from both Mrs Barnacle and Mrs Cronin, however, and towards D'Arcy's tenor tradition. Quite how such a voice could be capable of communicating the 'primal, elemental, passionate Ireland' or the 'more vital, dangerous territory of the national consciousness' as described by Terence Brown, however, is uncertain.

The fact is that 'The Lass of Aughrim' represents an extremely unlikely choice for a singer such as Bartell D'Arcy to attempt. The latter shows every sign of being, like Gabriel, an internationalist for whom the culture of his native land holds a limited attraction. He is in bad form throughout the evening; it may be the cold of which he complains later, or it may be the 'conceit' (150) of which he is accused by Gretta. Certainly, he is patronising towards his hosts and fellow guests alike during the discussion at dinner. D'Arcy claims not to be able to remember

'The Lass of Aughrim' when questioned by Gretta, but this in itself begs some vital questions: where, when and why would a singer trained in the European art style have learned a song from the vernacular tradition in the first place?[11] Would he not have been much more at home with one of the *Melodies* – Moore's 'Oh, Ye Dead!', for example?[12]

The most notable thing about Joyce's invocation of 'The Lass of Aughrim' in 'The Dead' is that it represents a failed performance, and as such a failure to register on the part of the culture that it supposedly embodies. D'Arcy does not know the song very well, and what he does know, he does not sing very well. This could be put down to his unfamiliarity with the song (both lyrics and melody), or to the cold from which he claims to be suffering. The true failure of his performance, however, resides in the fact that it is at odds with the performative model embodied in the song itself – the one encapsulated at a later date in the recording of a related ballad by Mrs Elizabeth Cronin. Ultimate responsibility for this failure lies not with the ballad or with the singer, however, but with Joyce himself.

Received critical wisdom has it that it was the power of the ballad tradition, as revealed to the author through contact with Nora Barnacle and her mother, that Joyce wished to invoke in order to throw into relief the compromised values of the dominant culture as depicted in the rest of the text and as embodied in the character of Gabriel. Bartell D'Arcy's performance does not *represent* that tradition, however; the latter, rather, is referenced in order to provide a moral presence without which the narrative could not function. Yes, Joyce invokes a vernacular musical tradition in order to expedite a critique of contemporary Ireland with its complex of Catholic, bourgeois and nationalist values; but that vernacular tradition is denied a coherent or meaningful representative voice within the text. It is, however, like Michael Furey (the singer with whom it is mistakenly associated), dead – available only as a memory that shadows the living. In bringing the radically inappropriate values of his own tradition to bear upon it, D'Arcy's performance represents a form of sonic tourism (very familiar in latter years) in which a marginal musical tradition is invoked for its supposed properties – exoticness, colour, authenticity – but in such a way as to deny that tradition an active role within the present.

ON LISTENING

Gabriel is *'gazing* up the staircase' at Gretta, who is *'listening* to something' (165, emphases added). Analytical theories relating to sight are plentiful and well-established: 'Vision', as Martin Jay suggests, 'has been accorded a special role in Western epistemology since the Greeks ... The role of vision in the imaginative history of Western man is no less important' (1986: 176). The notion of 'the male gaze' became a cornerstone of feminist critical theory in the 1970s, since which time it has been widely deployed in analyses of the ways in which the female figure is strategically – yet consistently – objectified by the gaze of the male subject. Before that (and contributing to the feminist development in some important respects), sight had figured as an important methodological consideration in various philosophical and psychoanalytical systems. Phenomenology, for example, is principally a philosophy of 'the seen', concerned with the immediate perception of the thing-in-itself as opposed to the intellectual abstractions of the Platonic tradition. 'The gaze' played an equally significant role for Jacques Lacan, in whose work it represents a central mechanism for the analysis of subject/object relations.

Figure 1 - Angelica Huston as Gretta

The image of Gabriel 'gazing up at his wife' offers a classic opportunity for sight-centred analysis. It is entirely characteristic, for example, that the male's initial impulse should be, firstly, to rationalise the sight by transposing it into an analytical discourse (Gabriel asks himself what the image of Gretta standing listening to music is a symbol of); and secondly, to objectify that image: 'If he were a painter he would paint her in that attitude.'[13] There is no image which cannot be imagined to symbolise something; by the same token, there is no image which cannot be artistically rendered. Symbols and paintings represent safe, familiar and, above all, *empowering* territory for Gabriel; they reside within, and at the same time confirm, a discourse of constitutive male agency with which, as an intelligent, educated male, he identifies. The act of self-interrogation ('He asked himself …' [165]) might appear to indicate uncertainty and/or loss of agency. In fact, such an act confirms both the presence and the agency of a subject – one prone, moreover, to subjecting material phenomena to regimes of abstract thought. The presence and the agency thus confirmed are then echoed in the imagined acts of painting and naming: Gretta's attitude is to be captured in a painting entitled *Distant Music*.

It is this objectified vision of 'his wife' that excites the powerful feelings which gradually overtake Gabriel. He continues to gaze at her as they make their way home from the party, culminating in the moment in the hotel room when he turns from the window to watch her undress. The language in the intervening time has become increasingly animated, not to say violent: he feels 'proud, joyful, tender, valorous' (168); 'He longed to defend her against something' (168); he experiences 'a keen pang of lust' (169), and imagines running away with Gretta 'with wild and radiant hearts to a new adventure' (170). As the narrative climax approaches, the language becomes more sexually charged:

> He could have flung his arms about her hips and held her still for his arms were trembling with desire to seize her and only the stress of his nails against the palms of his hands held the wild impulse of his body in check … He longed to be master of her strange mood … He longed to cry to her from his soul, to crush her body against his, to overmaster her … He was in such a fever of rage and desire … (170–1).

It is interesting to note that throughout this process Gabriel retains a measure of distance between his sense of self and the supposedly overpowering emotions that he is experiencing. He is aware, for example, of feeling 'proud' and 'joyful'; the 'new adventure' represents an attempt to narrativise his current attitude towards Gretta. The increasingly forceful vocabulary, meanwhile, represents an attempt to discover a discourse within which to express the advance of Gabriel's lust: he *feels* desire, certainly, but he also feels (as a writer and a critic) that 'desire' is a function of the discursive regimes within which it is activated. In other words, Gabriel is gazing not only at Gretta, but at himself. Her image has enabled him to become a desiring subject, a 'lover' – a role requiring an array of specialised gestures, emotions and languages. It is a role into which Gabriel throws himself with relish; the more he looks, the more he becomes the *subject who looks*, with all the power (and danger) encoded into such a position. There is another level to the relationship, moreover. For even as he gazes, Gabriel longs to be the object of someone else's gaze – a desire made explicit in his seduction fantasy, when he imagines that Gretta 'would turn and look at him' (169) as a prelude to sexual intercourse. This desire is overtly dramatised as Gabriel moves towards Gretta after her initial outburst:

> As he passed in the way of the cheval-glass he caught sight of himself in full length, his broad, well-filled shirt-front, the face whose expression always puzzled him when he saw it in a mirror and his glimmering gilt-rimmed eye-glasses. (172)

This moment – a classic mirror-scene in which the subject becomes the simultaneous object of his own gaze – is an extremely complex one. One thing it clearly represents, however, is a tacit acknowledgement of the reciprocity of subject/object relations instantiated in the moment of the gaze.[14]

An analysis based on looking can only take us so far, however. At some point we are obliged to acknowledge that the object of Gabriel's gaze is not passive; rather, she is engaged in a sensory act – listening – which stands outwith and in opposition to what Jay calls 'the empire of the gaze'. After millennia of marginalisation, 'listening' has emerged as a point of interest in a range of disciplines in recent times. If such interest was in part an effect of an 'anti-ocular' trend within twentieth-century French philosophy, it also represents an acknowledgement on the part of those with an academic interest in music of just how little is known about the cognitive processes, or indeed the philosophical implications, of listening.

A substantial literature now exists addressing the question (or rather, to the complex array of questions) of what occurs when we listen to music. One strand within the field of music psychology focuses specifically on an issue which is of particular relevance in the current context: the ability of music to excite strong emotional responses in the listener. We accept the evidence of the text that 'The Lass of Aughrim' has a profound effect on Gretta – indeed, it is crucial for the structure of the narrative (to say nothing yet of its meaning) that it should. Music psychology and music aesthetics encourage us to inquire into the cognitive and musicological processes whereby a particular sound precipitates a particular emotional response in the listening subject (Clarke 2005; Handel 1989; Levinson 1997). Is it somehow determined by factors intrinsic to the sound ('the old Irish tonality', perhaps)? If so, what role is played by the listener's familiarity with the sound, and their musical competence (or lack thereof)? Is Gretta responding primarily to the melody, the lyric, the 'grain' of the voice, or to some complex of all three? Does the 'meaning' of the sound emerge in the moment of hearing or is it the result of a subsequent (and separate) cognitive process? Is meaning dependent on an educated sense of the overall shape of the musical text? What part do memory and association play in the emotional response to music?

These are interesting and potentially enlightening questions. An analysis driven by such a methodology would be limited, however, and not least because (as one of the leading figures in the field has admitted) 'little is known about precisely what it is in the music that [listeners] are responding to', and further: 'There is no generally accepted theory of the emotions and how they interact with cognition' (Sloboda 2005: 209, 213). There is besides a rather more fundamental objection which relates to the appropriateness of speculating upon the cognitive processes of fictional characters. Like sight-based analysis, then, it seems that music psychology can only take us so far. We have to look elsewhere (and listen otherwise) if we wish to discover a more convincing interpretation of Joyce's famous scene.

In a short but suggestive study of the subject, Jean-Luc Nancy claims that philosophy has always worked to convert 'listening' into 'understanding'. What he means by this is that the listening subject is constantly invited to interpret 'sonorousness' as 'meaning' under the aegis of one or another philosophical system which is itself more or less adapted to the listening context. The act of listening is, in this sense, a confirmation of meaningfulness itself, and of the subjects who create and understand meaning: 'To be listening will always ... be to be straining toward or in an approach to the self' (2007: 9). According to Nancy, such a process precludes true listening, and this is because the traditional philosophical subject 'does not concentrate his ear on musical resonance but rather converts it ahead of time into the object of an intention that configures it' (20). The philosopher Husserl, for example, may have likened the awareness of time to the process of listening to a melody; according to Nancy, however, the father of phenomenology '[persisted] in "seeing" the melody instead of listening to it' (21).

In opposition to the 'hearing' subject of western philosophy, Nancy proposes what he calls a 'resonant subject', who is in fact not a 'subject' at all in the conventional philosophical sense, but a kind of constant deferral of subjectivity, of meaning, and of understanding. Such a subject may be identified by

> an intensive spacing of a rebound that does not end in any return to self without immediately relaunching, as an echo, a call to that same self. While the subject of the target is always already given, posed in itself to its *point of view*, the subject of listening is always still yet to come, spaced, traversed, and called by itself, *sounded* by itself ...' (21, original emphases).

The distinguishing characteristic of the resonant subject is its relationship to time. It is commonly accepted that music is the most time-oriented of the arts, in so far as it functions with reference to a past and a future which bear constantly upon the sound which fills the present. The discipline of musicology helps us, among other things, to understand the temporality of the musical text (it was with reference to this notion of temporality that Husserl theorised the phenomenological subject). There is a temporality beyond the musical text, however (which the text nevertheless gestures to), and it is to this temporality that the resonant subject attends:

> It is a question of hope: not a hope that promises itself possible futures, but rather an expectation that, without expecting anything, lets a touch of eternity come and come again (66).

The resonant subject who 'listens' rather than 'hears' is not approachable in terms of conventional temporality; instead, they temporarily inhabit a time-space outside time and outside understanding (whether considered in musicological or phenomenological terms).[15] That, after all, is what music is for:

> Music is the art of making the outside of time return to every time, making return to every moment the beginning that listens to itself beginning and beginning again. In resonance the inexhaustible return of eternity is played – and listened to (67).

My contention is that Gretta represents just such a resonant subject as she stands at the turn of the stairs, listening to a fragment of song drifting down from an upper floor; and further, that it is Gabriel's apprehension of this resonant subjectivity (or rather, his initial desperate misconstruction of it) that accounts for the vehemence of his response to her.

Critics have always responded to Gretta's experience as Gabriel himself does: by seeking to understand what she 'hears' – that is, the *meaning* of 'The Lass of Aughrim' as she apprehends it in the moment at which she becomes aware of the sound. Gretta's subsequent comments in the hotel bedroom serve as the basis for such a critical gesture; so, the song reminds her of a suitor from her Galway youth, which leads her husband to reflect on their relationship and in particular on his sense of self, which leads in turn to his epiphany regarding the relationship between the living and the dead. Gabriel is excited, and then frightened, by what he suspects Gretta to have heard in 'The Lass of Aughrim'; speculation regarding the reasons for these emotional responses have determined the critical parameters within which 'The Dead' is available for analysis. With this basic schema in place, any number of discursive emphases are then possible: political, psychoanalytical, aesthetic, feminist, religious, autobiographical – even musicological. All such discourses share an understanding of Gretta as a discursive subject – which is to say, a philosophical subject who 'hears' only the music's call to selfhood.

The insistence on 'hearing' represents an assault upon Gretta's right to listen, where the latter verb signifies not a *philosophical* action oriented towards the understanding subject, but a *musical* gesture oriented towards the non-subject who becomes the vessel, the instrument as it were, by means of which hope resonates. This is a gesture, moreover, which takes place (as remarked above) outside philosophical time; in which analysis, Gretta is neither in search of a 'possible future' (as Gabriel suspects at one point) nor lamenting the absence of a possible past which she might have shared with Michael Furey. Rather, the moment of pure listening locates Gretta within non-temporal eternity, and this is a moment about which philosophy can speculate but which it can never 'know' – hence, its fascination for a philosophical subject such as Gabriel. It is the eternal present within 'The Lass of Aughrim' to which Gretta responds – the moment of constant beginning, constant expectation, hope constantly resounding yet never realised.

It does not matter that Gretta subsequently rationalises her response to 'The Lass of Aughrim' in philosophical terms – as loss, sorrow, disappointed hope, frustrated desire, whatever. Her resonant (non-) subjectivity remains in potential within the various philosophical selves which circumstances made available to her, and which criticism has assigned to her. Neither does it matter that she is not (or not particularly) musical: the moment of her listening stands as a profoundly musical moment. As Nancy says: 'Music is the art of the hope for resonance … of making the outside of time return to every time' (67). It is this art – attractive, powerful, mysterious, frightening – which Gretta practises on the stairs as she listens to Bartell D'Arcy singing 'The Lass of Aughrim'; and it is this hope – so alien to his own mode of being in the world – which Gabriel senses in his wife as he gazes at her. No wonder he was impressed; no wonder he was terrified.

Paddy Sad and Paddy Mad: Music and the Condition of Irishness

'Our national music ... like our national character, admits of no medium in sentiment; it either sinks our spirit to despondency by its heart-breaking pathos, or elevates it to wildness by its exhilarating animation. For my own part, I confess myself the victim of its magic – an Irish planxty cheers me into *maddening* vivacity; an Irish lamentation depresses me into a *sadness* of melancholy emotion, to which the energy of despair might be deemed comparative felicity.'

Glorvina, from *The Wild Irish Girl* by Sydney Owenson (Lady Morgan), (1806: 73, emphasis added)

I

I began thinking about the affective powers of Irish music at the beginning of the 1990s when busy with other matters, but it was something that always fascinated me and something to which I felt I should return at some point. In particular, I was interested in the close association between certain aspects of Irish music – certain rhythms, instruments, keys, tempos, melodies, traditions, and so on – and certain emotional responses.[1] On a wider scale, I remain interested in the association of various stereotypical associations with various musical practices and effects – and particularly with the way in which these pertain to the ideology of national character. Such associations are usually evident from the context in which the music is encountered, although there is also the possibility – and this is perhaps the main point I wish to address here – that there is something inherent in the music itself, the way in which *these* particular sounds are manipulated in certain rhythmic, tonal and harmonic ways – which elicits the response that it does.

When I first broached these issues in articles in 1992 and 1995, I came up with the terms 'Paddy Sad' and 'Paddy Mad' as a kind of shorthand for some of the ideas about Irish popular music (and indeed Irish culture generally) that I had in mind. Let me try to unpack these terms in a little more detail here.

'Paddy Sad' connotes a history of dispossession and defeat. This is what might be described as the *declensionist* mode of Irish historiography, the tragic fall away from a Celtic Eden through a series of bitter dispossessions. This historical mode may be troped in many ways: in temporal terms, for example, we might regard island history as a series of moments in which an established order is always on the point of defeat by some form of modernity: the modernity of Norman invasion, of Tudor expansion, of republican zeal, of Restoration triumphalism, of Ascendancy paranoia, of Utilitarian industrialism, and so on. Among other things, 'Paddy Sad' is a character who is always *late*, always just about to be rendered obsolete by time; the nostalgia produced as a result of this condition can affect even the victors in the confrontation, emerging within the shared culture as a kind of Celtic melancholy which makes itself available whenever and wherever required. One of the most effective ways in which this melancholy may be expressed is through the medium of music.

The same is true of 'Paddy Mad' who, as his name suggests, is the comic counterpart to his melancholic relative. If 'Paddy Sad' might be regarded (in Northrop Frye's terms) as a localised expression of the autumnal tragedy which infuses the species at a deep archetypal level, then 'Paddy Mad' is his Bacchanalian other, given to pleasure and excess as a quasi-religious response to the disappointments of everyday reality.[2] He connotes an essentially festive identity, but one that I would suggest to be more associated with the irony of winter than with the comedy of spring; there is always something desperate about 'Paddy Mad', as if an implied subservience both to his environment and to his fellow men has driven him to give up on reality entirely and to embrace the oblivion for which nature has apparently pre-selected him.

These stereotypes circulate freely, making themselves available for invocation whenever and wherever the question of Irish identity is raised. My contention is that the musical articulation of these discourses in a variety of popular contexts and idioms (some examples of which I should like to consider below) has evolved as one of the principal means for the (mis) recognition and consequent reproduction of Irish identity in the modern era. Before that, however, it is necessary to consider a little more closely the relationship between music and emotion, both in general terms and with specific reference to Irish history.

II

Although joy and sorrow would appear to be fundamental human emotions, they are at the same time relative concepts, and resistant, therefore, to prescriptive discourses. The qualities of sorrow and joy, we might say, are extremely strained, functioning in different ways and to different ends throughout recorded history. This fact has not stopped people attempting to discover, or subsequently to describe (sometimes to *prescribe*), the essence of these emotions with reference to one or another set of practices or perspectives. On the contrary, the very elusiveness of an obvious system to ensure the presence of the one and the absence of the other has acted as a spur for a great variety of historical agents to develop just such a system. When confined to the realm of ideas, we tend to call these agents philosophers or poets; those whose principal aim it is to determine experience and modify practice we describe as scientists or politicians.

Although the scientific study of music's ability to excite emotions in humans is developing rapidly, even practitioners in the field admit that the process of mapping the brain's response to musical stimuli represents a dauntingly complex task, one that, in the absence of a 'generally accepted theory of the emotions and how they interact with cognition' (Sloboda 2005: 213), is unlikely to be completed any time in the foreseeable future. There is a general recognition, however, that factors both cultural and physiological bear upon the emotional impact of music – the former involving contextual considerations such as taste and competence, the latter connoting issues such as the pitch, pace and volume of an individual piece.

The neurologist/psychiatrist Oliver Sachs is particularly interested in music's curative powers, especially its ability (cited time and again throughout history) to relieve depression. In such cases, music does not embody or express a particular emotion, or at least its ability to do so is not of the first importance; attention is focused, rather, on the ability of music to modify the perspective, and thus to alter the mood, of the listening subject. Thus, a 'sad' piece of music (defined in relation to whatever set of conventions) might have the effect of lifting a listener's mood, depending upon the circumstances of the experience.[3]

The point relating to the conventionality of musical meaning is another matter to which scientists have addressed themselves. The psychologist Daniel Levitin suggests that the association of particular sounds with particular emotions is culturally determined, as for example with the association in western music of 'major scales with happy or triumphant emotions, and minor scales with sad or defeated emotions' (2006: 38). The contemporary force of such an association is felt in relation to two particular effects. Firstly, the west's continuing global hegemony (facilitated by the twin powers of technology and media) has had the effect of flattening the world's musical horizon: I suspect that in the early twenty-first century the minor chord of western tonality is likely to have 'sad' associations (or tending in that direction) at any point across the globe. Secondly, the coupling of certain sounds with certain emotions points up the persistence of ideology as a key political device in the modern world, especially the power of ideology to convert the identifiably cultural into the apparently natural.

There is evidence to suggest that the music familiar to ancient Irish society did not function with reference to the conventional associations of modern western tonality. Instead, it was based upon a series of modes which took the form of pentatonic scales, the latter determined, at least to some extent, by the technical limitations of the harp (Vallely 1999: 243).

If convention (and indeed ideology) help to account for the 'otherness' of modal music to modern ears, it is nonetheless interesting to note that despite their differences, the ancient Irish and modern western systems share a deference to human emotion as the ineluctable index of music's ability to 'mean'. We find reference to ancient Irish modes in the medieval text 'Cath Maige Tuired: The Second Battle of Mag Tuired (Moytura)', where at least two of them are, moreover, specifically associated with the particular emotional states that concern us here. In the political manoeuvring prior to the battle, the character Lug plays his harp for the Tuatha Dé Danann as evidence of his mastery of all the arts:

> Then the warrior played sleep music for the hosts and for the king on the first night, putting them to sleep from that hour to the same

time the next day. He played sorrowful music so that they were crying and lamenting. He played joyful music so that they were merry and rejoicing (Gray 1982: 43).

Later, another character (the Dagda) escapes the Fomorian enemy by playing 'the three things by which a harper is known':

> sleep music [súantraigi], joyful music [genntraigi], and sorrowful music [golltraigi]. He played sorrowful music for them so that their tearful women wept. He played joyful music for them so that their women and boys laughed. He played sleep music for them so that the hosts slept (71).

In *golltraigi* and *genntraigi* may be found the roots of the modern musical stereotypes of Paddy Sad and Paddy Mad.[4] The array of political, social and cultural processes whereby the latter emerged from the former demands prolonged study, but the reward would be invaluable: no less than a model of one of the most effective ways in which a national identity has been produced and reproduced for specific ideological ends over an extended period of time.

In the meantime, we note that one of the characteristics of the 'traditional' music that evolved in Ireland during the last two hundred years is its apparent ability to switch between modes during tune clusters, or sometimes even during the course of an individual tune. If this accounts for the music's resistance to western tonality, it also places a question mark over the conventional associations that arise from just such a perspective – in particular, the association of major scales with joy and minor scales with sorrow. Traditional music, we might say, exposes the illusion of ideal emotional associations, operating instead on an imaginary borderline where sadness and happiness segue imperceptibly into one another.[5]

Despite this, there can be no doubting the continuing force of emotional archetypes in Irish musical discourse, or at least in the responses emerging from an engagement with such music. Besides the comment from Lady Morgan which prefaces this chapter, modern Irish history is replete with 'analysis', the burden of which is the rapid emotional vacillation characteristic of the island's music. As in Glorvina's assessment, moreover, it is not uncommon to find a link between musical and political levels of engagement; Thomas Moore puts the standard case in his 'Essay on the Music of Ireland':

The tone of defiance, succeeded by the languor of despondency – a burst of turbulence dying away into softness – the sorrows of one moment lost in the levity of the next – and all that romantic mixture of mirth and sadness, which is naturally produced by the efforts of a lively temperament to shake off or forget the wrongs which lie upon it. Such are the features of our history and character, which we find strongly and faithfully reflected in our music (n.d: xi).

While noting Moore's characteristic movement between history and form – the manner in which the island's music articulates the cultural logic of a dispossessed people – we should also acknowledge that the contradiction between a resistance to conventional emotionalism (within the music itself) and a seemingly inescapable identification with certain emotional states (dominating the analysis which attends the music) arises from the fact that musical meaning is always dependent upon much more than the collection of sounds entering the ear.

III

Examples of the 'Sad/Mad' archetypes abound in each of the three major musical spheres: art, traditional/folk, and popular. A figure who links these different spheres is Seán Ó Riada. *The Banks of Sullane* (1956; Various Artists 1996: track 12) is a composition in which Ó Riada attempted to integrate certain aspects of the folk tradition (to which he was sentimentally disposed) with the European art tradition in which he had been trained. In effect, what this amounted to was the setting of a folk melody using techniques (harmony, orchestration and certain colouring effects) that had been developed in the discourse of European art music over a number of centuries, but especially in the so-called 'Romantic' phase of the mid-nineteenth century. This piece is a clear evocation of 'Paddy Sad': although lacking a 'programme' as such, its title alludes to the landscape of the composer's home county of Cork, and the arrangement – a slow dreamy melody (played on cello, oboe and harp) interrupted by a more 'modern' central section (angst-laden, syncopated, occasionally discordant) – creates an atmosphere of lost pastoral.

Ó Riada famously turned away from an art tradition which he came to regard as both emotionally and intellectually unsatisfactory, and began instead to imagine what a rejuvenated folk tradition might sound like (White 1998: 125–50). His work with Ceoltóirí Cualann during the 1960s culminated in a number of concerts in the Gaiety Theatre in Dublin during which the Irish folk tradition (or at least certain elements within that tradition) underwent a process of discursive repositioning (Ó Riada and Ceoltóirí Cualann 2005). There were two aspects to this process. In the first place, we observe the close association between traditional music and the expression of a limited number of rudimentary human emotions. This is not to deny the long coincidence within traditional music (noted above) between certain musical properties and/or effects (instruments, melodies, harmonies, rhythms, timbres, etc.) and certain emotional states. After Ó Riada, however, this coincidence achieved an official endorsement that disseminated out into the wider culture.

Secondly, Ó Riada's association with traditional music represented a significant moment in the bourgeois appropriation of local culture – that process (ongoing since the late eighteenth century) whereby the symbolic practices of everyday life throughout the island were systematically recruited as part of a national (and sometimes nationalist) narrative by licensed elites who were themselves both economically and emotionally mortgaged to the idea of the state. Once incorporated as part of the official 'story' of Ireland and Irishness, traditional music became a readily available means – indeed, perhaps *the* principal means – to articulate and recognise modern Irish identity.

Taken together, these two processes meant that: a) Irishness had a sound – a sound that was readily producible in a variety of contexts all of which were removed, to a greater or lesser extent, from the contexts in which that sound had emerged; and b) that sound was capable of being inflected in a limited number of registers which exhausted – apparently – the Irish emotional response to the world. 'Paddy Mad' and 'Paddy Sad' were now respectable and recognisable figures within the Irish cultural landscape. Ideologically over-determined to such an extent, it has in fact become difficult to 'hear' Irish traditional music in the post-Ó Riada era, despite the relatively vast amounts of music produced in that style.

Ó Riada's impact has been felt also in the realm of Irish popular music, and nowhere more so than in the music created by Horslips. The band's signature tune is 'Dearg Doom' from the 1973 album *The*

Táin (2005: track 6), a song based on a tune entitled 'Marcshlua Uí Néill (O'Neill's March)' which had been performed in a quasi-traditional arrangement by Ó Riada and Ceoltóirí Cualann at the Gaiety concert in 1969 (2005: track 1). The Horslips version sets the recognisably 'Irish' melody (played on a partially distorted electric guitar) within a typical rock arrangement which incorporates electric bass guitar, drums and keyboards. 'Dearg Doom' does not appear to immediately 'represent' any identifiable emotional condition; the lyrics are vague, while the music itself oscillates between D minor (driven by the urgency of rock rather than the pathos of the art tradition, however) during the verses and C major during the chorus. Heard on its own, one might hesitate to ascribe a definitive emotional significance to the song; when it is placed within the context of *The Táin*, however, and then within the wider context of the 'Celtic Rock' genre which Horslips inadvertently spawned (Smyth 2005: 41–5), 'Dearg Doom' begins to take on a tragic resonance which once again draws upon, even as it contributes to, the emotional economy of modern Ireland.

Another band who subscribed to this economy was The Pogues – in many ways, the limit case for modern popular articulations of 'Paddy Mad' and 'Paddy Sad'. In the early 1980s The Pogues cross-fertilised the energy of Irish traditional music with the energy of punk rock to create a unique sound within the canon of contemporary popular music. This 'uniqueness' was most clearly represented in the figure of Shane MacGowan who, as the main singer, songwriter and 'face' within the band, was also the main source of media attention. MacGowan embodied the dual aspect of the stereotype in exemplary fashion. On the one hand, in songs such as 'Waxie's Dargle' (track 4) and 'The Boys from the County Hell' (track 5) – both from the band's debut album *Red Roses for Me* (1984) – he appeared boorish and aggressive, 'mad' in ways that veered between carnivalesque festivity and alcohol-fuelled violence. If MacGowan could be regarded as the living incarnation of the mad (albeit expatriate) Paddy, however, on original compositions such as 'Kitty' (track 13) and on covers such as 'The Auld Triangle' (track 3) – written by Brendan Behan, the figure who was in many ways MacGowan's precursor as the embodiment of 'Paddy Mad' – he also articulated a darkly melancholic perspective which drew The Pogues back towards the tragic mode of Irish cultural history, the one characterised by dispossession, failure, exile and loss.

There can be no doubting that the stereotypes sketched here have proved remarkably resilient and flexible; the slightest exposure to Irish-related cultural activity – either *by* the Irish themselves or *about* them by others looking in – virtually guarantees their appearance in one form or another. A number of issues still need to be addressed, however, especially when one confronts the articulation of such stereotypes in musical form. Among all these issues, one principal – and apparently very simple – one persists: how *can* music express emotion, which is to say, how can mere sounds, sonic effects resulting from the strategic manipulation of various observable physical laws and properties elicit in the listening subject some of the most profound emotions that humans can experience: feelings of joy and sadness, triumph and loss, festivity and tragedy? Interestingly enough, the search for the answers to these questions takes us back to the period (and to the same nineteenth-century context) in which the stereotypes of the Irish character were beginning to emerge in their modern forms.

IV

During the nineteenth century the discourses attending the aesthetic structure of music and the archetypal condition of Irish identity were both in the process of consolidating. These apparently separate discourses were, moreover, locked into a shared intellectual regime (which in more systemic times might have been described as an 'ideology', a 'mentality', a 'politics of truth' or even a 'structure of feeling') in which certain cultural patterns, certain texts and even certain personalities recur.[6] This intellectual regime was known as Romanticism.

The question of the relationship between music and the emotions is over-determined in this particular case by the widespread, linked notions of the Irish as both extraordinarily musical and extraordinarily emotional (Smyth 1998: 61–4). These notions emerged and established themselves as part of a model of human agency which was self-consciously Romantic and unselfconsciously expressionist: to put it simply, the Irish had a special feel for music and this was both part of their identity and part of their attraction. Something definitive about the Irish could only be expressed (and experienced) through music. At the same time, the emotionality of music in general – and of Irish music in particular – rendered them unfit to deal with the modern world. Thus, the influential French philosopher Ernest Renan wrote in a famous extract from his 1859 essay on 'The Poetry of the Celtic Races':

> To them life appears as a fixed condition, which man has no power to alter. Endowed with little initiative, too much inclined to look upon themselves as minors and in tutelage, they are quick to believe in destiny and resign themselves to it ... Thence ensues its sadness. Take the songs of its bards of the sixth century; they weep more defeats than they sing victories. Its history is only one long lament; it still recalls its exiles, its flights across the seas. If at times it seems to be cheerful, a tear is not slow to glisten behind its smile; it does not know that strange forgetfulness of human conditions and destinies which is called gaiety. Its songs of joy end as elegies; there is nothing to equal the delicious sadness of its national melodies. One might call them emanations from on high which, falling drop by drop upon the soul, pass through it like memories of another world. Never have men feasted so long upon these solitary delights of the spirit, these poetic memories which simultaneously intercross all the sensations of life, so vague, so deep, so penetrative, that one might die from them, without being able to say whether it was from bitterness or sweetness (1988: 57).

For Renan (and indeed for those, such as the English cultural critic Matthew Arnold, who followed in his wake by transposing his speculative researches into a basis for politico-cultural practice) it would appear that the emotionality of Irish music – its capacity to excite feelings of joy and sadness in its participant subjects – lies inherent in a particular sound which itself arises as an expression of the character and the destiny of the Irish as a Celtic race. In a classic variation on 'the affective fallacy', the emotion is *experienced* by the composer, *interpreted* by the musician, and *transferred* to the listener. The music itself becomes almost incidental in this process; it is the feelings contained within the music that is of primary importance. Moreover, the conventional emotions associated with the sound accumulate over time, so that certain sounds may come to act as a convenient shorthand for certain stereotypical associations. Hence, some effects just 'naturally' sound joyful – both because they express an Irish response to the world, and because the listening subject has heard it or something like it before in contexts which they are routinely invited to associate with joy.

There is an alternative intellectual tradition running parallel to (or at least dissenting within) nineteenth-century Romanticism, one that affords a different way of addressing the affective properties of Irish music. This tradition might be described as a species of Aristotelian formalism, and is indeed related in certain key facets to the logical imperative which characterises the work of the ancient philosopher.

Eduard Hanslick was a German music critic (actually born and raised in Prague) who lived mostly in Vienna between 1825 and 1904, and he was one of the first figures to adopt (or at least to make a claim to the adoption of) what we would recognise as a properly philosophical approach to the question of meaning in music. In fact, his ideas about music were coloured by a profoundly conservative understanding, shaped in the main by the classical tradition which began (to his way of understanding) with Mozart and Haydn, continued through the likes of Beethoven, Schubert and Schumann, and survived in the contemporary composer whom Hanslick championed so vigorously in his own writing: Brahms. The counterpart of this classicism was his virulent antipathy towards the other great musical pole in late-nineteenth-century European art music: Wagner. Hanslick and Wagner (and their supporters) swapped insults for decades in the so-called 'War of the Romantics', the exchanges often couched in the anti-Semitic terms to which Wagner deferred so readily in all his cultural and critical dealings (Bowie 2007: 210–60).

Hanslick's mistrust of Wagner lay partially in what he regarded as the great composer's weakness for what were becoming known at the time as 'programmatic' effects, and which we, in our post-poststructuralist moment, might comprehend as 'a will to reference'. In 1854 – as Renan was beginning to ruminate on the significance of Celtic culture for the general cultural health of Europe – Hanslick published *The Beautiful in Music*, which began as an attack upon Wagnerianism but developed into something like a systematic statement on musical aesthetics. Over the course of his book, Hanslick attacked two versions of musical expressionism: firstly, the notion that meaning in music depends upon the accurate representation of the emotions of its creator (what would become known as the 'intentional fallacy' for a future generation of literary formalists); and secondly, the notion that music functions by reproducing in its participant subjects the dynamic psychological processes associated with certain corresponding mental states – the 'affective fallacy' we encountered above in relation to Renan's thesis on Celtic poetry (Wimsatt and Beardsley 1954: 3–18, and *passim*). For Hanslick, both these expressionist models led to a fundamental misinterpretation of musical meaning:

> The power which music possesses of profoundly affecting the nervous system cannot be ascribed so much to the *artistic* forms created by, and appealing to, the mind, as to the material with which music works and which Nature has endowed with certain inscrutable affinities of a physiological order (1974: 123, original emphasis).

So, Nature supplies us with an emotional soundtrack: certain sounds and certain emotions are 'naturally' affiliated – these sounds engender physiological responses in the hearing subject which are immediately transposed into an emotional register. When *sound* is subjected to artistic organisation during the process of composition, however, it becomes *music* – which is to say, it becomes susceptible to aesthetic analysis, to intellectually determined criteria of beauty. If sound impacts upon the emotions, it is music which affects the mind and which gives rise to the human sense of the beautiful. This in turn gives rise to different ways of responding to music, what Hanslick characterises at various times as the 'artistic' and the 'unartistic':

> The unartistic interpretation of a piece of music is derived ... not from the material part properly so-called, not from the rich variety of the succession of sounds, but from their vague aggregate effect, which impresses them as an undefinable [sic] feeling ... The sentiment pervading a piece of music is habitually regarded as the drift, the idea, the spirit of the composition; whereas the artistic and original combination of definite successions of sound is said to be the mere form, the mould, the material garb of those supersensible elements. But it is precisely the 'specifically musical' element of the creation of inventive genius which the contemplating mind apprehends and assimilates. These concrete musical images, and not the vague impression of some abstract feeling, constitute the spirit of the composition. The *form* (the musical structure) is the real *substance* (subject) of music – in fact, is the music itself, in antithesis to the feeling, its alleged subject, which can be called neither its subject nor its form, but simply the effect produced (127–8).

In a revealing comparison, Hanslick then goes on to claim that '[music] loosens the feet or the heart just as wine loosens the tongue.' In fact, the characterisation of the 'unartistic' response to music is couched in terms which will be familiar to anyone who has studied the representation of the Celt – and more specifically the Irish – since the nineteenth century:

> Music loosens the feet or the heart just as wine loosens the tongue. But such victories only testify to the weakness of the vanquished. To be the slave of unreasoning, undirected, and purposeless feelings, ignited by a power which is out of all relation to our will and intellect, is not worthy of the human mind. If people allow themselves to be so completely carried away by what is elemental in art as to lose all self-control, this scarcely redounds to the glory of the art, and much less to that of the individual ... As the *physical* effect of music varies with the morbid excitability of the nervous system, so the *moral* influence of sound is in proportion to the crudeness of mind and character. The lower the degree of culture, the greater the potency of the agent in question. It is well known that the action of music is most powerful of all in the case of savages (129–30, original emphases).

The language here – *loosen, weakness, vanquished, unreasoning, undirected, purposeless, elemental, morbid excitability, crudeness of mind and character, savage* – is especially revealing. And suddenly the Irish predilection for music begins to come into focus: the subject's 'elemental' response to music – articulated in the stereotypes of Paddy Sad and Paddy Mad – is locked into a wider politico-cultural narrative in which the Irish are regarded as led by predominantly material concerns; they are, moreover, intellectually unrefined and morally degenerate. In fact, they are not really concerned with 'music' – the human organisation of sound into meaningful discourses – at all; like children or savages they are too focused on the physical responses engendered by noise, and like children or savages they invariably mistake such responses for meaningful discourse. In such a discourse, the Irish are represented as being too caught up in the noise and the rhythm to worry about the music, too excited by the body to be concerned with the mind.

V

The story, then, goes something like this: the Irish enjoy a special relationship with music; it is one of their defining cultural characteristics – a source of pride for themselves and of envy and regard among many non-Irish people. The meaning of Irish 'music' tends to oscillate between extremes of tragedy and festivity, and most listeners are ideologically sensitised to recognise the particular sounds, styles and genres through which these stereotypes are capable of being articulated. According to one dominant aesthetic narrative, however, such stereotypes appeal to the most basic of physical human responses; the kind of 'music' that represents Ireland and Irishness is not really music at all but a rudimentary reproduction of various natural sounds which create resonance within the human body and which are subsequently transposed into one or another crude emotional registers.

Encompassing issues of psychology, aesthetics, politics and cultural history, each of the constituent elements of this story requires further research. And because music, as Jacques Attali has suggested, offers a super-sensitive guide to the prevailing cultural climate, I suggest that this is a research project of pressing importance for the wider Irish Studies community.[7]

Bringing It All Back Home? The Dynamics of Local Music-Making in The Commitments

The Commitments has been many things to many people since it was published in 1987. Most commentators appear to agree, however, that the principal theme of both book and film is the hybrid status of late twentieth-century Irish identity – the latter term apprehended with reference to some or other hierarchy involving the constituent discourses of (among other things) gender, race, class or age. This critical concern has by and large emerged from the perspective of postcolonialist and/or postmodernist literary theory, in both of which the category of identity is revealed to be strung out between centripetal (unified and localising) and centrifugal (dispersed and globalising) discourses.[1]

No analysis of either the Doyle novel or the film adaptation by Alan Parker (to a screenplay co-written by Doyle) has, so far as I know, engaged with what seems to me to be the text's most obvious frame of reference: the dynamics of local popular music-making. This is strange; after all, before it 'represents' anything else at a greater or lesser symbolic level, both the literary and the filmic narratives focus quite clearly on the formation, recruitment, interrelations, early success and precipitant demise of a group of local musicians playing a form of popular music to local audiences. Thus, most critical attention has focused on Jimmy's exorbitant claim that '[the] Irish are the niggers of Europe', rather than his immediately preceding sentiment, that '[your] music should be abou' where you're from an' the sort o' people yeh come from' (Doyle 1992: 13). Here, I suggest, is a rather obvious elephant in the room, roaring for attention from those preoccupied with some supposedly 'real' or 'primary' critical agenda.

The marginalisation of this aspect of the narrative is even less acceptable in light of the fact that there exists an extensive critical literature dedicated to explicating the processes of local music-making. True, this literature is located at some remove from Irish cultural criticism and its established array of interests and methodologies; but as someone steeped in those interests and methodologies, it has been interesting for me to learn that analyses of local music-making (emerging from the institutional-intellectual field of Popular Music Studies) tend to be concerned with issues of socialisation, authenticity, identity, and so on – concerned, that is, with many of the same things that animate contemporary Irish cultural criticism and its focus on the ambivalent status of modern Irish identity.

In this chapter I want to remove my Irish Studies hat, and try instead to discover what a reading emerging from popular music studies and its concern with local music-making might produce. To this end, I want to compare and contrast the experiences and practices of Doyle's fictional band with some of the experiences and practices described in three classic accounts of local music-making: *On Becoming a Rock Musician* (1980) by American sociologist H. Stith Bennett; Ruth Finnegan's anthropological study *The Hidden Musicians* (1989); and Sara Cohen's *Rock Culture in Liverpool* (1991). Each offers an extended ethnographic account of the beginning phase of the local musician's career – the same phase experienced by Doyle's fictional band. It is my impression that *The Commitments* warrants an analysis focused on its most obvious theme – local music-making; at the same time, I also believe that such an analysis will bring us back to many of the same concerns identified by established Irish cultural critique.

A LOCAL GROUP FOR LOCAL PEOPLE!

In the introduction to *On Becoming a Rock Musician*, H. Stith Bennett defines local music-making in three overlapping and interrelated ways: 'a local group (1) plays to a regional market, (2) is self-producing, and (3) plays live performances' (1980: viii). The Commitments fulfil all these criteria: (1) they orient themselves in relation to a specific kind of audience in a specifically defined area around the centre-north of Dublin city; (2) they do not rely on sources external to the band for the production of their music; (3) the band's music-making activities are (at least in the first instance) specifically geared towards live performance rather than any kind of electronically reproduced product which might circulate and thus signify in the absence of the musicians themselves.

Moreover, in the story of their formation, brief success and rapid disintegration, there is a clear model of Bennett's underlying premise, namely, that local popular music-making offers a salient example of 'the interpersonal problems that groups of any kind are now known to create' (1980: 4). 'Interpersonal problems' is an understatement of The Commitments' experience; as a group, they banter, bicker, argue and eventually fight themselves into oblivion. As they are doing so, however, they also engage in the activities that Bennett describes as evolutionary stages of the local music-making process. Without formally differentiating between novel and movie at this point, I want to spend a little time looking at these stages as they relate to the representation of local music-making activity in *The Commitments*.

Ignoring for the moment the crucial question of motivation (to which I shall turn in the conclusion), the first thing the aspiring musician has to do is acquire an instrument. This step has both practical and symbolic dimensions. Local musicians, no less than the stars they wish to emulate, invariably locate themselves and others in terms of a hierarchy of competence and seriousness. If the individual is to progress beyond the rudimentary stage, a significant initial financial outlay is necessary. Bennett found that once the commitment had been made to engage in local popular music-making, young musicians would beg, steal or borrow – even occasionally work – in order to find the money to acquire the necessary instruments. At the same time, different instruments connote different things in relation both to local music-making culture and to the plethora of popular genres that subsist within the wider culture. The six-stringed electric guitar, for example, performs a different function in rock than in soul, and this has implications for the guitarist's self-identity and his role in relation to the rest of the band.

The acquisition and status of a range of musical instruments play major roles in the evolution of The Commitments. At the outset, the core of the group – Outspan and Derek – do not possess adequate instruments to play the kind of music desired by their new manager, Jimmy Rabbitte Jr. Inspired by his enthusiasm and by the James Brown tracks he plays for them, however, Derek and Outspan decide to commit financially to the band. Derek borrows the 'odds' for a bass guitar and amplifier from his mother. Besides engaging in casual work (helping on a video round and selling stolen frozen chickens), Outspan also receives 'direct parental funding' (Bennett 1980: 19) – a gift from his mother – to acquire a guitar, not the 'really good one' (Doyle 1987: 22) he had hoped for, but a serviceable third-hand instrument and 'a bad amp and cabinet' (31). The rest of the band acquire or have acquired instruments in various ways: Dean inherits his saxophone from an uncle with a collapsed lung (24); in the film, Stephen 'borrows' a piano from his grandmother. Billy and Joey the Lips already own instruments (drum kit and trumpet), evidence of previous musical activity. Also in the film, Jimmy turns to Dublin's underworld to acquire some of the 'gear' needed by the band, a move that backfires when he is unable or unwilling to meet the repayments.

All this is typical of the activities described by Bennett. At the same time, it is interesting that the personality of each member of The Commitments accords at least to some degree with the instrument they play *and* with their style of playing: Billy is aggressive, for example, and this is mirrored by the fact that he '[blams] away at his drums' (33) in an aggressive manner. Billy cites '[your] man, Animal from The Muppets' (24) – a performer (albeit fictional) noted for his manic drumming style – as his main influence, and during rehearsals for one particular song he plays only a tin tray, beating it so hard in the process that its painted pattern disappears after a short time (33). The other musicians likewise possess or attempt to develop a homology between instrument, playing style and personality. The exception is Deco; one of the paradoxes of both novel and film is the discrepancy between the lead singer's crass personality and the emotion he can impart by virtue of his deeply expressive voice.

The symbolic significance of certain instruments also plays a part in the process of finding other musicians with whom to play. Jimmy's antipathy towards Ray (founder member of And And [fucking] And) is bolstered by his lack of regard for the latter's choice of instrument: the synthesiser. The notion of 'synthesising' sound is directly at odds with the kind of 'honest' or 'authentic' sound that Jimmy wishes to pursue with The Commitments. This is ironic, of course, in so far as the sound produced by soul bands is neither more nor less 'authentic' than that produced by any other kind of band playing any other kind of music. Music is the conventional organisation of noise, made possible through a greater or lesser exploitation of technology.[2] Jimmy is also suspicious of the synthesiser, however, because unlike 'real' instruments it diminishes (if not

The Dynamics of Local Music-Making in The Commitments   69

entirely eliminates) the need for group playing, a crucial aspect of rock discourse with which soul – with its heavy investment in notions of solidarity and shared emotion, and despite contrasting in many significant ways with the rock aesthetic – has strong affiliations. The synthesiser (and its higher-tech progeny) enables the musician to create the effect of group-playing without having to endure anything so potentially disruptive as real people.

'The design of rock instruments and equipment', on the other hand, as Bennett explains, 'points to a group music-making enterprise' (1980: 24). In other words, once the local musician comes into possession of a guitar, drums, saxophone, or whatever, he needs to find other like-minded individuals with whom to play. Different instruments, moreover, possess different connotations within local music-making culture. Generally, guitarists tend to proliferate, with many players making the transition from the acoustic instrument on which they learn during early adolescence to the electric model necessary for rock (or similar genre) group playing. The 'guitar hero' remains a potent symbol in many genres of popular music, while the instrument itself has been the mainstay of rock music and its derivatives (although not soul) since the 1950s. Because of the large number of guitarists, moreover, there tends to be a high turnover of instruments and equipment, as the local player either upgrades or 'retires' in response to factors such as success, age, commitment, and so on. Drummers, on the other hand, tend to be a much rarer animal on the local music scene because of the expense of their instrument and the relative difficulty of acquiring competence. Unlike the guitar, which can be bought cheaply and played effectively at an early stage, drums require the investment of both time and money, both rarer commodities in the predominantly working- and lower-middle-class contexts in which local popular music-making tends to thrive.[3]

The Commitments adhere to an established model in so far as most of the members (Jimmy, Derek, Outspan, James, Imelda and Bernie) already know each other before deciding to group together in this particular way for the purposes of music-making. If acquaintance alone cannot meet the personnel requirements, however, other means must be found. Jimmy uses one obvious social network – the workplace – to enlist Deco. Another route, familiar to local popular musicians the world over, is the advertisement – in this case, in Ireland's premier popular music magazine, *Hot Press* – for like-minded (at least musically speaking) people.[4] Billy and Dean are recruited in this way. Joey also responds to the advertisement, but his case is unusual in that he is re-entering the local personnel pool having (allegedly) 'made it' in the professional sphere to which local music-makers – such as his fellow band members – ostensibly aspire. Both his age and his international experience mark Joey out as different from the rest of the group, a difference which accounts both for his novelty attraction and at least some of the tensions that will eventually lead to the break-up of The Commitments.

Apropos break-ups, it is also significant that this particular group of musicians did not appear *ex nihilo*, but emerged from (even as it precipitated) the demise of another band. By the same token, when The Commitments do eventually fall apart the members go on, individually and in clusters of various size (and, no doubt, duration) to pursue alternative musical visions. In the film, Deco, Dean, Natalie, Bernie and Mickah (the band's erstwhile roadie-come-bouncer-come-drummer) all engage in post-Commitments music-making, while the novel ends with Jimmy, Derek, Outspan and Mickah forming a band with the intention of playing a kind of music described by Jimmy as 'Dublin country' (139). All these factors tie in with Bennett's thesis that local music-making is practised by pools of musicians who constantly form and reform – what he calls 'grouping and regrouping' (1980: 26) – according to a wide range of factors, including musical competence, friendship, geographical dispersal, aesthetic vision, and commitment.

Once the nucleus of the group has been formed, individual members need to improve their instrumental technique and to begin the process of ensemble playing. On a practical level, this initially entails finding places to practice, both individually and in clusters of various size up to and including the full cohort. Over the course of novel and film, the different members of The Commitments 'get friendly with their instruments' (as Jimmy puts it) in various locations: a train, bedrooms, workplaces, kitchens, playgrounds. (The practice stage provides further evidence of the extent to which local music-making is closely tied in to familial and other salient social patterns.) 'Practice' in this sense connotes not only technique but the development of what might be termed a 'disposition' – including language (both body and verbal) and attitude – which is attuned to the music itself. Thus, we see the Commitmentettes, Outspan and Deco practising the dance steps and poses they will strike to accompany the properly musical delivery; we also see Jimmy at different points explaining the group's 'philosophy' to various members and sub-groups. This is indicative of the fact that the actual *playing* is only one aspect of local music-making activity, and that membership of a band encompasses an array of attitudes and practices that informs the members' entire social experience.

In the novel, however, the band's principal rehearsal space is Joey's mother's garage, while in the film they use a large deserted room above a snooker club run by a friend. While the former represents *the* classic locus for this kind of activity, with that particular space even lending its name (the 'garage band') to one widely recognised kind of amateur music-making, the latter is a lucky and fairly unusual find. The architecture of Dublin, like most other western cities, was not developed with the demands of modern popular music and its peculiar sonic properties in mind. As with most other major conurbations since the onset of the rock era, however, Dublin did develop a semi-official network of rehearsal spaces to which generations of local music-makers such as The Commitments have had recourse.[5]

Bennett, Cohen and Finnegan all draw attention to the fact that the anticipated pleasure of successful group-playing is one of the experiences that attracts young people towards local music-making as a preferred leisure option in the first place. At the same time, all three also point out that rehearsal is the point at which tensions over competence, commitment and aesthetics usually begin to emerge. The Commitments are no different from other local popular music groups in either of these respects; they are also typical in so far as their career trajectory may be tracked in terms of the gradual overtaking of the former impulse by the latter. Thus, Jimmy criticises Bernie and Imelda for putting family concerns before the band, while Dean's wish 'to express meself' (122) with his saxophone is at odds with Joey's understanding of soul music's discipline. The main source of conflict, however, is Deco who, among other things, argues with Billy about the skill required to play the drums, continually harasses all three backing singers, resents any of them fronting 'his' group, plans a solo career while still with The Commitments, and manages to antagonise Mickah to the point of violence. It is he more than any other band member, displays the lack of commitment required to be a Commitment.

Gradually, however, technique improves, songs are chosen, rehearsed and learned, a set evolves, and The Commitments are ready to tackle the next step in the local band's evolution: the gig. Many commentators have noted that the aesthetics of post-war popular music-making are split between the *record* and the *performance*. The question is: wherein does the identity of the music lie – in the record that is mechanically produced in the rarefied atmosphere of the recording studio, or in the context of a live performance in which band, audience and music combine to create a specific kind of relationship?[6] This tends not to be an issue for most new popular music bands, however, as the chance to record (and the opportunities and difficulties it brings) only comes after an extended live career. The predominant unit of signification for the local popular band, therefore, remains the gig – a kind of event in which, as generations of local music-makers know only too well, the elusive pleasure potential is routinely outweighed by a ubiquitous pitfall potential.

Generally speaking, live performance remains an important element of popular music discourse in so far as it performs functions and provides experiences that recordings cannot. The recorded 'text' is the result of a multitude of procedures and contributions – musical, certainly, but also technological, artistic and economic – that are some way removed from either musicians' or consumers' perceptions of the music itself. And while few would disagree that these 'texts' have their place in the signifying economy of popular music, the experience of 'music in the raw' (as Cohen [1991: 93] describes it) plays a role of equal or in some cases greater importance for many musicians and consumers. Or to put it another way, '[performance] is the central ritual of local rock, a special setting for music for which the audience is as important as the performers' (Frith 1992: 175). The sense of occasion provided by live performance, the energy which must be invested in attendance and participation, the spatial and temporal collapse of the gap between production and consumption, the 'rough' quality of the music itself, the euphoric atmosphere ensuing from the spontaneous interplay of unpredictable factors – all these continue to be powerful elements of modern popular music discourse. And of the many factors bearing upon the 'meaning' of a live performance, it is this latter one – the euphoria (described as a 'buzz' or 'high' [Cohen 1991: 97] by members of the Merseyside bands) that ensues from a 'successful' performance – that tends to be the most elusive, and as a result, the most valued.

The 'buzz' associated with a good gig may be an ultimately recondite phenomenon, but certain practical measures have to be put in place before it may be even approached. Goalless rehearsal can accentuate internal band tensions, whereas the pressure of a gig deadline can galvanise a band into concentrated effort. So, among the first things that must be done are: (a) find a gig; and (b) get to it. The first live public performance by many local music-makers is *occasional*, with school or college socials, weddings, fund-raisers, parties and other local events providing the opportunity (Bennett 1980: 83ff). Again, family and colleagues tend to play a significant role in helping with transport and equipment preparation. Under-rehearsal, nerves, inadequate equipment and lack of technical knowledge are just some of the problems that can mar these early performances. All individual performers make mistakes; group-playing brings greater scope for error, and public group-playing extends the error margin considerably. One of the things that local groups have to learn, therefore, is to 'play the room' (Bennett 1980: 160), which is to say, to get a feel for the highly sensitive, yet ultimately inscrutable, relationship between atmosphere and architecture which constitutes 'success' in performance terms. Most popular musicians agree that the peculiar blend of technological expertise and self-discipline required for successful gigging is something that only comes with experience; and by 'self-discipline' I mean *preparing* the body to perform – in terms of musical competence, certainly, but also in terms of bringing the self to a state of readiness through a personal regime of emotional (being 'up for it') and physical stimuli (such as alcohol or mood-altering drugs).[7]

Despite all these problems, a proportion of local bands manage to survive the first gig, accumulating valuable experience regarding acoustics, stage organisation and set order in the process. The next stage is the steady gig, with the bar and the nightclub providing the most obvious locales. The winning of a loyal local following may represent the acme of many bands' desires, but this stage is no less fraught than the others. Who is in the audience? Are they strangers, fellow musicians, non-performing friends or family? What do they want? To dance? To look? To listen? To listen to *new* or to *familiar* sounds? To be entertained? For many local music-makers, the first time these issues are seriously considered is on stage during their first gig; it is only gradually, with repeated performances, that a band learns to 'read' an audience, and to bring their own (personal and collective) aesthetic criteria into line with the social factors bearing upon audience behaviour.

The Commitments experience variations on all the stages described above. Early in the story, Jimmy accepts a gig in the local church hall, despite Outspan's reservations as to both the quality and the quantity of material accumulated. The gig is part of a local church-sponsored drive against heroin (the drug that decimated working-class Dublin in the early 1980s), and they play to an audience of family, friends and acquaintances. Billy's van provides the main transport until he leaves the band, whereafter they 'borrow' the fast food van in which Bernie works. On the night of their first public performance, Derek suffers from nerves to the point of feeling ill, while Outspan refuses to perform because his mother is in the audience. Before this first gig, various members discuss the merits of wearing 'monkey suits'; their acceptance of Joey's argument that adapting a stage uniform lends dignity and identity to their performance is only temporary, however, and will eventually disappear as the band's gigging career progresses. Once on stage, more problems emerge, mostly centred on Deco: his antics knock over the Commitmentettes, the reference to 'his band' causes immediate resentment, and his microphone technique brings the gig to an abrupt end when he makes contact with Derek and blows the electric system. Although interpersonal, musical and technical problems persist, every performance brings improvement, so that by the time they reach what is to be their final performance, The Commitments are fully capable of achieving 'the buzz' characteristic of successful local music-making. Individual band members are 'familiar with their instruments' and with the material, as a band they know how to 'play the room', and the audience know the songs and the individual group members. The film editing during the rendition of 'Try a Little Tenderness' attempts to reproduce the excitement and euphoria of a successful live performance. The rapid cutting between various band members, the band as a whole, individual audience members and larger sections of the audience depicts a collective experience made up of consumers and producers; it is a moment in which the band's musical-performance aesthetic is completely at one with audience expectations and the sociocultural factors bearing thereon. Each performer appears completely identified with the music and with their individual and collective role in its production. Likewise, the audience appears completely absorbed

The Dynamics of Local Music-Making in The Commitments 75

with the music, gazing at the stage, swaying during the early part of the song, dancing, singing and clapping as it reaches its extended climax.

The euphoria that accompanies this successful performance is in stark contrast to the animosity that is pulling the band apart, however. Individuals who had been united on stage one moment are literally at each other's throats the next. And just as The Commitments are about to take the next step in the evolution of the local popular music group – recording – they disband. Although there are many reasons for this, as noted above, the principal cause of enmity among band members is identified by Jimmy at an early stage as 'that old rock 'n' roll demon: S.E.X.' This leads on to a set of issues regarding the function of gender in popular music-making discourse.

SHOW ME A WOMAN

In an earlier study of *The Commitments* I suggested that Imelda was a key figure, as she holds the male component of the band together through lust, and contributes significantly to its demise when she tells Joey that she is pregnant by him (which is untrue), thus precipitating his departure.[8] Roddy Doyle disagreed with this reading, and it is true that the point was under-developed. It did, however, have the virtue of touching upon an important issue concerning the role of women in local music-making culture. For it is clear that Bennett failed to appreciate one rather glaring fact thrown up by his research: by local music-making he actually means local *male* music-making. The kinds of practices, rituals and relationships he describes are heavily dependent on a particular model of masculinity, inherited from earlier contexts and adapted in various ways to suit the discourse of rock music. This is borne out by the fact that amateur rock music has tended to operate in terms of a hierarchical gender discourse in which each aspect of the process – from instrument acquisition and status to performance – is organised in terms of an implicit male priority.

Bennett's gender blindness is exposed by Cohen, who remarked upon the 'overwhelming absence of women in the rock music scene in Merseyside, not only in the bands themselves but in the audiences and many of their social activities' (1991: 202). This was not only to do with the fact that '[women] had different leisure opportunities from those of young men and more domestic commitments, and often lacked the access, encouragement, and freedom to indulge in a world of music-making' (202). It was also a reflection of rock's inherent gender bias and, more fundamentally, of the fact that the male-dominated local music scene continues to operate in large part as a response to a perceived 'threat of women' (201). To what kind of 'threat' is Cohen referring here?

In Liverpool, Cohen noted, adolescent boys tended to cluster together in groups of various kinds (sports teams offer another example) to pursue forms of male sociability defined over and against alternative forms (such as the family and the couple) organised specifically around the interaction of the sexes. 'Women and domesticity were associated with convention,' she writes, 'and thus seen to threaten men's creativity and independence' (221). Cohen suggests further that '[gender] differences are constructed, maintained, and negotiated not only by the way in which rock music is *used* but by the actual musical styles and their marketing' (202–3, original emphasis). On one level this is an allusion to the classic distinction between 'cock rock' – music made with reference to a mature, aggressive male sexuality – and 'teenybop' – in which the male persona is far less threatening, and the music itself is sonically and commercially designed to appeal to an adolescent and/or pre-pubescent female audience (Frith and McRobbie 1990). At a deeper level, however, Cohen was suggesting that the aesthetic animating the young Merseyside rock bands she studied functioned with reference to an opposition – occasionally articulated but always present – between *purity* and *impurity*; and furthermore, that although such an opposition could be inflected in any number of ways, in itself it relied upon a core distinction between masculinity and femininity.

Cohen advances the standard line that '[sexuality], as portrayed through rock music, has ... been predominantly masculine' (203). In the context of the local music scene, 'both sport and rock music offered young men, amongst other things, a respectable fantasy incorporating images of masculinity and power' (222). Cohen refines the point, however, by suggesting that the defining aesthetic impulse in this same context is the constant search by male band members for the 'buzz' (97), by which is meant (as we saw above in relation to the gig) an elusive combination of sound, expression and atmosphere. What her research clearly revealed was that the 'buzz' depended on solely male input and interaction, and that, in the context of its pursuit, 'women were seen in some way as polluting' (201). The irony here, of course (and it is an irony repeated throughout the popular music industry), is that one of the principal reasons for young men to join local music groups is to enhance their image with the opposite sex. Despite their exclusion from the local rock scene, Cohen wryly concludes, 'women [are] ... strongly present in their absence' (222).

It certainly seems to be the case that women's participation in rock culture has tended to be perfunctory and peripheral, and that such 'female' forms as have emerged (such as the guitar-playing singer-songwriter in the early Joni Mitchell mode) tend to reinforce the socially salient stereotypes regarding gender. As a rule, women rock musicians have to work harder and perform better to prove themselves in an industry geared towards their exclusion or their exploitation. However, the kind of music performed by The Commitments – soul – has traditionally functioned somewhat differently from the rock paradigm described at length by Cohen.[9] For one thing, it has not trafficked – lyrically, musically or commercially – in rock's standard cock rock/teenybop dyad. As a consequence, we should expect the gender relations experienced by the fictional Dublin soul group to function somewhat differently to those described by Cohen.

The Commitments are formed initially in terms of a rock aesthetic, and this is reflected in the band's internal gender relations which (for the males) is characterised at various points by (a) a desire to impress the women, (b) regret at their sexual unavailability, (c) disdain for their musical abilities, and (d) resentment at their incursion into the properly 'male' spaces of local music-making. At the outset, Outspan and Derek freely admit 'brassers' (women) and '[the] odd ride' (sexual intercourse) to be motivating factors behind the formation of the group (1987: 11). In a novel almost totally devoid of figurative discourse of any kind, Derek's memory of sticking his 'compass up Tracie Quirke's hole' (18) at school functions as a highly explicit sexual image, symbolic of the violence that characterises male attitudes towards the females throughout. Dean fantasises about a schoolgirl neighbour when he is learning to play the saxophone; James confesses to lusting after all three Commitmentettes; and although Deco may express the sentiments of a male adult in a mature voice when he is singing, for the rest of the time he behaves like the callow adolescent that he really is.

The exceptions to this are Joey and Jimmy, whose greater identification with the aesthetics of soul music is reflected in the extent to which they are willing to accept Imelda, Bernie and Natalie as legitimate band members. It is a struggle, however, because initially at least, the 'girls' appear to adhere to the stereotypes identified by Cohen. They are non-instrumentalists, seemingly incorporated into the band more for how they look than for their musical abilities. At the same time, their 'domestic commitments' (Bernie's care – including ironing and babysitting – of her pregnant mother) and 'different leisure opportunities' (Imelda's holiday in the Isle of Man with her 'folks') compromise their participation in the band. Some of the male members obviously feel that their very presence is a constant distraction from the proper pursuit of 'the buzz'. And all this fuels male prejudice regarding female unsuitability – at least in terms of competence and commitment – for local music-making activity.

As the group itself evolves, however, its internal gender relations also start to change, and this can be put down in some measure to the genre of material they are covering. The female persona presented in the soul songs (both male- and female-articulated) performed by The Commitments is related to, certainly, but also crucially different in a number of important respects from, her counterpart in the rock aesthetic. This is in large part a result of the gender relations of the African-American community from which blues, jazz, gospel, rhythm 'n' blues and eventually soul music emerged. Figures such as Billie Holiday, Ella Fitzgerald and Dinah Washington were significant contributors to that history, but it was the 'gutsy woman-ness' and 'joyful self-determination' of Aretha Franklin – 'Queen of Soul' – who established the archetype of the female soul singer (O'Brien 1995: 87, 89). The extent of The Commitmentettes' debt to the persona forged by Franklin following her move to the Atlantic label in 1966 is indicated by the inclusion of three of her definitive recordings from that period ('Chain of Fools', 'Do Right Woman Do Right Man', and 'I Never Loved A Man') on the film soundtrack.

Because of their own background in the working-class community of north Dublin, The Commitmentettes are highly receptive to the model of independent femininity encoded both in Franklin's music and in her persona. Socialised in the tough, unromantic milieu of Barrytown, they simply refuse to be the sexual and/or emotional victims that the majority of the band's male members so obviously wish them to be. One of the ways in which female independence may be exercised is through control of their own sexual activity. The gap between male expectation and female independence (and the tension caused thereby) emerges most clearly in respect of the sexual relations between Joey and all three female band members. On the one hand, the younger male band members are jealous of Joey's 'success'; on the other, because of their continued identification with an aesthetic derived principally from rock discourse they are unable to engage with the notion of active female sexuality in any terms other than 'slut'.

What all this points to is that whereas local music-making discourse appears to pull in one direction – towards a kind of (rock) practice in which women are marginalised or 'contained' – the soul music played by the band is pulling in another direction, one in which women are simultaneously more integrated and more independent. It is Jimmy's job as manager to try to reconcile these opposing discourses, but eventually the tension proves too much, the gap is too wide, and the band dissolves in misunderstanding and enmity. Of course, the misunderstanding regarding the role of women in the band is only one of the problems facing The Commitments as a group. By way of a brief conclusion, I want to suggest that all these problems (including that of gender) may be seen in terms of one over-riding issue: the motivation behind local music-making activity.

'WHY EXACTLY – D'YIS WANT TO BE IN A GROUP?'

Jimmy's question goes to the heart of local music-making discourse, and his answer speaks to many of the issues identified by the three scholars with whose work I have been engaging throughout this essay:

> Yis want to be different, isn't tha' it? Yis want to do somethin' with yourselves, isn't tha' it? ... Yis want to get up there an' shout I'm Outspan fuckin' Foster.
> He looked at Derek.
> An' I'm Derek fuckin' Scully, an' I'm not a tosser. Isn't tha' righ'? That's why yis're doin' it. Amn't I righ'? (1987: 11)

Bennett, Cohen and Finnegan each describe the desire for expressive individuality as the principal reason for engagement in local music-making activity. Jimmy goes on to refine his argument, however, by attacking the soon-to-be-defunct And And And for playing 'bad versions of other people's poxy songs' (11). For Jimmy, however, the problem does not lie with the fact that the band *played* other people's songs – functioning to all intents and purposes as a covers group – but rather that they played (what he considers to be) *bad* versions of *poxy* songs: functioning as a covers group but performing material he considers to be of lesser value and to a lower musical standard, according to the soul aesthetic he will shortly go on to define. As he says: 'It's not the other people's songs so much ... It's which ones yis do' (12).

The Commitments may be playing soul music, but the musical world in which they wish to make an impression is the pop/rock one which has produced successful Irish popular musicians such as U2, Bob Geldof and Sinéad O'Connor – artists name-checked (to Jimmy's delight) by a local journalist reporting on a Commitments gig. But the aesthetic vision shared by the journalist and Jimmy here is essentially incoherent, and it points to an incoherence at the heart of *The Commitments*. Consider this quote noted by Bennett during an argument between band members from one of the local American scenes observed by him:

> Man, I tell you I'm sick and tired of being a fucking juke box ... That's all this goddamned group is anyway ... one big juke box, and you know it. If you want to keep on playing this commercial bullshit then you're gonna have to do it without me ... Who wants to play other people's music, man, I want to play my music [*Angry guitar player*] (1980: 207).

As with Jimmy's vision for The Commitments, this local musician has both a desire to 'express himself' and an aversion towards 'other people's music'. It is clear, however, that his desire for self-expression ('I'm fuckin' me', in Jimmy's idiom) should take the form of an original, creative expression – 'my music'. And as Ruth Finnegan points out, of all the motives for engaging in local music-making activity, it is the realisation of individuality through creative self-expression that is most consistent:

> Perhaps the most prominent single characteristic of the preoccupations of rock players in Milton Keynes ... was their interest in expressing their own views and personality through their music-making ... [Playing] in a band provided a medium where players could express their own personal aesthetic vision and through their music achieve a sense of controlling their own values, destiny

and self-identity (1989: 129–30).

Finnegan found that young people invest heavily in popular music production because it provides important formative experiences – namely, self-realisation through creative endeavour. Such experiences are, by and large, unavailable elsewhere in society. Local bands occasionally play cover versions, but as Cohen points out, they do so in order to claim influence and to help audiences locate the band's original music in terms of particular sub-genres of what is a highly differentiated popular music tradition. But again, too much reliance on 'other people's music' – irrespective of 'quality' – is felt to threaten the fundamental motivation for playing in a local band:

> Most rock bands started off playing and rehearsing covers but progressed on to their own material. Thereafter many were against performing a lot of covers because they felt that to do so showed a lack of creativity and initiative. 'It's very easy to copy someone,' said a member of one, 'but it's the hardest thing to be original.' [One musician regarded] the performance of covers as an indulgence that pleased audiences but some musicians didn't like the idea of 'playing entirely for an audience' and saw covers as 'entertainment' and thus demeaning, as opposed to the creation and performance of original material which was integral to a band's self-respect (Cohen 1991: 184–5).

All in all, then, these studies reveal that the principal impulse behind local music-making based in the pop/rock idiom is self-expression, and the principal criteria for successful local music-making tend to be creativity and originality. *The Commitments* – novel and film – emphasises the first but disregards the second. Individual members live the life of the local group – acquiring instruments, learning songs, rehearsing, gigging – but without the potential reward of self-expression through original composition. For someone so immersed in popular musical culture, and with such a strong vision of music-making as a means to self-realisation, Jimmy is actually pretty dogmatic in his opposition to any spark of originality, describing Outspan as a 'tosser' when he expresses an anxiety about the band's direction, and accusing Dean of 'musical wanking' when he wishes to pursue his hard-won musicianship around the 'corners' laid down in Joey's soul aesthetic. The disparaging sexual connotations here obviously reflect the gender politics addressed in the previous section; but Jimmy's avowed antipathy towards the principal motivating factors of local music-making – originality and creativity – also highlights a fundamental incoherence underpinning *The Commitments*.

The problem facing Doyle and Parker was to depict a group of young people coming together in search of self-expression, but without a plausible motivation. In the novel, Doyle describes The Commitments' most successful song as a Dublin version of James Brown's 'Night Train'; yet he never broaches the possibility of the band composing original material that would express (in a soul idiom) something of their own individual and/or collective identity. This would no doubt have necessitated a different kind of writing in which the exigencies of popular music composition would have had to be engaged, and the entire ethos and tenor of the book altered as a consequence. As a high-investment, profit-seeking concept, the film functions somewhat differently. The material performed by The Commitments already exists; no new songs needed to be commissioned or composed. Drawing on a canon of soul classics, Parker's cinematic text offers the viewer an experience in which pleasure oscillates between exoticism and familiarity: for those unfamiliar with the songs, they may be temporarily 'passed off' as original engagements with working-class Dublin life; for those who know this material, however, pleasure is available in observing the discrepancy between its original African-American context and its charming revisitation in the anomalous context of a white, working-class Dublin environment. Either way, the possibility of original composition is eschewed.

In short, *The Commitments* succeeds as novel and film, but fails as a representation of local music-making practice. In reality, as more or less accurate reproducers of a kind of music still valued by a niche audience, The Commitments would be successful within the limited world of the tribute or 'authentic covers' band; they are, however, entirely out of place in the local music-making world where they are located in the texts produced by Doyle and Parker. The Commitments are essentially a showband – those notorious covers groups demonised by early purveyors of Irish rock tradition, which nevertheless provided both the personnel and the music-making context from which an 'authentic' Irish rock tradition emerged.[10]

There are deep ironies here. Showbands provided the seedbed for an alternative aesthetic organised in terms of *production* (originality and creativity) rather than *reproduction* (accuracy). One important subgenre to have emerged from this new aesthetic was soul; which is to say, bands based in the capital have been composing and performing original material that could be described as 'Dublin soul' since at least the mid-1960s.[11] During the same period, Van Morrison achieved worldwide success composing and performing a kind of music that might be described as 'Irish soul' – music that engages with the African-American soul aesthetic but which incorporates both/either Irish lyrical and/or Irish musical influences. His first experience of local music-making was with the showband The Monarchs, a Belfast group which made a name for itself in the early 1960s performing covers of James Brown. Yet Morrison was peculiarly amenable to soul music because, as his own theory puts it, he believed 'that soul music originally came from Scotland and Ireland' (quoted in O'Connor 1991: 6). Questionable though that claim might be, Morrison's career helps to reveal the incoherence of The Commitments' engagement with the two traditions which inform their music: the Irish one on their own doorstep, and the African-American one they attempt to reproduce.

Celtic Music: From the Margins to the Centre (And Back Again?)

Celtic music emerged in the latter decades of the twentieth century as a branch of the world music phenomenon. This form of music functions as marketing terminology for an array of sounds, practices and attitudes emanating from the so-called 'Celtic' regions. Among other things, the phenomenon represents an attempt on the part of various critical and economic institutions to posit a connection between diverse musical practices – not only Irish, but a wide diversity of regions and nations, including Ireland, Scotland, Wales, Brittany and Gallicia.[1] The key to the genre's ideological status, however, is encoded in the seemingly unproblematical use of 'Celtic', a word with a long and troubled career in Irish cultural history. Despite its undoubted novelty status in commercial terms, much of the time this form of music is composed, performed and received in terms of long-established discourses which emphasise 'Celtic' difference from mainstream or normative experience. Especially in relation to Ireland, Celtic music in fact serves to reconfirm certain ideological assumptions regarding an essential national recalcitrance towards modernity, and an innate (indeed, often a biological) difference from other musical formations.

To contextualise such an analysis, it is necessary to recognise Ireland's traditional dual status as a stereotypically 'troubled', yet 'inherently' musical, nation. This latter is a 'fact' seemingly evidenced throughout the island's cultural history, from Giraldus Cambrensis, through figures such as Turlough O'Carolan and Thomas Moore, and on to the wealth of music activity practised in contemporary Ireland. There can be no doubting that music has emerged as a central element of modern Irish culture, supporting historical interpretations of a supposedly unproblematical 'Irish' identity, *and* modern creative initiatives which attempt to trade upon such interpretations. At the same time,

Celtic music is invariably figured (both in commercial and in critical terms) as a marginal or peripheral discourse, the articulation of a culture that is somehow at a tangent to 'the real world'.

Passing over the irony whereby Celtic music is represented as at odds with the marketing system which created it, my contention in this chapter is twofold: firstly, that engagements which make reference to an inherent Irish musicality remain deeply suspect, depending as they do upon notions of cultural identity which are themselves heavily mortgaged to the ideology that, in many accounts, they were constructed to oppose; and secondly, that it is neither sensible nor profitable to approach cultural discourse in terms of a spatial model (such as the one based on notions of marginality and centrality) which clearly no longer reflects the ways in which culture is produced and consumed in the modern world.

WHAT IS 'CELTIC MUSIC'?

'Celtic music' has two principal fountainheads: Ernest Renan, a French philosopher and historian; and Matthew Arnold, an English poet and cultural critic. As one of the leading British intellectuals of his day, Arnold's self-appointed task was to co-opt Britain's Celtic margins into a peaceful political arrangement with the archipelago's dominant power: England. In a series of essays and lectures beginning in the latter part of the nineteenth century (1867, 1891), Arnold attempted to flatter the Scots, Welsh and Irish into acquiescence, proposing that they were delightful people possessed of qualities without which the British imperial project could not advance (Smyth 1996). In his 1867 study of Celtic literature, Arnold produced a critical model in which the eponymous race contributed a range of identifiable tendencies to the English poetic tradition. Arnold deployed a specific array of pseudo-scientific and cultural discourses to hypothesise a wistful, melancholy, sentimental, passionate identity; the Celt is 'keenly sensitive to joy and to sorrow'; at the same time, however, he is 'always ready to react against the despotism of fact' (1900: 82).

Arnold's understanding of the Celt relied heavily on the work of Renan who, just a few years earlier, had described Celticness in this way:

> Its history is itself only one long lament. If at times it appears to be cheerful, a tear is not slow to glisten behind its smile; it does

not know that strange forgetfulness of human conditions and destinies which is called gaiety. Its songs of joy end as elegies; there is nothing to equal the delicious sadness of its national melodies. Never have men feasted so long upon these solitary delights of the spirit, these poetic memories which simultaneously intercross all the sensations of life, so vague, so deep, so penetrative, that one might die from them, without being able to say whether it was from bitterness or sweetness.[2]

The qualities supposedly 'identified' by Renan and Arnold have had a profound influence on the emergence of modern Irish culture, especially during the period of the so-called 'Celtic Revival' (Deane 1985: 17–27). Ultimately, both men characterise Celticism as a kind of spirit – one that might be approached through close study of pan-Celtic culture but which because of its nature must remain ultimately impervious to rational analysis. When incorporated into the British racial mix, such qualities, Arnold averred, would help to humanise what he perceived to be the Anglo-Saxon's characteristic gifts for worldliness and pragmatism. Basically, in Arnold's vision, the Celts were ideally suited to entertain the English after a hard day at the empire.

A century or so later, and it seemed as if not much had changed. Despite energetic resistance during the revolutionary period of the early twentieth century, the discourse of Celticism survived and re-emerged in some rather odd places throughout the twentieth century, one of the most unexpected of which was the vogue for 'Celtic music'. But what exactly is 'Celtic music'?

That is the question June Skinner Sawyers sets herself in *The Complete Guide to Celtic Music: From the Highland Bagpipe and Riverdance to U2 and Enya* (2000). The author evinces a wide knowledge of Celtic matters, the result of a lifetime's immersion in the field. As the title suggests, the book offers to 'guide' the reader through a number of historical and geographical aspects of Celtic music, while also providing a number of useful resources (including bibliography, discography, webography, glossary, events guide, and institutional listings) for those interested in learning more about the subject.

Problems emerge from the opening chapter, however, in which Skinner Sawyers attempts to address the question: 'What is Celtic Music?' The author attempts initially to define the field in quasi-scholarly terms, quoting linguistic, geographical and historical authorities to establish a link between those parts of western Europe washed by the Atlantic. However, the 'meaning' of the music remains ultimately obscure, and not because of inadequate research but because such is its essence, its nature, its inalienable character. The opening pages of the book introduce a rhetoric that pervades the entire volume:

> When all the techniques are checked off, the element that the music of the Celtic lands most commonly shares is *something* a lot more intangible and certainly less quantifiable – a feeling or quality that evokes emotions of sadness or joy, sorrow or delight. Some of Celtic music's qualities, it is true, derive from the modal scales of traditional music, but others are hard to pin down. All share, for want of a better word, a Celtic spirit, a unique bond with one another that transcends time, distance, and political units (2000: 5, added emphasis).

This 'something' (a classic mystificatory term) animates the culture not only of the disparate 'Celtic' nations of Europe, but also of the Celtic diaspora, whether it surfaces in Nova Scotia, Chicago or Sydney. Such a notion – the existence of a transhistorical 'feeling', 'quality', 'spark' or 'spirit' infusing an arbitrarily defined body of music – appears alien to the modern critical imagination. Here, however, it underpins an entire world-view. We are back, in other words, in the world of Matthew Arnold, where the Celt functions as light relief from the rigours of the real (in this instance, western) world, endowed with qualities characterised as valuable yet at the same time categorically disempowered vis-à-vis the critical and economic discourses in which they are recruited. Just as Arnold incorporated the Celt in order to consolidate late Victorian British identity, so the modern phenomenon of Celtic music performs specific ideological tasks within a global popular music market. The phenomenon of 'Celtic music', in other words, represents a lucrative niche market in which certain unique experiences are offered to those willing to invest – emotionally, certainly, but also financially – in the notion of some inherent Celtic spirituality which is supposedly non-compliant towards the modern world.

'Essence' segues irresistibly into this volume's other discursive touchstone: authenticity. This is another concept with an extremely troubled heritage in Irish history, responsible – when harnessed to one or another ideological agenda – for all manner of outrageous prescriptions and dangerous proscriptions (Graham 1999). *The Complete Guide to Celtic Music* is organised around a central opposition between the authentic and the inauthentic, with the author self-elected to differentiate between these categories. Time and again, artists, performances and individual musical texts are celebrated or dismissed in the name of an 'authenticity' which, like the 'spirit' which animates it, is ultimately unlocatable. Like style, you either have it or you do not. Recourse to such rhetoric bespeaks a degree of overconfidence, itself borne of the elitism that has come to inform at least some aspects of the traditional music revival (O'Shea 2008: 119–34).

Of course, the so-called Celtic music scene is not the first to adopt such a tendentious aesthetic. 'Keep it real' has been the vainglorious war cry of jazz, rock, punk and hip-hop in their day. All those genres learned the lesson that popular music invariably emerges from a complex matrix of business interests, creative energy and audience engagement; over-investment in the latter two categories in the name of some putative 'real', 'true' or 'authentic' moment located outwith the former invariably leads to fruitless attempts to sort out the worthy from the unworthy. These efforts always bring disappointment, and for two reasons: firstly, because in the realm of popular culture the *idea* of the authentic is in itself a product of the inauthentic – that is, of the capitalist imagination within which it is evoked; and secondly, because the authentic *per se* has no existence in reality – it is the site of something that cannot be located, the name for something that never happened.

Skinner Sawyers is not entirely to blame for the turn to 'something'. Many of the artists she evokes have at one time on another alluded to a Celtic presence within their music. In a *Time* article from 1996 about the worldwide success of Irish music, Enya referred to her music's 'melancholy', Mary Black discussed the 'passion' of Irish culture, and Christy Moore accounted for the success of Irish artists by pointing to the 'very interesting and colorful way' in which they use the English language (Walsh 1996: 80). Indeed, there are specific reasons – commercial and ideological – for the continuing attraction of the 'Celtic note', as Noel McLaughlin and Martin McLoone explain:

> the need to mark difference, especially in the global discourse of popular music, might also require the 'strategic' mobilisation of aspects of this 'Irishness' precisely to identify and mark out a space in the global 'noise' where the experience of being peripheral

might be articulated (and a firm political belief or sense of cultural identity asserted) (2000: 182).

Whether this explains the continuing vogue for Celtic music (a vogue that remains especially marked among the diasporic communities) is a moot point. What we can say is that with its touching faith in the persistence of an all-informing 'spirit' and its presumption of an ability to identify that spirit whenever and wherever it manifests itself, *The Complete Guide to Celtic Music* attempts to establish a range of diverse musical tendencies as a discrete cultural tradition. If there are 'spirits' in this book, however, they belong to Ernest Renan and Matthew Arnold, and it is about time those particular ghosts were laid to rest.

MARGINAL CULTURE – MARGINAL SPACE

Another critical route along which to approach the phenomenon of 'Celtic music' concerns the possibility of marginal culture – an idea (like Celticism itself) with a significant genealogy in the history of ideas. The idea of marginal culture emerges from a spatial imagination, one in which certain notions regulate and determine the various models of culture and power which circulate in any given society. This spatial imagination runs like a seam through western thought during the modern period. It is adapted during the early modern period in Newtonian science and Cartesian philosophy; it is refined during the Enlightenment by the likes of Locke and Kant; and it is brought to a position of discursive dominance during the nineteenth century in the philosophical systems of Hegel and Marx. It is, arguably, still the dominant way in which we make sense of the world, for it is still setting the limits on how human subjects imagine themselves to fit into society as well as into the natural world.

What are the distinguishing characteristics of this spatial imagination? Well, it is essentially a rationalist, positivist and scientific model of the world and of those who occupy it. One of its dominant cultural articulations is 'realism' – the notion that art can 'express' with greater or lesser accuracy the events of the 'real' world. It is linear, chronological and consequential. It is a model of existence in which observable causes give rise to observable, and more or less predictable, effects; likewise, it is a conception of existence in which the world is answerable to a set of observable and more or less predictable physical laws. And it is in terms of these observable, more or less predictable, physical laws that the entire range of discourses that we use to organise life on the planet is developed (Harvey 1989; Soja 1989).

Among the many elements of this scientific model, the one I wish to emphasise here is that of *structure*. The dominant spatial imagination encourages an understanding of the world in terms of the spatial relationship between phenomena.[3] The world is made up of objects which are organised into structural relations with each other; these structural relations, moreover, provide us with the dominant ways of making sense of the world. Consider, for example, the absolutely fundamental nature of the following sets of binaries: here/there; near/far; big/small; up/down; depth/breadth. Consider also the ineluctable influence on all aspects of human experience of concepts such as perspective, dimension, size, distance. These are the concepts which enable us to negotiate our way through the flux of time and space. At the same time, these are all effects of a spatial imagination that emphasises structure – a particular understanding of the world that has been so dominant for so long that we have come to consider it entirely natural. It is in fact extremely difficult to apprehend 'structure' as the ideological imposition it so clearly is; we must rely on theory to alert us to the entirely conventional nature of what might be described as 'the experience of experience'.

CENTRE AND MARGINS

One of the principal effects of the structural imagination is that of 'centre and margins', and this is the point at which a number of recognisable cultural and political traditions hove into view. A cursory glance reveals that the idea of 'centre and margins' animates a great deal of cultural and critical activity – so much so, in fact, that one might even claim it to be the single most significant idea informing humanistic and social scientific research in the modern era. The idea of centre/margins is at the heart of all oppositionalist analyses, including those organised in terms of what has been the dominant triumvirate of institutional research in the humanities: class, gender and race.

In terms of class, for example, there is the familiar Marxian critique of the domination of the means of production by an elite cadre of capitalists who form the centre of the civic, social and political world.[4] The category of culture (including that of art) is subject to the same spatial logic: 'true' art (as opposed to debased 'popular' forms or exotic 'primitive' forms) is defined in terms of a peculiar historical outlook which answers the needs of the western bourgeoisie during a particular phase of its evolution. To introduce a metaphor which is not quite a metaphor, bourgeois art moves to the centre of the stage, leaving other models of artistic production on the margins. 'Popular' and/or 'working-class' culture is relegated to the peripheries of meaningful discourse; its value, such as it is, is anthropological or historical or scientific. Whatever pleasure it might afford, it can tell us nothing useful about what it means to be a real subject; and this is precisely because the category of subjectivity has been so entirely and so successfully appropriated by the bourgeois world view.

So, class is a profoundly spatial notion, and this is just as true of the models imagined by progressive late-Marxist thinkers such as Antonio Gramsci and Louis Althusser. It is also the case with the category of gender which, as considered by generations of feminists since the late eighteenth century, clearly relies on an implicit spatial model of central/marginal relations.[5] Biological *Man* is at the centre; he has presence, agency, responsibility; his way of understanding and relating to the world is the real way – perhaps not the only way but certainly the preferred option for all parties and all contingencies. Because she sees the world differently, because she is not answerable to the demands of rational, linear, positivist, scientific thought, biological *Woman* is relegated to the margins – an exotic, charming yet dangerous alternative to the proper (which is to say, most effective) way of being in the world. The points introduced above pertain also to the consideration of race and ethnicity. The dominant paradigm of race studies in recent times has been postcolonialism, and this is a critical-theoretical practice which is implicitly founded on the spatial notion of centre and margins. Though refined in any number of ways by its principal exponents (including the so-called 'Holy Trinity' of Edward W. Said, Homi K. Bhabha and Gayatri Chakravorty Spivak), the principal object of postcolonial criticism has always been the ideological organisation of the world into a western centre and its margins (Said 1978, 1993). Much of the time, the various tactics and strategies (sometimes even the languages) relating to this spatial relationship have been adopted from class and gender politics. As with those other discourses, moreover, the racial subject is always already 'related' – which is to say, always already situated in a structure which is itself regulated by the prevailing array of political, moral and legal discourses.

A range of critical-theoretical initiatives – all operating more or less from a broadly poststructuralist/postmodernist perspective – have broached the possibility of a spatial imagination alternative to the one which has set the limits on traditional models of power. That alternative brings us back towards the 'Celtic', albeit via a detour through the strange beast that is 'Irish music'.

IRISH TRADITIONAL MUSIC

The roots of Celtic music lie in the twentieth-century folk movement and, in particular, in the revival of Irish traditional music which began in the 1960s. 'Traditional' music was in fact a relatively recent invention, a product of the socio-cultural practices of post-Famine Ireland. The genre was in effect a folk music that had evolved as an accompaniment to dancing; while other elements (ballads and slow airs, for example) had been incorporated over the centuries as an effect of changes to the fabric of Irish social, economic and political history.

Although infused with commercial considerations at every turn, Irish traditional music functioned by and large in isolation from 'properly' commercial music. It was also distanced from the art tradition which (as elsewhere in Europe) held an attraction for the established and the upwardly mobile classes. Traditional music was associated with the countryside; although widespread throughout Ireland, traditional music was in fact a marginal discourse in a country that was itself (both politically and geographically) on the edge of Europe.[6]

During the latter part of the eighteenth century, Irish music had become an object of interest for folklorists, anthropologists and musicologists. This was part of a European-wide pan-Celtic movement which was itself linked to the onset of Romanticism (Snyder 1923). Irish music was considered a significant object of scholarly interest both for what it could reveal about the island's cultural history, but also (and more importantly) for what it could contribute to a developing sense of what it meant to be Irish. The music embodied what was peculiar about such an identity; its existence necessitated an array of intellectual and institutional responses, and it was in terms of these responses that the identity would be enabled to make a social (and eventually a political) impact. Irish traditional music became politicised, in other words, and it has remained so ever since.

Shortly after the identification of music as an issue of crucial importance within Irish history, academic interest segued into commercial interest. In all manner of ways (composition, collection, performance, interpretation, competition, and so on), this particular form of music entered the marketplace, where it has remained ever since – or at least the *idea* of this particular form, for contention raged, then as now, as to its essential elements. Questions proliferated: What did 'real' Irish music sound like? Where did it come from and to whom did it belong? Was it primarily a racial or a musical category? Who was competent to distinguish it from other forms, both deserving (such as art music) and undeserving (rock or pop)? More significantly: who was empowered to make such distinctions?

Controversy notwithstanding, one of the earliest figures to exploit Irish music's commercial possibilities was the writer/composer Thomas Moore (see Chapter 2). Moore adapted existing scholarship for the demands of the contemporary market, producing a highly successful brand of 'Irish music'. Indeed, in some ways it is possible to regard Moore as the progenitor of the contemporary form of 'Celtic music', for he it was who adapted traditional forms and effects for a mass (in his case, mainly British) market. While definitions of the form have come and gone since Moore's time, the *idea* of Irish music – as both a political and a commercial prospect – has remained. And it was this idea that in time gave birth to the strange hybrid creature that has become known is modern popular music discourse as 'Celtic music'.

After the political revolution of the early twentieth century (a revolution that was largely inspired by, and eventually came to be dominated by, the ideology of nationalism), folk music was incorporated – along with sport, language, as well as certain economic and social practices – as part of a state-sponsored vision of what an essential Irish identity should entail. Irish traditional music was believed to articulate a very local sense of identity, in other words; even when it was transported (along with the great Irish diaspora) to all corners of the earth, the truth it spoke was a peculiarly 'Irish' truth.

When Irish society began to liberalise during the 1960s, one of the first ways in which that process was articulated was through the social organisation of music (Smyth 2005). New kinds of noise began to be heard – some of it loud, electric, discordant, 'unnatural' (a sort of euphemism for 'un-Irish'); some of these noises became mixed up with familiar, already established noises to produce revolutionary new sounds. It is here that one may locate the beginning of the revival of Irish traditional music, the period during which a particular musical discourse is wrested from one prevailing dispensation and begins to be re-articulated by new generations in terms of their concerns and desires. It would have been difficult for any young musician to play traditional music in the received ways once they had heard, say, Jimi Hendrix play the electric guitar; likewise, it would be difficult for any listener to respond to a traditional style of singing in the prescribed manner once they had heard Aretha Franklin sing a torch song. All in all, it is difficult for anyone interested in one form of music which features canonicity as a fundamental aspect of its discourse not to be affected by another form of music in which creativity is the predominant feature.

What I would like to suggest (and this is not a radical or controversial suggestion by any means) is that Irish traditional music since the 1960s has been profoundly influenced by developments in the wider field of popular music. Changes in technology; changes in economic practices regarding recording, distribution, playback, and so on; changes in fashion regarding instrumentation, sound, consumption; changes in the iconography of music and musicians; changes in the wider social function of music – all these and more have indelibly impacted upon the idea of Irish traditional music. Moreover, certain aspects of the music have been accentuated and distorted while other aspects have been either de-emphasised or completely silenced. The fact is that what passes for Irish traditional music today is very different from what was produced even two generations ago. Some people believe that this is a good thing; some people most definitely do not. Regardless of one's standpoint, the fact is that the function and meaning of the music have changed, and this has necessitated a change in the scholarly response to it.

What I would also like to suggest is that at some point this kind of music (which, it is important to remember, was once a 'marginal' cultural practice) was incorporated into the global mainstream so that it became one of a range of sounds that would be recognisable all over the world: not only in terms of its provenance (*where* it supposedly came from) but also in terms of a range of distinctive associations – by which

I mean the emotional, cultural and political effects that it supposedly solicits. Subjected to all that modern technology could throw at it, and cross-fertilised with other genres, this music also underwent a name change and emerged into the modern marketplace as a fully fledged genre in and of itself, one capable of attracting audiences, creating effects and influencing opinion: 'Celtic music'.

IT'S COOL TO BE A CELT

What does Celtic music sound like? Clannad are a family band from Donegal who developed a style of music during the 1970s incorporating elements of traditional, pop and jazz. In 1982 the band released the theme song from a television programme called *Harry's Game*, becoming the first act to have a hit in the UK charts with a Gaelic lyric. The sound of 'Theme from *Harry's Game*' was one that was to become very familiar in subsequent times: its lush, layered textures, its non-standard structure, its enigmatic content – all these became hallmarks of Celtic music. That breakthrough recording was followed by 1985's collaboration with Bono (lead singer with the Irish rock band U2) entitled 'In A Lifetime', by which time Clannad had established their own sonic identity within a much wider soundscape (see Chapter 8).

Other significant moments include the first appearance of former Clannad member Eithne Ní Bhraonáin (Enya) on the BBC programme *Top of the Pops* with her number 1 hit 'Orinoco Flow' (1988). Enya went on to become a global phenomenon, selling millions of records and appearing whenever a particular kind of 'Celtic' effect was required. Two of her highest-profile impacts in recent years were as singer of one of the theme songs from Peter Jackson's *Lord of the Rings* trilogy (2004), and as musical accompaniment – with a song entitled 'Only Time' from her 2000 album *A Day Without Rain* – to the emotive footage of the events of 9/11 in New York. Such evocations reveal a great deal about what has come to be expected of the version of Irish traditional music that has segued so irresistibly into this phenomenon called Celtic music. Other evidence is provided by the worldwide success of *Riverdance* (2005) and *Lord of the Dance* (1998) (both of which incorporate elements of Irish traditional music) and the use of so-called Celtic elements in the theme music of worldwide blockbuster movies such as *Braveheart* (1995) and *Titanic* (1997).

There was a point during the 1990s when it was a definite career advantage in all sorts of fields to be able to boast an Irish heritage, or failing that, at least some Celtic blood. Scots or Welsh might do at a pinch, but Irishness was the trump card. It was during this period that Enya came to personify a kind of Celtic cool – sophisticated, attractive, engaging and yet slightly remote at the same time. The Republic was doing very well economically; diasporic Irish culture (especially in Great Britain and the United States) was as confident as it had ever been; postcolonial theory was encouraging the notion that the Irish were all recovering victims of malevolent British imperialism; the Peace Process was creating a cultural dividend in Northern Ireland while also revising the image of the Irish as a benighted, unforgiving race. Most significantly, Celticism became associated with a discourse of spirituality which was widely touted to be at odds with prevailing western social values stressing material success as the measure of happiness and achievement. All things considered, it was a good time to be Celtic; and music was a crucial – perhaps the single most important – element of that condition.

CELTIC MUSIC: A MARGINAL DISCOURSE?

Bringing together these two elements: on the one hand, there is a powerful tendency established within western thought – perhaps the overriding tendency (arguably since the Renaissance, certainly since the Enlightenment) – to organise phenomena in particular spatial configurations which align, apparently, with a positivist model of human agency. Everything relates to everything else in terms of their spatial location: thus we can speak meaningfully of centres and margins, and of a huge array of accompanying terms and concepts which allow us to cognitively map the world and to come to a sense of our own place within it. As an instance of that kind of thinking, we have the phenomenon of Celtic music which, while attempting to retain some of the glamour associated with the marginal practices (Irish traditional music) from which it evolved, clearly embodies the values of the centre, if considered in economic, political or social terms.

The standard political-economy critique of contemporary Celtic music would go something like this: the global music industry is a capitalist business, and as such it needs (to adapt a metaphor from the natural world) to feed and protect itself in order to keep alive and growing. Capitalism is always hungry, but it is important that it feeds judiciously, with an eye to the future, if it is to continue to dominate the local environment. In this case, of course, the local environment just happens to be the whole world.

Celtic music might be regarded as one element of the 'World Music' phenomenon, which many commentators saw as the latest stage in an age-old process whereby the western centre remakes itself in relation to the exotic culture of the southern and eastern peripheries (Bohlman 2002: 150–81). What this entails is the identification and monitoring of emerging musical genres and scenes by the global music industry, in order for new trends to be tapped, adapted, even nurtured to some extent – but always within the terms which reproduce the industry in its established form. What does this mean? It means that any new music genre or scene is subject to macro-discursive processes determining issues such as production, distribution, marketing and so on – processes that have evolved to ensure the continuing dominance of the industry in its established form, and to maximise profits. But also, and more insidiously, it means that any new music is subject to micro-discursive processes which profoundly affect what the music sounds like: instrumental technique, recording technique, length, volume, regional style, the prevalence of sub-genres within a recognisable genre, and so on. It is possible to observe an instance of this micro-discursive impact in the changing status of the slow air within Irish traditional music, for example, and its re-orientation for specific affective purposes within the discourse of contemporary Celtic music. But this is just one of countless ways in which a genre such as Irish traditional music is subsumed within the global culture industry.

Dominated by a small number of major record companies (themselves affiliated to media conglomerates located in centres of activity such as Los Angeles and London), contemporary popular music emerges from the global–local interplay of economic and cultural processes. So much so, in fact, that at some point it becomes difficult to conceptualise (and mistaken to try to do so) the relations between local and global in terms of a centre/margins relationship. Local culture provides the substance, the raw material, which the culture industries will convert into a global product; but the culture industries are themselves surrounded by a dense matrix of institutions and practices without which no product would be available, and in the absence of which no subjective engagement with the product would be possible.

The fact is that the contemporary cultural industries no longer adhere to the received spatial model of centre/margins relations. Such a model evolved in response to an earlier political-economic dispensation which was locked in to nineteenth-century industrialisation and modernist economics (Harvey 1989: 125–40). As far as music is concerned, the centre-periphery model is especially associated with the Marxist critic Theodor Adorno who, having fled to the United States from Nazi Germany in the 1930s, was concerned about the way in which culture – especially art, and even more especially music – was being warped by capitalist economics (1973).

Such a model does not answer the demands of postmodern capitalism, however, with its mobility, its quest for synergy, its speed, and its economies of scope (Harvey 1989: 141–72; Jameson 1991: 154–80). The traditional model which both depended upon and supported the notion of a distinction between inside and outside, between centre and margins, has been superseded; in its place is a much more fluid, much more flexible notion of interdependent interest groups operating from a great variety of locations. It no longer makes sense to speak of 'centre and margins' – and it certainly no longer makes sense to mount a critique of contemporary capitalist practices in terms of these concepts – if the target of that critique no longer functions with reference to that old spatial model.

In other words, if the object for analysis has changed radically, then so too must the analysis of the object. As theorists such as Fredric Jameson (1991, 2000), David Harvey (1989) and Slavoj Žižek (2006) have argued, it is inappropriate for critical discourse to adhere to the standard spatial imagination of centre and margins if culture itself no longer functions in those terms. What is required is a different way to conceptualise contemporary cultural practices if we are to make sense, for example, of a phenomenon such as Celtic music and the way in which it functions.

OTHER SPACES, OTHER MEANINGS

As one means by which to begin to think beyond the limitations of received spatial thinking, I would just like to mention the work of the French philosophers Gilles Deleuze and Felix Guattari, and in particular

Celtic Music: From the Margins to the Centre (And Back Again?) 99

their deployment of the 'rhizome', which is a term described in their 1980 book *A Thousand Plateaus: Capitalism and Schizophrenia*. Before proceeding any further I should explain that the introduction of this concept here is not intended as a solution to anything; it is merely a way to begin the process of thinking about unfamiliar issues and rethinking familiar ones. It points towards a conceptual experiment which may or may not have implications at a methodological level; therein lie its limitations, but also its potentially fruitful uses.

The 'rhizome' is an audacious rhetorical concept which refers to any non-hierarchical network in which established practices of logic, causation, filiation, and so on cannot function. In the introduction to *A Thousand Plateaus* Deleuze and Guattari describe rhizome with reference to a number of characteristic principles: connection, heterogeneity, multiplicity, rupture:

> [Unlike] trees of their roots, the rhizome connects any point to any other point, and its traits are not necessarily linked to other traits of the same nature; it brings into play very different regimes of signs, and even nonsign states ... A rhizome has no beginning or end; it is always in the middle, between things, interbeing, *intermezzo*. The tree is filiation, but the rhizome is alliance, uniquely alliance. The tree imposes the verb 'to be', but the fabric of the rhizome is the conjunction 'and ... and ... and ...' (1987: 21, 25).

Rhizomatic thought is anti-systemic, contingent and improvisatory; it does not follow established narrative principles, it does not proceed ineluctably along pre-established lines towards pre-determined goals. It proceeds, rather, by way of connections between different, seemingly incommensurable, parts of the system; it is chaotic, polymorphous and metamorphic, forging temporary links between different languages and different categories only for them to disintegrate as new pathways are mapped and new connections forged. Above all, the rhizome is always and everywhere opposed to binary thought, always and everywhere opposed to an ordered, hierarchical model of reality in which everything is (and can only ever be) itself.

If rhizomatic thought is brought to bear upon the phenomenon of contemporary Celtic music, a different kind of critique begins to emerge. What this entails in effect is the impossibility of approaching the field as a political and/or commercial practice with reference to an outmoded spatial model founded on the relations between the centre and the margins. It is instead necessary to think of this contemporary genre in terms of system, of flow – as a web comprised of many different agents: musicians, producers, business personnel, consumers, and so on. These agents, moreover, occupy many different spaces and pursue many different goals – uncertain and changing goals; they form temporary alliances between themselves, they operationalise different value systems, they *use* the music differently. Likewise, contemporary 'Celtic music' comprises a web of many different, related and overlapping activities: writing, performing, deciding, recording, marketing, selling, consuming. Such activities also occur in many different locations: the home, the pub, the concert hall, the office, the factory, the shop, and so on.

In short, it is necessary to recognise that the music – as well as all the attendant activities surrounding the music – are simply not answerable to an increasingly outmoded model of cultural production based on the spatial concept of centre/margins. Seán Ó Riada famously likened

> the progress of tradition in Ireland to the flow of a river. Foreign bodies may fall in, or be dropped in, or thrown in, but they do not divert the course of the river, nor do they stop it flowing; it absorbs them, carrying them with it and it flows onward (1982: 20).

Embedded within this image is what Deleuze and Guattari describe as a 'conception of voyage and movement' (1987: 25), a narrative of primacy and privilege, a structure of belonging and identification. Against such an image, rhizomatic thought provides us with an opportunity to understand Celtic music as 'a stream without beginning or end that undermines its banks and picks up speed in the middle' (1987: 25).

The related point is that critics are obliged to think about their own analyses in respect of this situation. The complexity of the secondary critique, in other words, must respect and resonate with the complexity of the primary source. There is little point in continuing to talk about centres and margins if the object of analysis has left that particular model of spatial relations far behind. Considering Celtic music as a rhizomatic phenomenon necessarily changes the emphasis of any critical approach; indeed, returning to an earlier point, such a re-orientation may mitigate the hermeneutics of suspicion which tend to dominate analyses based on the classical structural model. The critic Timothy D. Taylor alludes to this when he claims Celtic music to be 'caught up in myriad commodifying, noncommodifying, and uncommodified practices at any one time and in any particular place'. This should not be regarded as a source of pessimism, however, but as a call upon commentators to understand and to respect cultural practices that

> permit consumers to find a moment of stability in the otherwise fragmenting nature of today's hustle bustle world, to find an identity, however temporary, that offers a sense of self rooted in both place and community marked by ethnicity or race (2003: 282).

Only the most cynical could doubt the force of this search for a rooted self, even in the face of the rhizomatic economics characterising postmodern capitalism. It may be, then, that Celtic music is best approached as a discourse that functions along a continuum between rootedness (on the part of musicians and consumers) and rootlessness (on the part of those attempting to understand how it works).[7]

Listening to the Novel: The Role and Representation of Traditional Music in Contemporary Irish Fiction

How can one 'listen' to a novel? Although prose narratives are still occasionally read aloud, and although the audio book has emerged as a viable commercial prospect in the early twenty-first century, most would agree that the contemporary novel is a form usually consumed alone and in silence. Moreover, the novel does not produce any remarkable sound of itself, other than perhaps a rustle of turning pages or a dull thud as it is set down. In fact, silence appears to be built in to the novel's historical, sociological and commercial heritage. In this sense, anyone wishing to 'listen to the novel' is going to be disappointed and will, moreover, appear a little foolish.

By 'listening to the novel' I mean addressing to the ways in which music has impacted upon the formal and conceptual organisation of a particular literary form; reflecting upon the value accorded thematic material that is noisy by definition within a medium that is predominantly silent; most importantly, I mean attending to music's representation in relation to a variety of discourses within a particular socio-political formation over an extended period of time. By 'listening' to the novel in these ways I suggest it is possible to identify some of the most potent issues bearing upon Irish society, past and present: both the ways in which it has been organised, and the means by which it may be understood.

As mentioned in the introduction to this volume, the existence of formative links between music and literature in Irish cultural history has begun to be acknowledged. As a contribution to the development of that process, in this chapter I want to consider some of the theoretical and methodological issues pertaining to the study of music in fiction, before going on to look at a number of contemporary Irish novels in which one particular style of music features. Given the key status of the words 'Ireland', 'music' and 'fiction' within my general remit here, I may be forgiven for taking a short detour through the example of James Joyce before commencing towards my primary goal.

Before that, however, the question arises as to the disciplinary context within which an analysis of the role and representation of traditional music in contemporary Irish fiction could proceed. On this I have two related points to make. Firstly, I subscribe to a materialist position which insists that *general* categories must always and everywhere be considered in relation to *specific* historical experience: both 'music' and 'fiction, that is to say, are always qualified by the geo-political formations within which they subsist. If postcolonial theory has taught us anything, it is that 'perspective' represents the key element in all cultural discourse – including most centrally those which claim objectivity in some or other terms. The music with which I am concerned here is a particular form of Irish music; the literary form in which that music is represented emerges from a tradition of Irish prose fiction; it seems axiomatic to me that the representation of the former in terms of the latter should be determined to a formative extent by the specifically national (although not nationalist) element with these traditions.

Secondly, I admit that I am neither a literary critic nor a musicologist, but a cultural historian by training, inclination and profession. In principle I am oriented towards *all* forms of writing, although for present purposes I restrict myself to texts that qualify to be described as 'prose fiction'. At the same time, and for the same reasons, I find myself drawn towards an understanding of music which, as described by the American cultural historian Lawrence Kramer, attempts to destabilise 'firm distinctions between cultivated and vernacular forms, and in principle takes all music as its province' (2003: 126). The engagement with a 'vernacular form' (Irish traditional music) within the terms of a 'cultivated form' (the Irish literary novel) represents one of the key issues broached in this chapter.

Reference to Kramer leads me to claim the 'cultural musicology' associated with him as a formative critical influence. I identify closely with his premise that music is above all else 'worldly': both *in* and *of* the world – composed of, referring to and influenced by matters which have observable consequences for a range of subjects in what, for better or worse, tends to be known as 'the real world'. This understanding is opposed to a more traditional one which sees music as being 'otherworldly' – as John Shepherd puts it:

> Because the sounds of music function in a non-denotative fashion and do not refer to the external world, music is thought of as being devoid of worldly significance, either 'empty', or replete with formal properties, but none that would speak to the material and therefore social worlds (1999: 162).

One of the clearest ways in which music might be seen as worldly is its *wordiness* – that is, its amenability to linguistic, as opposed to purely musical, treatment. Music is always being talked about and written about, always being described in languages of various kind. Crucially, music is always being *reconstituted* in language. Music may possess the ability to 'speak for itself' – 'on its "own" terms', as Kramer puts it (2003: 124); I have no wish to dispute this, and am indeed keen to avoid the claim that musical meaning can *only* exist as a function of linguistic ascription. I do contend, however, that music inevitably speaks the language of those discourses within which it is invoked – which is to say, the linguistic discourses within which the sound of music is constantly encountered and re-encountered. 'Words', Kramer writes,

> situate music in a multiplicity of cultural contexts, both those to which the music 'belongs' in an immediate sense and those to which it stands adjacent in ways that often become apparent only once the words are in play ... Musical meaning is produced less by the signs of a musical semiotics than by signs about music, signs whose grounding in historically specific forms of subjectivity is the source of their legitimation, not of their – literal – insignificance (2003: 125, 130).

In reconnecting music with the wider cultural contexts within which it is composed, performed and consumed, cultural musicology provides an imprimatur for interventions such as the present chapter. For it turns out that music looms surprisingly large in the history of Irish fiction. Novelists from every generation, working within every subgenre, have responded to the power of music by incorporating it into their narratives, by trying to harness its techniques and effects, and by attempting to recreate the emotions that come to be associated with particular musical styles, forms and/or texts. In fact, music represents a recurring feature of the tradition, one ranging from those texts in which it plays a seemingly incidental (although usually strategically significant) role to those in which it permeates the formal and conceptual fabric of the entire text.

MUSIC AND THE NOVEL: A THEORETICAL OVERVIEW

In his essay 'Musical Form as a Problem in Literary Criticism' William E. Grim claims that '[generally] speaking, there are three ways in which music may influence the creation (and by extension, the critical reception) of literature' (1999: 237). These three ways are: the inspirational; the metaphorical; and the formal.

Of the 'inspirational' level of influence, Grim writes:

> A writer of fiction or poetry may simply be inspired by a particular piece of music in the act of creating a work of literature. This is a case of music being the writer's muse. At this level of influence the work of music is not utilized as subject matter or thematic material for the work of literature it inspires (1999: 237).

It is an unfortunate person who has never been 'inspired' by music; such, indeed, has come to function as one of the principal 'meanings' of music in society – its ability to *inspire* certain emotional responses among its listeners, responses which may in turn lead to observable consequences. It has been a commonplace of Western culture for over two hundred years that listening to the music of Beethoven, for example, can change the way you understand the world – can *inspire* you, in fact, to re-orient yourself in relation to the world, to act and behave differently as a result of the sounds that have penetrated your brain by way of your ear.

At the same time, Grim's definition seems far too narrow to encompass the many and varied ways in which music may impact upon either the composition or the interpretation of the literary text. When one considers the seminal role that music has played in the development of a range of philosophical systems since the eighteenth century, and when one notes the impact of those systems upon generations of writers and readers, then it is necessary to acknowledge that music has indeed 'inspired' the novel – but often in ways that are far from 'simple', far from acting as an occasional 'muse' for the writer in search of a spark. We need to acknowledge, in other words, that music is linked to the novel first and foremost in as much as they are both part of an ancient and ongoing process of inquiry into 'the human' – a process that encompasses issues such as the special role of language in the evolution of the species, the question of consciousness, the historical development of a moral imagination, and the role of creative culture in the apprehension of the human.

Turning to Grim's second influence, we find that with music so central to a range of humanistic and social scientific disciplines, it was inevitable that it would begin to feature at the thematic level in various artistic media, even those that were primarily non-musical in orientation. Because they were born of the same philosophical matrix – the one focused on the relationship between language, experience and consciousness – literary discourse proved especially receptive to music, incorporating it (as Grim puts it) 'as the subject matter, point of departure, or intertextual reference within the work of literature' (1999: 238). This might seem a natural adaptation in relation to poetic discourse; after all, poetry and music shared a common concern with rhythm, and they had been locked together through the practice of singing from an early point in the evolution of the species. Music as metaphorical presence also made a strong and enduring impact on the novel, however, and nowhere more so than in Ireland where the history of both media is so enmeshed with the wider question of national identity (Smyth 1997; White 1998).

Grim extends music's influence to 'the critical reception' of literature, and this becomes significant when we consider the work of the single most important theorist of the novel. Stephen Benson (2006: 73) has pinpointed the passage within *Problems of Dostoyevsky's Poetics* in which Mikhail Bakhtin transposes musical concepts – specifically, polyphony and counterpoint – into literary critical discourse. Against Bakhtin's contention that such a transposition represents 'a graphic analogy, nothing more', Benson argues that a particular understanding of music (or at least of certain musical effects and properties) was in fact vital to Bakhtin's imagination of novelistic discourse in every aspect, from its (pre) historical evolution to its consummation in 'the multi-levelledness and multi-voicedness of the polyphonic novel' as exemplified by the work of Dostoyevsky.[1] The fact is that music in one way or another informs the work of *the* leading modern theorist of the novel; that it provides him with concepts and tools for tracing the evolution of the genre and for explaining its workings; that it locates the novel at the nexus of an ongoing, multidisciplinary debate incorporating issues of language, meaning, history and consciousness; and that this both justifies and demands a dedicated critical discourse focused on the role and representation of music in the novel.

The final element in Grim's tripartite model relates to the problem of form. The question occurs: supposing you are a novelist 'inspired' by music, and supposing further that you do wish to incorporate music into your writing: *how* are you going to do it? One response, both obvious and valid, might be: by introducing it at the thematic level – that is, by making it an element of greater or lesser narrative significance within the plot. But such a response raises another question: might not *what* you say about music have implications for *how* you say it? In other words, is it possible that *fiction about music* always has a tendency towards *musicalised fiction*, that is, towards a kind of writing which attempts to recreate some aspect of the musical material which has been invoked at a thematic level?

These questions arise in the context of a consideration of how a novelist's concern with music as inspiration or metaphor impacts upon the formal structure of the text – how 'the work of literature utilizes or attempts to imitate musical forms and/or compositional procedures within a literary context' (Grim 1999: 238). All art embodies a negotiation between *what* it represents and *how* it represents it; but this is complicated in the case of the music-novel because music has traditionally been regarded as the art wherein form and matter, theme and expression, are most thoroughly enmeshed. Walter Pater's famous dictum regarding the pre-eminence of music is worth quoting at length:

> It is the art of music which most completely realises this artistic ideal, this perfect identification of matter and form. In its consummate moments, the end is not distinct from the means, the form from the matter, the subject from the expression; they inhere in and completely saturate each other; and to it, therefore, to the condition of its perfect moments, all the arts may be supposed constantly to tend and aspire ... Therefore, although each art has its incommunicable element, its untranslatable order of impressions, its unique mode of reaching the 'imaginative reason',

yet the arts may be represented as continually struggling after the law or principle of music, to a condition which music alone completely realises ... (1910: 138–9).

According to this theory, any novel approaches 'the law or principle of music' in so far as it attempts to 'obliterate' the division between form and content; the novel *about* music functions as a special case, however, in as much as its subject matter (music) is precisely the practice wherein the form/matter division is (according to common perception) always already collapsed. What this means is that every such text realises a tension between different (possibly opposing) levels of musical influence: one general, emerging from what may be regarded as an historical tendency among all the arts towards a specifically musical effect (the 'perfect identification of matter and form'); one specific, emerging from the textual event-in-progress, in which the music represented at the level of plot is revealed to have a bearing on the organisation of the narrative.

The situation with regard to the musical novel is complicated still further by the impact of yet another tier of significance: textual criticism. For the question insists: must the occurrence of musical effects and features in the novel always be the result of authorial intention, or may it appear without the intention or even the knowledge of the writer? For example, a novel might incorporate any number of formal techniques – rhythm, repetition, counterpoint, leitmotif, theme and variation, and so on – that could be identified as having a musical function. Is it legitimate, if the author was not aware of or did not intend those functions, to interpret the text with reference to musical discourse? Put another way: to what extent is the presence of music in the novel a matter of critical *ascription*, as opposed to authorial *inscription*? The likelihood is that anyone, depending on their taste and/or competence, could 'discover' musical effects and influences in a novel. For example, it may seem bizarre, or just plain wrong (it is certainly anachronistic), to describe *Finnegans Wake* as a 'punk' novel, but it seems clear that in some respects Joyce's text does offer itself up for such an interpretation. It seems equally clear, however, that such a characterisation would raise more questions – regarding value, legitimacy, method, and so on – than it could ever answer.

All in all, the question of form in the music-novel is extraordinarily complex, because there are a number of different forces operating constantly (although not equally) upon the text: the forces of history, of narrative, of criticism. Moreover, the apprehension of form introduces a self-reflexive element into any critical discourse which takes as its object the musical novel, in so far as every individual project will be obliged to incorporate, with a greater or lesser degree of self-consciousness, a theory of how musical content might be related to literary form. Likewise, every such project will be obliged to acknowledge that the critical separation of form from content is either conventional (which is perhaps acceptable), illusory (which is not), or (and this is the worst of all) contrary to the spirit of the literary text under analysis.

THE EXEMPLARY CASE OF JAMES JOYCE

Joyce has emerged as the quintessential Anglophone modernist in a number of ways; none more so, however, than in his recalcitrant attitude towards received literary discourses, and more specifically in his attempt to bring literary and musical discourses into some kind of fructifying relationship. Building on the insights and achievements of previous experiments, Joyce was intent on re-animating the field of prose fiction so that it was answerable to his understanding of art and its role in human experience. As a talented amateur singer, moreover, he was well disposed towards a consideration of music as an aesthetic system through which such a radical project could be broached. Together with Marcel Proust and Thomas Mann, Joyce was responsible for 'musicalising' the European novel in ways, and to an extent, with which the genre is still coming to terms (Smyth 2008).

A number of stories in *Dubliners* (1914) signal the emblematic role that music will come to play in Joyce's art. Sometimes – as with the seemingly throwaway references in 'Eveline' and 'After the Race' – music appears incidental, although as generations of dedicated researchers have shown, every reference is thoroughly enmeshed in the complex narrative webs woven by the author. In other stories ('A Painful Case' and 'A Mother', for example), music assumes a more central narrative role. It is in the final story, 'The Dead', however, that Joyce's obsession becomes apparent (see Chapter 3). The significance of music for the group gathered in a house in Dublin on a winter night at the beginning of the twentieth century is signalled in a variety of ways: it is an accompaniment to dancing, one of the main activities of the evening; all three hosts are involved in music in some form or other – as performers, organisers or teachers; it forms the major topic for discussion during dinner, as different styles, periods and performers are introduced and evaluated. As Joyce shows, music is woven into the fabric of contemporary Dublin life in a manner that both reflects and comments upon a supposed innate national proclivity.

Music is incorporated as part of Joyce's critique of contemporary Ireland and its bland, disappointing imitation of the English culture from which it was ostensibly attempting to separate itself. It would be erroneous to maintain, however, that 'any discussion of Joyce's "musical" technique in fiction writing need not concern itself with references to actual music, heard or performed in his novels, but with the musical experience as a metaphor for life and for the novelist's attempt to translate this metaphor into words' (Aronson 1980: 39). On the contrary, Joyce is one of the few writers for whom thematic references to music are at least as significant as experiments with transposing musical into literary discourse, something that is borne out in his most daring and most elaborate experiment with musical fiction.

Incorporated as Chapter 11 of *Ulysses*, 'Sirens' is generally recognised as an extraordinary achievement, '[containing] remarkable analogies to musical microstructures and general compositional techniques as well as some fine word music' (Wolf 1999: 138). The story of Joyce's ambitions for this piece of writing has been told often enough; critics since Stuart Gilbert have followed the author's direction in regarding the chapter's 'art' as music, its 'organ' as the ear, and its 'technic' as the '*fuga per canonem*' – this latter term translating as something like 'fugue according to rule' (Joyce 1993: 875). Basically, in his desire to incorporate Ulysses' encounter with the Sirens in the Homeric original, Joyce produced an extended piece of writing in which he attempts to render written language according to the precepts of music – using techniques (such as onomatopoeia, puns, neologisms, and extensive repetition) which militate against language's traditional signifying function. The result, as Gilbert wrote, was a chapter 'which both in structure and in diction goes far beyond all previous experiments in the adaptation of musical technique and timbres to a work of literature' (1952: 239).

Various critics have devised ingenious ways of interpreting the product of Joyce's musical imagination.[2] Among all the critical responses 'Sirens' has elicited, however, two points are worth stressing for present purposes. Firstly, even as Joyce was extending the possibilities of literary music, he was at the same time exposing its limitations, and revealing (by example if not by intention) the referential powers of language and narrative above and beyond 'pure music'. It may be, as Wolf suggests, that 'the higher the degree of musicalness the less a text is recognizable as narrative fiction' (1999: 78). Nevertheless, as the editor-critic Jeri Johnson writes, with reference to the famous quote cited earlier:

> If Joyce takes Pater seriously in pushing narrative as far as it might go toward imitating the form/matter dissolution in music, he also parodically pushes Pater into an admission that the sensible words formed into narratives which are novels necessarily refuse the decomposition into pure sound required in music. For *Ulysses* (and no less *Ulysses*) resists the Sirens' song (1993: 876).

It would appear, in other words, that written language retains an ineluctable 'will-to-signify', no matter the extent to which such a will is deliberately alienated as the artist pursues some form or level of experience which cannot be expressed by means of 'normal' language. It seems clear that Joyce belonged (with critical retrospection, perhaps, but also self-consciously to a certain extent) to a modernist movement which was intent on deconstructing not only an entire range of received narratives, but the very category of narrative itself. Nevertheless, narrative subsists within 'Sirens' – with familiar characters and locations, dialogue, themes, plot developments, and so on. Time moves, characters meet, the story advances – all the stuff of the traditional mimetic novel is present, even if remotely. Joyce, it seems, retained an investment in 'story', no matter the pioneering lengths to which he was willing to go to mitigate the effects of traditional mimesis.

The second point is a general critical-theoretical one, but one which, I maintain, has its origin in musicological discourse. The attempt to render human consciousness as fully and as honestly as possible led many modernist writers – either by deliberate analogy or by accident – to attempt to replicate musical effects in their work. As William Freedman writes:

> Simultaneity, the impingement of past and future on present and vice versa, the interrelationship, repetition, and overlapping of ideas, the intricate and mysterious associations of those ideas, and the sudden or prepared transitions between thoughts, attitudes,

and emotions – all are characteristic of the processes of interior experience, all are characteristic of the processes of musical development (1978: 49).

As a writer dedicated to capturing inner consciousness in novel ways, Joyce turned – sometimes deliberately (as in 'Sirens'), sometimes without apparent purpose or intention – to a cultural medium which both his education and his inclination led him to believe was equipped for the task by Nature itself. In doing so, he advanced the possibilities of the music-novel beyond anything previously attempted, and his impact on future experiments has been inescapable. I want to suggest, however, that the influence of *Ulysses* in general, and of 'Sirens' in particular, extends forwards *and* backwards. If since its publication the text has obliged every musically inclined novelist to re-assess their motivation and their method, its presence may be discerned in *all* musical fiction, including that which pre-dates it – as a kind of imagined ideal 'Text', as yet unwritten but providing sanction and example for every new experiment in the field. As the full development always resides within the musical note or phrase, so the music-novel always resides within the first tentative uses of musical effects to mitigate narrative discourse. Thus, novels such as *Tristram Shandy* (1760–7), *The Wild Irish Girl* (1807), *The Lake* (1905) and *The Crock of Gold* (1912) resonate more clearly *after* 'Sirens', because the former were 'composed' in anticipation of the latter – in anticipation, that is to say, of what a fully dedicated music-novel would be.

Bearing all this in mind, I wish now to look briefly at a selection of novels in which Irish traditional music is represented in order to consider how such representations draw upon (and in doing so necessarily modify) the meaning of the music that circulates in the wider cultural context. The over-riding issue for such an analysis, as Stephen Benson points out,

> is not the success or otherwise of the evocation, but the nature of the performance: the question of how and why music is staged, and to what desired end. Reading music in the novel allows us to see, literally and literarily, how music is received *as music*. Fiction serves as earwitness to the role of music in everyday life, a record of why, where and how music is made, heard and received (2007: 4).

TRADITIONAL MUSIC IN CONTEMPORARY IRISH FICTION

The Bodhrán Makers (1986) takes place in and around Listowel, the small rural town in County Kerry in which John B. Keane grew up and lived for most of his life. Keane's attitude towards his native parish accorded with the division which Patrick Kavanagh (another writer with an acute sense of his rural roots) observed at large throughout Irish cultural history: that between a positive parochialism and an insidious provincialism. 'The parochial mentality,' wrote Kavanagh, 'is never in any doubt about the social and artistic validity of his parish ... In Ireland we are provincial not parochial, for it requires a great deal of courage to be parochial' (quoted in Smyth 1998: 108).

Part of the 'social and artistic validity' that Keane wanted to celebrate in his novel was the ancient custom known as 'Hunting the Wren'. Groups of outlandishly dressed people, many of them playing musical instruments, would travel around the parish on St Stephen's Day, ostensibly in pursuit of a bird which had the misfortune to become associated in folklore with betrayal. Although its roots lie in long-established beliefs and practices (some of which are common across Europe), latterly the Wren became an important event in the cultural calendar of many parts of rural Ireland. The 'hunt' frequently ended with a party at which food and alcohol would be provided, paid for by donations collected during the course of the day. Both the procession and the ensuing party provided opportunities for public performance, play-acting and sociability up to and beyond the point of flirting with the opposite sex.

Because of its association with music, masks and humour, it is possible to regard the Wren as an example of what Bakhtin famously and influentially theorised as 'the carnivalesque'. This term refers to a tradition, with roots going back at least as far as Roman times, in which everyday reality is temporarily suspended and the normal precepts of established power are mocked.[3] As a form of carnival, it is not surprising that the Wren should become a target for the representatives of authority in Dirrabeg – those agents with an investment in 'hierarchical rank, privileges, norms, and prohibitions'.

In specifically musical terms, and equally suggestive for an analysis of the political aspect of the Wren, is Jacques Attali's characterisation of 'a subversive strain of music [that] has always managed to survive, subterranean and pursued' (1985: 13). This strain is an 'inverse image' of the perennial attempt on the part of established power to control music's subversive potential through three specific 'channelling' techniques which Attali describes as 'forgetting, believing, and silencing': 'Make people Forget,' he writes, 'make them Believe, Silence them. In all three cases, music is a tool of power' (1985: 19).

Authority in *The Bodhrán Makers* is embodied most clearly in the figure of Canon Tett, a bully and a martinet who browbeats his staff and threatens summary excommunication for anyone opposing his rule. The principal target of his anger are the two poor farmers who lead the Dirrabeg Wrenboys: an older man named 'Bluenose' Herrity (an expert bodhrán maker) and his younger neighbour Donal Hallapy (an expert player of that unique percussive instrument). In their different ways, these two characters embody an alternative form of power within the parish – the power of a traditional music which, subterranean though it may be, must be 'pursued' and silenced by established authority.

The struggle over the Wren ritual accumulates symbolic weight during the course of the text. With reference to Attali's third channelling technique, we observe that traditional music is depicted as a defence against the silence which both the state and the Church are seeking to impose (or to re-impose) over the landscape: the state by its inept economic performance, the Church by its intolerance towards any instance of vernacular culture which deflects attention from its own agenda. The novel opens with a brief preface set twenty-five years after the main action of the story; and the main thing that strikes the character who is taking his grandson on a tour of the area is 'the mortifying silence' (1986: 8) into which it has slipped. The dialectic between silence and sound is repeated in a scene which constitutes the crisis of the novel, when Canon Tett and his curate Father Donlea interrupt the Wren party. After abusing and threatening the revellers, the Canon turns his attention to the musicians:

> 'If you have any sense now,' the Canon addressed himself to Bluenose and the others, 'you'll stop this tomfoolery and go to your beds. It's past two o'clock in the morning and you'll be entering the Church of God in a few short hours. Do not, under pain of excommunication, enter my church with the sign of drink on you. Go on along with you now and prepare yourselves for the Sabbath.'
>
> Nobody moved. From the stairs the drumming of the bodhrán

increased in volume. The Canon turned, anger flashing in his eyes, his face contorted.

'Stop that infernal sound,' he shouted. 'Stop it at once or I'll put God's curse upon you.'

Donal Hallapy placed the cipín behind his ear and placed the palm of his right hand on the surface of the bodhrán. Still the sound persisted, infinitely fainter now, almost inaudible.

'Put that thing from you!' the Canon commanded. There was no response from Donal Hallapy. His eyes were fastened on the hand which covered the surface of the bodhrán. There was no movement from the hand but if one drew close and peered intently one might see that the fingers rippled almost inperceptibly on the goatskin. From a distance the rhythmic beat must seem to be generated by the instrument itself.

Father Donlea wondered at Donal's expertise. There was no movement from the hand that he could see and yet the muted, haunting, rippling tattoo persisted. Sometimes it seemed to come from a distance, yet all the time, vaguely sinister, it pervaded the kitchen, creating a strange tension. He noted too that the eyes of the man who held the bodhrán had closed. Yet he wasn't asleep. His body was too taut for that. A look of uncertainty had crept over Canon Tett's face. For once he was speechless. The uncertainty became transformed into puzzlement and from puzzlement once more to anger.

'Put that infernal contraption from your hand!' he called.

Donal reacted by snatching the cipín from behind his ear and belting the bodhrán with a ferocity and speed which alarmed Father Donlea. From where the curate stood the man with the bodhrán seemed to be possessed. The vibrant drumming filled the kitchen; it was almost deafening. The Canon placed both hands over his ears as Donal Hallapy with unbelievable dexterity wrenched the fury through the medium of the drumbeats from his being. Suddenly the drumming stopped. Donal opened his eyes and placed the cipín once more behind his ear.

The silence which followed was unnerving. The Canon removed his hands from his ears, the anger once more dominating his features.

'Throw that barbaric instrument away from you at once,' he

called out to Donal.

'It is not a barbaric instrument,' Delia Bluenose flung back. 'It's a drum made by my man Bluenose and the likes of it was never made before.'

'It is barbaric,' he thundered, 'and as well as that it is the devil's drum.'

The devil's drum. The phrase was whispered by Delia Bluenose in awe and terror. It was here that Bluenose intervened for the first time: he stepped into the middle of the kitchen and faced the Canon.

'Listen to me, Father O'Priest,' he cried with his fists clenched. 'Listen wrendance-wrecker and joy-killer. Just as sure as your Christ and mine is the King of Kings so is the bodhrán the drum of drums!'

'Drum of devils,' Canon Tett shot back unchastened. 'Come on!' he turned to Father Donlea, 'our business here is finished' (Keane 1986: 231–3).

What emerges from scenes such as this is the extent to which music appears to be embedded organically within the community; in some ways it *constitutes* the community, fulfilling a natural function of embodying and expressing a connection with Nature, with the landscape and with the past. Donal's skill in playing the bodhrán, Bluenose's skill in making it: these constitute a vital part of the way in which this community knows itself, both in relation to its own past and to the outside world. These characters represent the community representing itself through cultural expression; the attempt to deny or alienate that right to self-representation is revealed as an act of violence on the part of privileged power: violence economic, cultural, political and personal.

One wonders what Canon Tett would have made of the following passage from the opening page of Dermot Bolger's *Father's Music* (1997):

> My lover lowers his headphones over my hair, then enters me. He thrusts stiffly and deep. Irish music swirls into my brain, a bow pressing down across a fiddle, teasing and twisting music from taut strings. My breath comes faster as his hands grip my buttocks, managing to rub his shoulder against the walkman's volume

control. The tune rises, filling me up. I close my eyes so that I can no longer see Luke, just feel his penis arching out and in. The set of reels change and quicken. I listen to a gale blowing across a treeless landscape, see a black huddle of slanted rooftops and drenched cows dreaming of shelter. The beat is inside my head from childhood, imagining an old shoe strike the stone flags and the hush of neighbours gathered in.

Luke pulls my legs higher, positions a pillow under my tensed back. I don't want to ever open my eyes. The music is so loud and quick it seems sweet torture. It courses through me. I can see his old face playing, that capped man with nicotined teeth and tufts of greying hair in his nostrils. His eyes are half closed, his breathing laboured. He looks so infirm that he could hardly shuffle across the room, yet his hand flicks the bow back and forth without mercy. He squeezes the wild tune loose, an old master in utter control, coaxing out grace-notes and bending them pitilessly to his will, while the wind howls outside along sheep tracks known only to mountain foxes and to him. He is my peddler father, the wandering lone wolf tinker my mother would never speak of, whose restless soul must now be constrained in some isolated graveyard (Bolger 1998: 3).

In some ways Bolger's novel takes up where Keane's left off, with the traditional community forced from the land, displaced to England where it begins to develop new forms of hybrid culture. With an English hippy mother and an Irish itinerant musician father named Frank Sweeney, Tracey, the narrator of *Father's Music*, is a product of that displaced history. Her mother's death precipitates a crisis of identity for Tracey. The only memory she retains of her father (who disappeared from England soon after she was born) is of an old man playing the fiddle – the image she describes in the second paragraph above. This memory, she will learn, derives from a time when he – drawn back to the life of itinerant musician in Ireland, yet heartbroken to be separated from his child – kidnapped her and took her back to Donegal with him. Reclaimed by her English grandfather, Tracey grows up in England feeling rootless, alienated and displaced.

As she wanders aimlessly through her life in London, Tracey meets and becomes the lover of an exiled Dublin gangster named Luke Duggan who introduces her to Irish traditional music. She begins to respond to a kind of power she perceives within the music, a dialectic of energy and control that seems to speak to her in ways that 'normal' music (as represented by the rock and techno that she occasionally listens to) cannot. Traditional music, sex and violence thus become enmeshed in Tracey's life, leading her on a seemingly downward spiral towards depression and, so it seems, death. The only redemption that is available is provided by the music itself, as at the end of the book, Tracey and her father, through a series of complex plot machinations, finally come face to face in a shebeen somewhere in the wilds of Donegal.

The portrait of Tracey's father is loosely based on Johnny Doherty, a travelling fiddle-player from Donegal to whom Bolger dedicates his novel (along with trad. 'stars' Séamus Ennis and Joe Heaney). The author's depiction here of the latent power of a semi-submerged tradition is fully in keeping with his other work in which, typically, a complacent Irish present is exposed by the eruption of a supposedly dead past. Just so in *Father's Music*, in which traditional music embodies a positive, organic culture that is being eroded under pressure from a 'fallen' modernity. The music itself, however, is revealed to be possessed of a kind of natural energy that channels itself through the individual performer by dint of his closeness to the land. Indeed, 'Father's Music' is a highly suggestive description of a kind of music that survives through inheritance, and yet has to be remade by each generation. Within the moral economy of the novel, Tracey's itinerant father embodies a valued way of life that is just about to disappear, whereas Luke Duggan represents a perversion of the spirit of the music, an attempt to recruit its natural energy for exploitative purposes. Only Tracey – the British-Irish hybrid raised in Greater London – can redeem the music and access the true power that it embodies.

The novels of Keane and Bolger hinge on traditional Irish music's implicit worth – its ability to embody and to express positive values in relation to Irish history and Irish identity. *The Bodhrán Makers* celebrates the music's expressive powers while at the same time lamenting the loss of the geo-social context from which it emerged. *Father's Music* likewise recognises traditional music's role as both symbol and embodiment of the organic community. Tracey's search for her father is in effect a search for the essence of the music: the *proper* tune played *properly* in the *proper* context. At the same time, that role is mitigated by the association of music throughout the text with a discourse of excess. This quality is implicit within the music itself – hence the use of words such as 'wild', 'pitilessly' and 'restless' in the extract above. It is also an effect of the music's decontextualisation, however: the fact that a tune performed in a rural northern county, for example, must *mean* something different when heard outside its 'natural' milieu – in a foreign country (such as England), for example, or even in a different part of the same country (such as urban Dublin).

For Patrick McCabe, traditional music was always possessed of dangerous energies; it always concealed a kind of menacing power beneath the façade of community and conviviality. The world of *Winterwood* (2006) represents classic McCabe territory. The story is told by Redmond Hatch (also known as 'Little Red'), who gradually reveals himself to be a profoundly unreliable narrator. Hatch tells the story of his acquaintance with a fiddler named Ned 'Pappie' Strange who runs traditional music classes for the local community. This character is 'strange' by nature as well as by name, as the reader discovers when it is revealed that Pappie uses his position to indulge paedophile activities. This strand is interwoven with the story of Hatch's marriage, its breakup, *his* breakdown and subsequent murder of his wife and daughter. The reason for this psychotic behaviour is (as with so many of McCabe's dysfunctional characters) rooted in the past, as Hatch slowly reveals that his mother was beaten to death by his father, and that he himself was a child victim of sexual abuse by his Uncle Florian.

Winterwood is very much a text of what might be described as the 'Tribunal Phase' of modern Irish history, in so far as it too is anxiously focused on the continuing impact of the sins of the past upon the present. Music, it emerges, is a seminal component of that relationship. The deeply romantic songs of the late Scottish singer-songwriter John Martyn are referenced throughout, for example, as is the country and western music of Hank Williams and Charley Pride. It is the traditional music associated with Pappie Strange and Uncle Florian, however, which dominates the narrative's soundtrack. In a scene towards the end of the book, the adult Redmond relates how his younger self – sent to an orphanage after the death of his mother – would be visited by the seemingly charming Florian:

> The sisters loved to see him coming. They asked him to play 'The Last Rose of Summer', the Thomas Moore song. And it must be admitted that he played it quite magnificently. It wasn't like the

other tunes. It was softer, more lyrical and gentle and mellow. With the notes like drops of water falling slowly into the stillness. Which was why they liked it so much. And why they probably thought that Florian's soul was something similar in texture to its sad drifting heart. They said he was the nicest man who'd ever visited the orphanage. They knew about the rumours but they didn't believe a word ... Uncle Florian was like something from their dreams. Secret dreams about which they never dared to tell anyone. Never a word about the night-time visitors who would slip from the shadows with dark eyebrows and teeth and something they had which pleasured you and of which most emphatically you could never speak. That's what they thought when Florian arrived, lifting up his bow to play the 'bowld' Tom Moore. That's what they were thinking of when he'd stroke his chin, stroke his chin and give them a wink. Saying he liked hornpipes – especially with Little Red. They were afraid if they listened to Little Red's stories, especially the ones about being 'scared of the hornpipe', that Florian would disappear and never come back for as long as they lived. So they said to Little Red:

— Button your lip, you moaning little minnie!

And demanded that in future he look forward to Florian's visits. Those Sundays when Florian would say:

— Right, sisters. Me and me nephew is going off for a ramble. I might have a few things to tell him about the goings-on at home. A few little bits of private business, you understand.

— Very good then, Florian, the good sisters would say, but make sure you come back to say goodbye before you go.

— I will indeed, sisters, have no fear of that, my dears.

Throwing his arms around Little Red's shoulders as off they went down the slopes into the meadow. Where Florian stamped out his stogie and grimaced. Before grabbing a hold of him and muttering with a grunt:

— Right so, Redmond. In here with us now behind the big tree. This is as good a place as any, for you and me to dance our hornpipes. We can dance it here till our fucking heart's content! Get over there now till I get out my fiddle! Till I get out my fiddle, well boys – ah – dear, ha, ha!

And such sawing and scrapings as would fill the woods then, as the leaping music screeched above the tops of the tall pine trees (McCabe 2006: 189–91).

The nuns make a classic interpretive error when they equate the emotionality embodied in the music with the man who plays it, as if Florian's ability to reproduce certain musical patterns and effects somehow endows him with the benign programme encoded within the music. The hornpipe and the fiddle, so familiar from the discourse of traditional music, are here invested with brutal, bestial power. McCabe subverts the image of traditional music – a discourse with almost uniformly positive connotations in modern Irish cultural history – by associating it with some of contemporary society's most sensitive notions of horror, in particular the notions of child sex and child murder. If traditional music was possessed of a subtle and mysterious power (although ultimately always benign) in the novels of Keane and Bolger, in scenes such as this that power is revealed to be sinister and murderous. As always with McCabe, the comfortable stereotype masks a dark truth – the host of negative experiences which subsisted beneath the façade of Irish society in the twentieth century: sexual exploitation, violence, betrayal, murder, psychosis. And as always with this author, the narrative works to resonate at a wider level, so that it is not only the characters who stand indicted but the society which produced them, and deeper still, the ideology upon which that society was founded.

Whatever the nature of their understanding of Irish traditional music's role and worth, none of these texts could be said to be particularly successful in their representation of that cultural form. Although the question of 'appropriateness' is relative, it may be that literary fiction in the established sense is on the whole not an appropriate means through which to attempt an intermedial representation of Irish traditional music. It is more likely, given their shared parentage, that traditional music's most apt literary partner is poetry rather than any of the prose or dramatic forms (Crosson 2008).

If one were in search of a more sympathetic prose form for the representation of Irish traditional music, however, one could do worse than Ciarán Carson's *Last Night's Fun* (1996). Although this book is not a novel as such, it is a brilliant example of the possibility of communicating the dynamics and characteristics of one cultural form (music) using those of another (writing). There is, moreover, a quasi-novelistic theme running through *Last Night's Fun* which concerns the relations between the detail and the pattern, the personal and the communal – or, described in musical terms, the phenomenology of the individual performance and the immanence of the tradition.

What emerges throughout *Last Night's Fun* is the enormous subtlety of the practices surrounding every aspect of traditional music discourse. The task Carson sets himself is nothing less than the development of a literary style that might do justice to that subtlety. It seems clear, for example, that traditional narrative fiction's reliance on the individual subject is questionable in the context of a form in which communal experience figures so signally. Thus, the central character of *Last Night's Fun* is a composite 'we' persona who thinks, drinks, eats, smokes and plays music together. Instead of story there is anecdote, instead of narrative there is digression, instead of reference there is allusion. As with the serendipitous logic underpinning tune clusters during a session, one section picks up in seemingly random fashion on some detail and uses it as a point of departure for the next, determined by the immediate context as much as by tradition, and communicated to fellow players/readers by the merest of physical/textual signs.

Traditional music is represented here as a living, vibrant order of experience, entirely relevant and perfectly attuned to modern 'Irish' life, whether it be encountered on or off the island. In contrast to narrative fiction's focus on the significant detail, Carson's writing is attuned to what Michel de Certeau (1988) describes as 'the practice of everyday life' – those seemingly inconsequential moments which inscribe a particular mode of being-in-the-world: ash falling from a cigarette, a figure rosining a bow in the dark corner of a pub, the supposedly 'dead' time when a pint is settling. Individual tunes are shown to be mere structures used by players as the point of departure for their own creative explorations. The music is simultaneously repetitious and singular, confirming the possibility of shared historical experience (the pattern recognised by the community of performers and listeners) while at the same time providing a space for individual innovation and interpretation (the moment which eludes all attempts at pre-emptive categorisation). It is, in other words, a radically performative discourse, resisting realism, closure, coherence – all traits, as it happens, associated with the traditional novel.

It seems that Irish traditional music is still awaiting its great novelistic realisation (which will not necessarily be 'great', just sympathetically responsive to its theme). It may be that when it finally arrives that text will be closer to the providential ramblings of *Last Night's Fun* (and thus more truly novelistic in a Bakhtinian sense) than to the 'proper' examples supplied by the likes of Keane, Bolger or McCabe.

No Country for Young Women: Celtic Music, Dissent and the Irish Female Body

On 31 January 1984 a 15-year-old girl named Ann Lovett left school after morning lessons and made her way to a field outside the small town of Granard in County Longford in the Republic of Ireland. In the field was a shrine to the Virgin Mary. At around 4.00 p.m. she was found by a passing schoolboy, lying in the grass beside the dead body of a baby she had attempted to deliver alone and unaided. Ann Lovett died later that day from blood loss and exposure.

The event shocked the local community and the island as a whole. One of the interventions within the ensuing debate was made by a Dublin-based performance artist named Nigel Rolfe, when he presented a lyric entitled 'Middle of the Island' to Christy Moore, one of Ireland's most popular and most successful folk singers. Moore set the lyric to music and included the song (with vocal accompaniment from Sinéad O'Connor) on his 1989 album *Voyage*. This is the lyric:

> Everybody knew, nobody said
> A week ago last Tuesday
> She was just fifteen years when she reached her full term
> She went to a grotto, just a field
> In the middle of the island to deliver herself
> Her baby died, she died a week ago last Tuesday
>
> It was a sad, slow, stupid death for them both
>
> Everybody knew, nobody said
> At a grotto in a field in the middle of the island

The death of Ann Lovett was immediately acknowledged, and has continued to be regarded in the years since, as an important moment in modern Irish history. The event encapsulates a struggle between modernity and tradition which many perceive to be the island's central ideological conflict throughout the modern era. That struggle, as well as the debates attending it, is also to be found in 'Middle of the Island' – in its musical and lyrical discourses as well as in a number of other factors bearing upon the 'meaning' of the song. In short, the scandal of Ann Lovett's tragic death, as well as this particular musical response to it, are locked in to some of the most compelling moral, political and cultural issues besetting modern Ireland. It is the task of this chapter to describe those issues, and to identify the nature of the relationship between the 'primary' event and the 'secondary' response which it generated.

THE FEMALE BODY AND THE STATE

On 7 September 1983, when Ann Lovett would have been about seventeen weeks pregnant, the people of the Republic of Ireland approved by referendum a constitutional ban on abortion. The relevant clause of the Eighth Amendment of the Constitution Act (enacted on 7 October 1983) was this:

> The State acknowledges the right to life of the unborn and, with due regard to the equal right to life of the mother, guarantees in its laws to respect, and, as far as practicable, by its laws to defend and vindicate that right.[1]

The ambiguity of this statement ensured that the controversy would continue, as indeed it does to the present day. Of course, it is not possible to know the extent to which Ann Lovett might have been affected by the furious debates which raged during the course of her pregnancy, and especially in the month or so leading up to the day of the vote. We do know that 75 per cent of the Longford–Westmeath constituency in which she lived voted in favour of the amendment (Hesketh 1990: 400), and that typically of the country at large, the debate in all its aspects would have permeated the local community, including the Catholic secondary school in Granard that she attended. In other words, it seems reasonable to assume that Ann Lovett would have been bombarded with a range of discourses concerning the role and status of the Irish female body just as she was becoming aware of her own pregnancy.

In fact, the abortion referendum of 1983 represents just one moment within a much longer history in which the Irish state (both before and after independence) attempted to assert control over the female body (Flynn 1993; Ward 1991). Despite a tradition of female political activism throughout the revolutionary period, the state ushered in by the Treaty of 1922 by and large adhered to imperialist precepts regarding the categorical subordination of women. This implicit gender divide was ratified by the Constitution of 1937, which declared:

> The State recognises the family as the natural primary and fundamental unit of Society, and as a moral institution possessing inalienable and imprescriptible rights, anterior and superior to all positive law ... In particular, the State recognises that by her life within the home, woman gives to the State a support without which the common good cannot be achieved. The State shall, therefore, endeavour to ensure that mothers shall not be obliged by economic necessity to engage in labour to the neglect of their duties in the home. The State pledges to guard with special care the institution of Marriage, on which the Family is founded, and to protect it against attack.

The feminine ideal encoded into the Constitution was enormously influential on life in the Irish Republic in the ensuing decades (Nash 1996, 1997). Despite the advent of feminism in the 1960s and 1970s, that ideal (constructed from a combination of orthodox Catholicism and bourgeois nationalism) represented the 'reality' into which children such as Ann Lovett were born and socialised. As the above extract reveals, the ideal setting for the ideal woman was the house: as wife, mother and home-maker, she was the rock upon which the family (and hence the state and 'the common good') was built. Attempting to step outside that domestic domain – for purposes of salaried work, education or public life, for example – was, at best, 'unusual', at worst, an assault upon the 'natural' order of things (Daly 1997; Harford 2008).

The Church–state partnership claimed jurisdiction over all matters relating to the female body, including sex, sexual health, reproduction and legal status. Failures to adhere to the Irish feminine ideal were strongly sanctioned, both officially and in vernacular culture. There were strong taboos against pre-marital sex and adultery. Single motherhood could have especially dire ramifications – at least for the mother. Divorce and 'artificial' contraception were banned, although the more 'liberal' wing of the establishment pointed to the sops of legal separation (once duly sanctioned by the Catholic hierarchy) and the so-called rhythm method (a 'natural' contraceptive system to which many Irish people of the late twentieth century owe their existence).

Feminism and bourgeois revisionism began to make inroads into Irish life during and after the 1960s, although this was predominantly an urban, middle-class (at this stage, Dublin-centred) development (Foster 2005). Typically, the principal effect of this was to excite strong establishment reaction, which in turn precipitated the abortion and divorce referenda of the 1980s and 1990s. These issues were forced by elements (sponsored, once again, by the institutions of Church and state) which retained an investment in enshrining once and for all a set of values which (so they believed) constituted an immemorial Irish identity, especially the role and representation of the female body in relation to that identity. If, during the late summer of 1983, the debate throughout the Republic of Ireland on the Eighth Amendment was both rancorous and far-reaching, the outcome was never really in any doubt: the people voted to accept it by a majority of two to one (Hesketh 1990).

This was the context within which Ann Lovett lived her short life. Even as her own body was in the process of changing, she would have been confronted – in the media, at school, in the community at large – with an array of frighteningly prescriptive discourses relating to the use and disposal of the Irish female body. Eventually, the state into which she had been born decided (without consulting her – as a 15-year-old she had no vote) that it retained control over her body, its functions, disposition and capacities. If, as the poet W.B. Yeats famously proclaimed, the Ireland of his day was 'no country for old men', sixty years later the fate of Ann Lovett was a disastrous demonstration that the same place was not a particularly salubrious country for young women either.

MUSIC IN IRELAND IN THE LATE TWENTIETH CENTURY

'Middle of the Island' is clearly *about* the death of Ann Lovett, and thus by extension *about* the array of socio-cultural discourses (religious, familial, educational, medical, etc.) which created the context within which that execrable event occurred. It is also a very particular kind of cultural event in itself, however – a song – and as such, it is necessary to approach it with an awareness of the traditions within which certain musical discourses emerge and develop. There are in fact three recognisable musical discourses (overlapping and intertextual) discernible within 'Middle of the Island'. Before going on to examine the song itself in detail, I would like to offer some suggestions as to the function of these discourses in relation to Ireland and Irish identity in the late twentieth century.

Since its 'discovery' and institutional ratification in the late eighteenth century, traditional music had emerged as one of the principal cultural signifiers of Irish identity. 'Traditional music' in this context comprehends an identifiable body of material which includes dance tunes of various kinds (with the reel and the jig predominating) and a song canon combining influences from an ancient Gaelic poetry tradition with a ballad repertoire accumulated over centuries of international exchange (O'Boyle 1976). Traditional music also comprehends a particular set of musical values which determine instrument selection and technique, text structure, the dynamics of ensemble performance, etc., as well as a set of extra-musical precepts which impact significantly upon how the music is produced and consumed (O'Shea 2008; Vallely 1999).

Traditional music's position as an easily recognisable sonic representation of Irishness was consolidated by the development of a complex infrastructure throughout the nineteenth and twentieth centuries (including various amateur and academic initiatives) which guaranteed it a crucial role within Irish cultural life. After 1922, it became one of the tasks of a newly independent state to nurture this cultural practice in which, so it was widely believed, some inalienable sense of Irish identity was embodied (Smyth 2005, 18–24; White 1998).

As with so many other areas of Irish life, this model of traditional music began to come under pressure with the advent of mass media during the 1960s and the emergence of a general revisionist sensibility within the public sphere. As the meaning of Irishness changed, in other words, so the function of those cultural practices which embodied Irish identity were obliged to change also. It was one of the signs that things were changing (and not necessarily for the better) that a widely practised and much-valued 'traditional' discourse was fusing in all sorts of ways with various elements (musical and otherwise) which, precisely because of their 'foreign' status, were categorically suspect to a Church–state establishment which was ideologically indisposed towards offshore interests.

Music is particularly amenable to influence; ultimately it refuses to adhere to the prescriptions laid down in non-musical agenda (those geared towards state or subject formation, for example). Music is always adapting, anticipating, remembering, welcoming, suggesting, gesturing, metamorphosing – it is always somewhere and something other than we would wish it to be. That in large part constitutes its perennial fascination. It should thus come as no surprise that traditional music provided a crucial site for the contention between tradition and modernity which came to characterise Irish life during and after the 1960s, nor that such debates should be understood to have implications which impact upon every aspect of Irish life, both contemporary and historical.

The singer-songwriter Christy Moore was exposed to Irish traditional music as he was growing up in Kildare during the 1950s and 1960s. At the same time, like so many other young Irish people of the period he would have been aware of the folk movement which was gathering pace in the US and the UK. At an early stage, the idea of North American folk music connoted the performance of material (traditional ballads in the main) adapted from the immigrant Celtic and Anglo-Saxon communities. During the first half of the twentieth century, however, the idea of folk music had incorporated a number of identifiable influences (acoustic blues, for example) and modifications (an emphasis on topicality and vaguely leftish leanings) (Mitchell 2007; Reuss 2000). By the 1960s the iconic figure of the international folk movement was the hard-travelling, guitar-toting white male, a figure upon whom Woody Guthrie was the defining historical influence, and for whom early Bob Dylan was the modern avatar (Cohen 2002).

As an Irish folk singer, Christy Moore could be expected to perform material from the native tradition with which he was so familiar. So it proved on an early album entitled *Prosperous* (1970), which included a range of traditional material including adapted British ballads such as 'The Raggle Taggle Gypsies' and 'The Dark-Eyed Sailor' as well as indigenous ballads such as 'Spancil Hill' and 'The Cliffs of Dooneen'. However, the album also included new songs by Moore ('I Wish I Was in England') and by friends ('Letter to Syracuse' by English songwriters

Dave Cartwright and Bill Caddick), one song by Dylan ('Tribute to Woody') and one by Guthrie himself ('Ludlow Massacre').

In fact, Moore's career profile (including his association with the seminal bands Planxty and Moving Hearts during the 1970s and 1980s) has by and large adhered to the template laid down on *Prosperous* in as much as he has continued to record and release a blend of traditional and topical material – the latter a combination of self-penned and purpose-written ballads. He has also become identified as a kind of contemporary protest singer, something once again which has been adapted from the folk profile of Guthrie, early Dylan and the American folk movement of the 1960s. Over the course of a forty-year career Moore has performed a range of material characteristic of what might be described as a generally left-wing engagement with the modern world. He has sung about 'dissident' topics ranging from nuclear power to witches, from the Spanish Civil War to American industrial relations. Moore has performed material by 'left-field' artists such as Morrissey, Elvis Costello, Jackson Browne, Willie Nelson, Joni Mitchell and Bono, while also being claimed as an influence by various younger Irish musicians possessed of a vaguely dissenting profile (such as Shane Mac-Gowan, Damien Dempsey and Sinéad O'Connor).

Over the years, Moore has tended to gravitate towards any situation in modern Ireland in which (so he understands) power is being abused and resisted. He affiliated himself with republicanism during the so-called 'Troubles' in Northern Ireland, supporting those actively involved in the conflict and regularly performing material directly relating to it. While remaining a nominal republican (and socialist), Moore distanced himself from the armed struggle after the infamous Enniskillen bombing (1987), however, and his focus turned to other causes. His extensive canon includes material on a variety of subjects sensitive in modern Ireland: emigration, immigration and racism, urban poverty and drugs, the itinerant community and vigilantism, industrial relations, landscape despoliation, religious hypocrisy, and political corruption.[2] He is, to all intents and purposes, the nearest thing contemporary Ireland has had to a high-profile protest singer.

Part of this identity is constituted in terms of a specifically sonic discourse. In musical terms, that is to say, Moore retains an identity that is 'folky', by which I mean lo-tech and oriented towards live performance. He plays most of his material on acoustic guitar, using a capo to enable him to perform the songs using chords derived from his favourite G shape. Although occasionally employing acoustic accompanists (such as his friends Declan Sinnott on guitar and Donal Lunny on bouzouki), Moore's recorded repertoire clearly adheres to a 'folk' aesthetic in as much as the foregrounded lyrics are mediated by his distinctive vocal style, while the modest musical arrangements constantly gesture towards the ideal of live solo performance.

The one occasion on which Moore deviated significantly from that aesthetic was *Voyage*, the album containing 'Middle of the Island'. Moore's own comment on this record is instructive:

> I got my head turned here by Warner suits. They came to my home and sat there telling me I should remix the album. An A&R wanker who fell asleep during the meeting, a big shot from London, the head of WEA Ireland, my manager and me. I listened to these shysters and took their counsel and allowed my album to be remixed. It was a rash and regrettable move on my part and to this day I regret it – but I learned.[3]

One of the reasons why Moore may have allowed his head to be turned from what he believed to be his core values was the emergence of a new style of 'Irish' music during the 1980s. In 1988, Moore's label WEA released an album entitled *Watermark* by the Irish artist known as Enya. The latter was in fact Eithne Ní Bhraonáin, onetime member of the family band named Clannad who became well known in Ireland during the 1970s performing an attractive (if sometimes controversial) blend of traditional and jazz music, and who had scored a Top Ten hit in the UK in 1982 with a single entitled 'Theme from *Harry's Game*'. If that track introduced the possibility of a new form of sonic Irishness, it was the worldwide success of *Watermark* a number of years later, spearheaded by the single 'Orinoco Flow', that may be said to have brought the genre known as 'Celtic' music to a mass market.

'Celtic' music constitutes an important subgenre of the 'world music' marketing phenomenon that emerged in the latter decades of the twentieth century (Stokes and Bohlman 2003). (Interestingly, the release of 'Theme from *Harry's Game*' coincided with the inaugural WOMAD [World of Music, Arts and Dance] Festival.) The version of Celtic music represented by the Brennan family is possessed of a highly distinctive sonic signature, characterised by lush, layered soundscapes which are themselves the result of intense studio work involving a combination of 'real' and synthesised instruments. These technical values support a thematic function which is generally at a distance from the modern world. The lyric of 'Orinoco Flow', for example, invites the listener to 'sail away' in order to experience the different values associated with a range of exotic locations removed in space and time from 'normality': the Yellow Sea, Avalon, Fiji, Babylon, the Coral Sea, and so on. Music and lyrics combine to produce a mood that is clearly intended to be ethereal, other-worldly and New Ageish – a species of Celtic spirituality, in fact, understood by its adherents to be at odds with a prevailing Western system in which material success is the implicit index of happiness.

Christy Moore was not the only artist (Irish or otherwise) to feel the force of a sound that has become perhaps the foremost sonic signifier of Irish identity in the years since 'Theme from *Harry's Game*' and *Watermark*. Such a development has been subject to widespread criticism, however, and on a number of grounds. In some accounts 'Celtic music' encompasses everything from Alan Stivell to U2, rendering any attempt to describe a cogent impetus informing the music as highly questionable (Melhuish 1998; Skinner Sawyers 2000). The style has also been critiqued as an attempt on the part of various critical and commercial institutions to posit a connection between quite diverse musical practices – not only Irish, but a whole range of supposedly affiliated regions and nations, including Scotland, Wales, Brittany and Gallicia.

The main problem with this style of music, however (as pointed out in Chapter 6), is the seemingly unreconstructed use of the word 'Celtic', and the subsequent wholesale incorporation of a range of stereotypes which are locked in to specific discourses of power that have their roots deep in Irish–British history. It is no wonder that Moore felt both uncomfortable and resentful.

'MIDDLE OF THE ISLAND'

By the time Moore came to record *Voyage*, traditional, folk and Celtic music were established elements within Irish popular music. Like all his albums, *Voyage* contains a mixture of material.[4] It was, nevertheless, a departure for him – one which (as we observed in the previous section) he came to consider as a false step. The title track (written by Johnny Duhan) is a slow, sentimental love song organised around an increasingly strained nautical metaphor.[5] The inclusion of another love ballad (Ewan McColl's 'The First Time Ever I Saw Your Face', widely perceived as a modern popular 'classic') is perhaps another indication of record company pressure. There are also topical interventions such as 'Musha God Help Her' (about Dublin's contemporary underclass) and 'Farewell to Pripchat' (about the Chernobyl disaster). The album contains four songs – 'Mystic Lipstick', 'The Mad Lady and Me', 'Missing You' and 'Bright Blue Rose' – by Jimmy McCarthy, a well-known songwriter from Cork and a popular performer in his own right. Of these four only 'Missing You' – on the theme of Ireland's latest lost generation of emigrants – is a 'typical' Moore song; the others are more ambitious (lyrically, structurally and musically) than had been his wont up until this point. The same is true of 'Deportees' Club' – purpose-written for the album by the British-Irish rock artist Elvis Costello, and a song which contributed to Moore's reputation as a serious artist possessed of crossover potential.

The track 'Night Visit' is based on an Irish adaptation of a traditional English ballad about an illicit nocturnal encounter between a guest and the landlord's daughter. The version performed on *Voyage* bears little resemblance to a 'traditional' ballad, however, with its rock rhythm section of drums and bass guitar, and its whining harmonica played by well-known Irish blues artist Don Baker. In Moore's adaptation, moreover, after having her pleasure the empowered woman rejects the nagging man who, in an unlikely reversal of the traditional structure, only wants to get married as soon as possible. 'Night Visit' is in fact one of a number of songs performed by Moore over the course of his later career in which, as part of a broadly dissident agenda, he attempts to recover and/or assert female agency.[6] With its attempt to walk a fine line between maintenance and renewal, it also stands as a clear example of the clash between tradition and modernity in modern Ireland.

Moore's changing persona is already established in a paratextual sense by the album's artwork. The cover image features a soft-focus black-and-white headshot of the artist cross-faded with a brooding 'Celtic' landscape. Moore gazes seriously into the distance off right, one side of his face lit by watery sunlight, the other half partially hidden by cloud and mist rolling off the hills just discernible to the bottom left of the shot. The resonance of the image – with its evocation of times and places removed from the here-and-now – is distanced from

Moore's hitherto predominantly realist visual identity. He is no longer the 'ordinary man' of the 1985 album title; like all 'Celts', rather, he appears to be implicated in deeper and graver matters. A cover image further removed from his first album *Paddy On The Road* (1969) – featuring a colour photograph of the young bearded Moore sitting against a tree with his guitar case by his side – is difficult to imagine. The artwork on *Voyage* invokes the idea of a mystical, ethereal Irishness, and as such it was a clear attempt on the part of WEA to associate Moore with the discourse of Celtic music which had been developing throughout the decade.

The signature status of 'Middle of the Island' in relation to *Voyage* is established by the fact that it is the last sequenced track on the album. Before the advent of downloading (a practice in which consumers can cherry-pick their favourite album tracks), there was a general belief in the significance of the final track on multi-part texts such as long-playing albums. This, after all, was the sound with which the listener would be left, and was therefore an important consideration when determining the impression created by an album as a whole.

The song lasts for four minutes and five seconds. Its B flat minor key is unfriendly for the acoustic guitar (even one with a capo on the first or the sixth fret). Twelve seconds of electric slide guitar (0.06–0.18 – played, untreated apart from slight reverb, by Moore's long-time collaborator Declan Sinnott) help to establish a yearning, melancholic atmosphere from the outset. Besides this, however, the track is comprised of only four distinct 'voices'. The first is that of a Prophet-5 synthesiser played by Donal Lunny (who also produced the album). This is an analogue keyboard instrument developed in the US during the late 1970s, and capable of sophisticated polyphonic effects. Lunny has used it extensively since the early 1980s whenever he wishes to introduce drama and texture into what would otherwise stand as standard acoustic ballads. Such was the effect it had when he played it on 'Ride On' (another Jimmy McCarthy composition), the seminal track from the album of that title released in 1984 and still Moore's most successful release. Such was the effect, also, when Clannad used the Prophet to create the brooding, eerie soundscape of 'Theme from *Harry's Game*'. This instrument's use in Irish music stands as a clear indication of the way in which innovative technology can be deployed to create discursive effects which are in some respects opposed to technology, both in terms of their ethos and their wider cultural impact.

The melody of 'Middle of the Island' is not, as suggested by Moore on his website, 'sung a cappella to a drone', as there are in fact clearly discernible chord changes (provided by the Prophet) from B flat minor to F major and E flat minor, as well as harmonic overtones throughout. Nevertheless, the melody clearly seeks to evoke something brooding and primordial, and it is interesting to observe how the musicians set about creating this effect. Research has revealed that the melodies of the ancient Gaelic civilisation (ostensibly part of the great Bronze Age Celtic diaspora) were produced for the most part on the harp (O'Boyle 1976: 30). Because of the particular tuning of that instrument a modal system emerged, which in time (and with the added influence of rhythmic considerations) led to the classification of three main melodic types: *Goltraige* (meaning Sad), *Gentraige* (meaning Joyful) and *Suantraige* (meaning Sleep). The melody of 'Middle of the Island' is modal (Aeolian) and obviously belongs to the first category (Sad); while this resonates with the theme of the lyric, it also contributes to the track's overall 'Celtic' feel (see Chapter 4).

The melody of 'Middle of the Island' also alludes to the traditional Gaelic singing style known as *sean-nós*, which translates (misleadingly, as it happens) as 'old style'. *Sean-nós* is rooted in the social, cultural and linguistic systems of the Gaelic world (Vallely 1999: 336–45). It refers in the first instance to a style of unaccompanied singing which is characterised by a great number of technical and contextual protocols, the complexity of which only prolonged exposure and study can comprehend. These include subtle tone quality, rhythmic variation, phrasing and (most recognisably to an outsider) pronounced melodic ornamentation. Despite this, it is a style in which communication is valued above technique, and in which emotion and personality are the yardsticks of a successful performance.

So-called 'Celtic' music has developed a kind of vulgar *sean-nós* element which endeavours to invoke the emotionality and intimacy of a traditional performance through the use of various studio techniques. On 'Middle of the Island' this is provided by the 'drone' from the Prophet (although, as suggested above, the sound produced by that instrument in this instance is in fact no such thing), by the 'close miking' of Moore's voice (creating a breathy, uncomfortably intimate performance), and through certain vocal techniques on the part of the singer himself. Moore's singing voice is recognisably Irish, both in terms of his accent – on words such as 'years' (53) and 'herself' (1.33) – and his pronunciation, as for example when he sings about 'de middle of de island' (1.21). Indeed, it is an important aspect of his 'folk' persona that Moore refuses to modify his accent for the purposes of singing, and that the 'Irishness' of the vocal medium through which the text is communicated accords with the 'Irishness' encoded with the lyrical and musical content of the text itself. Beyond this, however, at various points throughout 'Middle of the Island' Moore introduces vocal trills – on the words 'Tuesday' (42), 'for' (2.18), 'knew' (2.30) and 'island' (3.02) – the effect of which is to claim intertextual allegiance with *sean-nós* and its specific socio-cultural dispensation.

A third 'voice' is provided by a bell which is actually comprised of two clearly discernible sounds – one a deeper and more resonant 'gong', the second a brighter ringing note. The bell, which enters after seven seconds and repeats thereafter at approximately five-second intervals throughout the track, has a programmatic function in as much as it is intended to invoke a sound (a 'passing bell') which has been associated with death since medieval times.[7] Despite Celtic music's alleged recalcitrance vis-à-vis 'the real world', the intention here is clearly realist and mimetic: the song is *about* death, therefore the musicians produce sounds which *signify* death for a listener who will be more or less familiar with its sonic conventions.

The final 'voice' on 'Middle of the Island' is provided by Sinéad O'Connor, a singer well-known for her outspoken views on a wide range of issues. O'Connor has in particular become noted as a critic of the Catholic Church in Ireland and what she understands to be the repressive moral regime under which generations of Irish people, and Irish women in particular, have suffered. In 1989 (the same year as the release of *Voyage*), O'Connor appeared as a minor character in *Hush-a-Bye Baby*, a film which tells the story of a schoolgirl from Derry who becomes pregnant.[8] O'Connor's role in relation to this film (a public figure known to have an interest in the theme of the story) anticipated many of the issues that bear upon her performance on 'Middle of the Island'. On this song, O'Connor's presence oscillates between two related yet distinguishable discursive functions – one oriented towards her extra-textual public persona, the other towards her role as a character 'inside' the song, as it were. This in turn is linked to certain key aspects of O'Connor's wider identity.

In iconographical terms, O'Connor operates between two recognisable paradigms: one sensitive and vulnerable, the other aggressive and militant. These paradigms, moreover, are directly related to O'Connor's singing style, which, as Keith Negus describes it, is characterised by

> the use of two distinct voices: a more private, confessional, restrained, and intimate voice; and a harsher, declamatory, more public and often nasal voice that she frequently slides into a snarl or shout. There is often a tension present throughout many of Sinéad's vocal performances, between a more vulnerable and uncertain voice, and a more imperative and assertive voice (1995: 221).

This tension may be heard on many of her recordings, including the version of 'Nothing Compares 2 U' which was a number 1 hit in the UK and the US in January 1990. On 'Middle of the Island', O'Connor restricts herself by and large to the former voice – one that is, as Negus says, 'private, confessional, restrained, and intimate'. When she enters on the line 'It was a sad, slow, stupid death for them both' (2.09), doubling Moore's melody line an octave higher, her voice is located quite far back in the mix. The purity and thinness of her voice at this stage, when contrasted with the foregrounded resonance of his, suggests the idea of female vulnerability which is a central element of the lyric. At such points, I suggest, she becomes discursively identified with Ann Lovett herself. Something of O'Connor's more aggressive public persona emerges in her delivery of the emotive words 'sad, slow, stupid death' when she repeats that line on her own a little later (3.10). Once again, however, the anger subsides and the voice fades into a kind of 'girlishness' during the words 'for them both' (3.22). The voice which articulates the final line (and it is instructive that Moore has withdrawn by this stage) – 'Everybody knew, nobody said' – is both mimetic (Ann Lovett) and diegetic (Sinéad O'Connor), both part of the world *inside* the story, and part of the world trying to make sense of that story (see Chapter 10).

I have been quoting lines from 'Middle of the Island' throughout the above analysis without really discussing their meaning, but of course words represent a crucial aspect of this (and indeed every) song. The first thing to note is that, in apparent contrast with the complex musical discourses at work throughout the piece, Nigel Rolfe's lyric sounds disarmingly simple and straightforward. The words relate the tragic story of Ann Lovett in a few lines, describing how the 15-year-old went to a shrine in a field somewhere in the midlands to deliver her own baby, and how she and her baby died there. The language is predominantly descriptive rather than interpretative or analytical; it uses simple, relevant words and structures to relate what happened rather than metaphor, analogy or other rhetorical devices. The partial exception is the line 'It was a sad, slow, stupid death for them both' which employs alliteration to emphasise the point. Even then, however, the opinion is all the more striking for the relevant straightforwardness of its expression. The words 'sad, slow [and] stupid' have no great resonance here beyond their primary signification; they are all relative terms (how sad is 'sad'? etc.), yet they have a currency which renders them perfectly serviceable in everyday discourse. The lyric of 'Middle of the Island' is thus on one level fully in keeping with the banal reality of Ann Lovett's needless death.

There may appear to be a tension, then, between the music and the words of 'Middle of the Island' – the former multi-dimensional and allusive, the latter one-dimensional and realist. There are, however, at least two aspects of the lyric, which complicate such an interpretation; moreover, the relative importance of these aspects to the text as a whole (the opening line of the lyric and the title) points to an underlying complexity which belies the impression of linguistic realism.

The opening line of the song – 'Everybody knew, nobody said' (0.20–0.34) – is repeated twice later in the track, the first time (2.26–2.42) by both singers singing an octave apart, the second time (3.27–3.46) – and with a slight melodic variation – by O'Connor. Such repetition signals the importance of this utterance within the linguistic economy of the song; it also establishes a discursive binary between 'everybody' and 'nobody', and between *knowing* and *saying*. On one level, 'everybody' refers to the local community among whom Ann Lovett lived and died; likewise, 'nobody' refers to the absence of anyone from that community who was willing to address the situation before it reached its crisis. The listener recognises this indictment, and acknowledges the moral culpability of those who 'knew' but refused to 'say'. As it is repeated a second and then a third time (the latter, as we have observed, by a voice identified with the victim), however, the indictment extends beyond the local community. Now it encompasses not only a mimetic subject located within the world of the song, but also an extra-narrative subject – the listening community, located ostensibly 'outside' the drama described in the lyric, but in fact fully implicated in its moral failings. 'Everybody' *means* everybody – those who were blamed and those who did the blaming, those represented within the text and those consumers protected by the privilege of the 'off' switch on their playback system.

The same point obtains with reference to the spatial discourse which structures the lyric. The words 'grotto' and 'field' defer to the discourse of localism noted above. It was, after all, 'just a field' in which Ann Lovett died. It appears as if the listener is being invited to observe and enjoy the irony of the fact that such a shocking event could take place in locations which have a benign (and occasionally a comic) cultural resonance.[9] With the introduction of the line 'In the middle of the island', however, there is a shift from a local perspective (one limited to the apprehension of the senses) to a much larger one in which, once again, the listener is implicated. As the focus zooms out, moreover, geography segues into morality. The words 'the middle of the island' register in a geographical sense, certainly, in as much as the town of Granard is located in a part of the Republic known as 'the midlands'. However, it also registers in a moral sense, invoking a kind of imaginative heartland in which the core values of the whole community have been tested and found wanting. Thus, to entitle the song 'Middle of the Island' is to signal not only the geographical centrality of the event (with all that that entails in terms of traditional values), but also, and more importantly, the significance of Ann Lovett's death as an indictment of the moral health of the wider community.

CONCLUSION

'Middle of the Island' stands as an exemplary instance of the troubled relationship between popular music and human rights. Its primary resonance has a particular geopolitical focus, however, in terms of modern Irish history. As suggested at the outset of this chapter, many of the issues which have animated the debate regarding post-revolutionary Irish identity may be observed within this particular song. On one level the text invites interpretation as part of a clearly dissident discourse, opposed to many fundamental aspects of traditional Irish identity. Moore, O'Connor and Rolfe may be said to inhabit the broadly revisionist public sphere which emerged within Ireland during the last decades of the twentieth century, and which was intent on deconstructing the precepts, as well as exposing the silences, of the world into which they had been born. Most centrally, the song appears to be an indictment of the attitude which allowed, indeed encouraged, a patriarchal Church–state establishment to define the role and representation of women within that world. The artists draw on different cultural traditions and utilise different musical techniques to expedite their (re)vision. These traditions and techniques carry their own ideological resonances, however – some of which support the dissident stance, some of which undermine it. While the debates as to strategy and the effectiveness of cultural interventions continue, however, one fact remains: Ann Lovett would have been forty by the time this book will be published.

'The same sound but with a different meaning': Music, Politics and Identity in Bernard Mac Laverty's Grace Notes

Recent years have witnessed a proliferation of novels in which music is of central importance. Any starting point is arbitrary, but one might date the commencement of this trend from Toni Morrison's *Jazz* (1992), a typically opaque novel which attempted to reproduce the elaborate systems of early twentieth-century African-American music in literary form. In the UK alone, there followed high-profile examples by an army of literary *galacticos*: Louis de Bernières (1994), Jeanette Winterson (1994), James Kelman (1994), Hanif Kureishi (1995), Kazuo Ishiguro (1995), Alan Warner (1995), Nick Hornby (1995), Ian McEwan (1998), Jackie Kay (1998), Salman Rushdie (1999), Vikram Seth (1999), Rose Tremain (1999), Jonathan Coe (2001), Michel Faber (2002), Janice Galloway (2002), Zadie Smith (2005), Russell Hoban (2007) and A.N. Wilson (2007). As this list demonstrates, moreover, music was very liberally understood by these writers, encompassing a wide array of styles and traditions from art to jazz to rock and pop. Taken in conjunction with a host of other titles by lesser known authors, this list represented the latest impulse of a long trans-national tradition: the 'music novel' – by which I mean the engagement with musical matter through the medium of extended prose fiction (Smyth 2008).

Another such novel is Bernard Mac Laverty's *Grace Notes* (1997), a book which is not only *about* music on a number of levels, but which also attempts to invoke musical effects and to incorporate musical form into its own structure. Besides representing a clear example of the music novel, moreover, *Grace Notes* is also a story about the 'Troubles' in Northern Ireland. As such, it engages with a long tradition of Irish fiction in which questions of representation, resistance, identity and voice are to the fore. In this chapter I shall suggest that Mac Laverty's novel is located in the interstices between linked, though distinguishable, cultural-critical narratives: one concerned with a (supposedly) generalised politics of representation; the other with a specific national-historical tradition. *Grace Notes* is organised in such a way that the latter is resolved in terms of the former; the 'problem' of Northern Ireland, in other words, is represented as a specific historical instance of a deeper human problematic, one focused upon the relations between the unique and the general in human affairs, and more suggestively upon the function of *repetition* at both a cultural-historical and a phenomenological-individual level. The music novel, as we shall see, is the ideal medium for this kind of artistic treatment, for it enables the theme of repetition to be engaged at both the formal and conceptual levels, thereby fostering a quasi-organic cycle of theme, repetition and variation within the text.

I would also suggest, however, that *Grace Notes* withdraws from the radical implications it sets in motion, that its musical (and, by extension, political) vision is circumscribed by the classical bourgeois frame of reference within which it operates, and that despite its incorporation of significant musical elements into its form, Mac Laverty's novel eventually succumbs to a 'modernist' aesthetic which offers the reader 'matter for solace and pleasure' rather than 'a stronger sense of the unpresentable' (Lyotard 1997: 81).

MUSIC AND FICTION

What could account for the rise (or rather the re-emergence) of the music novel during recent times? One might speculate that the trend represented a response to the *fin de siécle* growth of interdisciplinarity in the critical languages which service the creative arts (Moran 2001). Cultural Studies is one such obvious language, less concerned with traditional disciplines (whether creative or critical), it seems, than with the organisation and dissemination of power across a range of discursive practices and institutional sites. Cultural Studies – indeed, modern cultural criticism in general – is by and large theory- rather than text-driven; it tends to 'read' the text in terms of a range of *a priori* precepts rather than granting it the courtesy of an immanent response. The provenance and effect of such a practice is the subject of ongoing debate; but in the meantime, the currently dominant critical mood might be described as *holistic* rather than *discrete*, and this may have created, or at least contributed to, a general intellectual/academic *zeitgeist* in which the music novel can flourish.

Rather than representing some entirely new departure, however, the admixture of artistic concerns in the musical novel in fact partakes of a long-established tradition. The novel, it turns out, has always been fascinated with music, and at some points in its history this fascination has become an obsession (Aronson 1980; Benson 2006). Perhaps this should not come as too much of a surprise: the modern form of the novel and the tradition of classical art music developed alongside each other from the early eighteenth century, although for much of their shared history, the latter represented a far more respectable pursuit (understood in the bourgeois terms which set the standards for artistic decorum) than the former (Brown 1948; Freedman 1978). The novel in fact suffered something of an inferiority complex with regard to what is widely seen as its more developed, better patronised, and frankly more popular sister art. With its invocation of ritual elements such as rhythm, rhyme and repetition, poetry may have been a reminder of language's link to music; fiction, however, remained primarily story-oriented, mortgaged to the remorseless logic of the bourgeois realist narrative and its attendant discourses: character, plot, plausibility.

Jealous of their poetic and musical rivals, novelists made a virtue of the verbal medium within which they worked, with the consequence that the novel developed into a mass form during the nineteenth century. Novelists clinging to an image of themselves as artists rather than 'mere' storytellers, however, continued to envy what they perceived to be the more favourable medium of their musical counterparts. This helps to account for the ubiquity of musical references in the writings of a host of modern(ist) novelists, of whom the most notable are Forster, Joyce, Proust, Woolf, Huxley, Beckett and Mann (Smyth 2008: 16–86). The attraction of music for these writers, as Alex Aronson suggests in his extended study of the subject, was that it was both *transcendent* and *historical* at the same time. Specifically, music alerted the writer to 'the existence of a non-verbal reality more expressive than speech and conforming to the dictates of inner time beyond anything that the novelist's language could communicate' (1980: ix). At the same time, it enabled the writer to dramatise much more fully than language ever could the tension (supposedly essential but actually consequent upon the evolving bourgeois imagination) between individual expression and social compulsion. I shall return to this duality presently. In the meantime, the significant point to note is that music became much more than a mere device for the development of narrative or the explication of character; in many cases it replaced verbal language-narrative as the principal expressive medium. By the time of the high modernist *avant-garde*, in other words, the time seemed ripe for some kind of rapprochement between fiction and music.

Unfortunately, western art music has been undergoing its own agonies throughout the nineteenth century, and was in no position to entertain the offer. Two related problems beset the composer during the Victorian era: on the one hand, what could he (almost invariably 'he') do but construct elaborate yet essentially limited glosses to the harmonic, melodic and structural creations of the dead masters: Bach, Mozart and Beethoven? On the other hand, the world had changed so rapidly over the course of the century that those creations seemed less and less appropriate for any meaningful expression of the human condition. Haunted by an anxiety of influence on one side, and a fear of redundancy on the other, it is no surprise that twentieth-century western art music existed in perpetual crisis, characterised by a series of determined efforts to 'leave home'. It is in this context that one may begin to understand the appeal of serialism, as well as the various challenges – for example, electronic and aleatory music, as well as the use of a range of 'noisy' effects such as syncopation, chromaticism, dissonance and atonality – that proliferated both within and outwith the academy since the latter decades of the nineteenth century.

The effect of such developments was curious, to say the least. While fiction was turning to music as relief from the banalities of verbal language-based narrative, many composers and music critics were rejecting the kind of music (and the effects it supposedly generated) coveted by these writers, and were instead searching for what they considered to be more appropriate modes of 'musical' (now sufficiently problematical so as to be worthy of scare quotes) expression.

Such seemingly abstract critical negotiations are linked to one rather obvious creative problem, which is the fact that 'language is a singularly inept vehicle of expression when it is called upon to say something adequate about the content of a musical work' (Aronson 1980: 21). How can the novelist convey a form of expression that is aural by definition in terms of a medium that is principally visual (the written word as it appears on the page)?[1] Although initially presenting itself as a problem to do with medium, the stand-off between music and language might be regarded as one between different types of music novel: those in which the description of music is central to the narrative, and those in which music assumes a more incidental role in the contextualisation of a character or event. Interesting in this respect is the fiction of Roddy Doyle, throughout whose career (popular) music has formed an essential element of the literary imagination. Whereas music's centrality to human experience is overtly thematised in *The Commitments* (1987) and *Oh, Play That Thing* (2004), however, in novels such as *Paddy Clarke Ha Ha Ha* (1993) and *The Woman Who Walked Into Doors* (1996) music functions to illustrate the central character's relation to the various collectives – family, community, state – in which they find themselves (see Chapters 5 and 7).

It might be argued that the novelist's invocation of musical discourse in this way is in danger of missing the point entirely: that music represents a *qualitative* difference in the signifying economy, and that such an appropriation violates its essence. But this in turn begs the question of music's 'essence', its fundamental property and condition as a mode of human expression. This is the issue broached by a second category of writer who, accepting the novel's debasement before music, chooses to focus on what is widely perceived to be the latter's 'essential' function as an indication of truth beyond the ability to represent. In Vikram Seth's *An Equal Music*, for example, the writer seems concerned to celebrate music (and to invite the reader to share that celebration, both by reading the book and by purchasing the accompanying CD) as the primary human medium to the degree that it intimates mysterious levels of meaning which must remain impervious to rational engagement.

But such an understanding brings its own problems. On one level, the postulation of music as an ultimately recondite discourse obviates the validity of any historical (and thus effective) explanation of its impact. The result, as one reviewer of *An Equal Music* put it, is 'to imprison music in a sentimental idealism – ahistorical, anti-intellectual and fundamentally uncreative' (Spice 1999). There are other ways, especially for the novelist, to write about music which highlight its effectiveness as opposed to (or at least as well as) its ineffability. More significantly for present purposes, however, problems accumulate around the issue of representation, and more specifically around what Jean-François Lyotard, in his description of the difference between the modern and the postmodern, terms the 'unpresentable'. Lyotard writes:

> modern aesthetics is an aesthetic of the sublime, though a nostalgic one. It allows the unpresentable to be put forward only as the missing contents; but the form, because of its recognizable consistency, continues to offer to the reader or viewer matter for solace and pleasure ... The postmodern would be that which, in the modern, puts forward the unpresentable in presentation itself; that which denies itself the solace of good forms, the consensus of a taste which would make it possible to share collectively the nostalgia for the unattainable; that which searches for new presentations, not in order to enjoy them but in order to impart a stronger sense of the unpresentable (1997: 81).

An Equal Music is obviously 'modern' in these terms, because although Seth is quite clearly alluding to the 'unpresentable', he does so within the terms of a straightforward realist narrative in which a linear plot is driven forward by discourses of 'recognizable consistency' – which is to say, causal plausibility and character identification. Here, indeed, we have 'matter for solace and pleasure' as music's numinous beauty is set against the narrator's loss of youth and love to create an atmosphere of wistful nostalgia.

Music performs specific functions within the novelistic tradition, then, focusing issues to do with the relationship between reality and representation in ways that literary discourse alone cannot. *Grace Notes*, as we shall see presently, is addressed to the dialectic described above in its representation of, on the one hand, a specifically historicised music (music, that is, which emerges from and impacts upon specific sociopolitical contexts); and on the other, a music which speaks to (supposedly) transcendent human truths. It is, moreover, self-consciously responsive to the ways in which the formal aspects of one medium mitigates those of another. But Mac Laverty's celebrated novel is not only *about* music; it is also *about* Northern Ireland. Another set of issues arises, therefore, in relation to Ireland's traditional dual status as a 'troubled', yet 'inherently' musical, culture.

MUSIC AND IRISH IDENTITY

While the late twentieth century witnessed the re-emergence of the music novel, it also saw the development of an institutional/intellectual formation in which issues of race, ethnicity, space and power came to exercise a powerful influence upon both creative and critical practices. Many of the writers mentioned at the beginning of this chapter qualify to be described as 'postcolonial'; many of them also focus quite self-consciously on issues of identity, ethnicity and gender. This alerts us to the possibility of a connection between the politics of resistance (including quite centrally postcolonialism) and the systematic utilisation of music as an alternative mode of expression within novelistic discourse.[2] The status of Ireland (which Ireland?) as a postcolonial country (island? republic? province?) remains a point of contention. Nevertheless, it remains a commonplace of one school of critical thought to say that Irish fiction represents a discourse in perpetual crisis, and that this crisis may be seen as a reflection of a violent, disrupted history.[3] Although describing both a coherent cultural concept and a recognisable social practice, in other words, the phrase 'Irish novel' is one under erasure, comprehending a discourse in which each term constantly interrogates and mitigates the other. With its connotations of displacement and fragmentation, there is something about the word 'Irish' which disrupts any normative model of novelistic discourse; conversely, there is something about the word 'novel', with its drive towards heroic self-possession and narrative closure, that threatens the 'Irish' qualifier. Without exoticising the situation, one may appreciate how this created the context in which specifically non-novelistic practices – in effect, a peculiar Irish modernism – could emerge and thrive.[4] This in turn provided a space for the exploitation of signifying systems alternative to the traditional novelistic conventions of narrative, language and character. One such signifying system, as is clear from an overview of the tradition, is music.

If the 'Irish novel' is an inherently unstable prospect, the phrase 'Irish music' is similarly problematical. To understand the crucial role that music has played in modern Irish cultural history we have to turn to the beginnings of cultural nationalist discourse in the latter half of the eighteenth century (see Chapter 2). For it was during that period that the notion of an inherent Irish musicality – a notion extant but never fully politicised during the medieval and early modern periods – was consolidated.[5] This notion of the Irish as an essentially musical race continued to grow throughout the nineteenth century. Irish music, as Neil McLaughlin and Martin McLoone argue, became locked in to 'a specific ethnic category based on the assumption that there was an identifiably Irish musical style that existed as an expression of the people, a reflection of their innate feelings and sensibilities' (2000: 181). As they go on to suggest, moreover, this assumption continues to impact upon modern Irish culture:

> In terms of music, the essentialist notions that underlie dominant conceptions of 'Irishness' (and which are most characteristically applied to Irish traditional music) can be seen on the one hand as ideologically conservative and analytically restrictive, privileging 'nature' over culture and alluding to a deep essence of Irishness that withstands historical change. On the other hand, the need to mark difference, especially in the global discourse of popular music, might also require the 'strategic' mobilisation of aspects of this 'Irishness' precisely to identify and mark out a space in the global 'noise' where the experience of being peripheral might be articulated (and a firm political belief or sense of cultural identity asserted) (182).

The latter 'hand' is a postmodernist variation, enabling a range of musicians from the popular and art traditions to 'quote' their Irishness without being implicated in any form of essentialist politics (Keohane 1997; see also Chapter 6). But even a brief glance at the contemporary Irish cultural landscape shows us that it is the former 'hand' which remains dominant. There can be no doubting, in other words, that music has emerged as perhaps *the* central element of modern Irish culture, supporting historical interpretations of a supposedly unproblematical 'Irish' identity, and modern creative initiatives which attempt to trade thereon. But if postcolonial theory has taught us anything, it is that critical engagements which turn on 'inherent' cultural capacities (such as musicality) inevitably reproduce the systems of thought which they were constructed to oppose; such, indeed, has been the burden of many of the major Irish critical engagements with postcolonial theory (Deane 1997; Lloyd 1993; Gibbons 1996; Kiberd 1995).

Music, Politics and Identity in B. Mac Laverty's Grace Notes 149

Although it is possible to observe these two factors cross-fertilising throughout modern Irish cultural history, the primary arena where the notion of a crisis-ridden literary tradition meets the notion of an 'inherently' musical race is the work of James Joyce – especially 'The Dead' (1914) and the eleventh chapter ('Sirens') of *Ulysses* (1922).[6] As mentioned in Chapter 7 of this volume, Joyce sits at the centre of this particular subgenre, casting a shadow on practitioners of the music novel both before and after him. That shadow is doubled when such an attempt is located in a specifically Irish context. To shift the metaphor slightly, the post-Joycean music novel is threatened on two sides: once by dint of its invocation of an alternative signifying system (music), and once by dint of the fragmented national tradition within which it is located. Such, nevertheless, was the task that Bernard Mac Laverty set himself in *Grace Notes*.

Grace Notes

Mac Laverty's novel is an unusually structured work, being divided into two almost exact halves. Part One (which in plot terms actually post-dates Part Two) introduces us to Catherine Anne McKenna, a young composer living in Glasgow. At the outset of the narrative Catherine is returning home to small-town Northern Ireland for her father's (Catholic) funeral. We learn of her troubled relationship with her parents, her current depression, her musical education in Belfast, Glasgow and Kiev, and her encounter with different characters in various contexts. Part Two takes the reader back to the period preceding the death of her father, during which time Catherine lived on the small Scottish island of Islay with Chris, a feckless English charmer with whom she has a baby. Narrated largely in free indirect discourse, we read of Catherine's pregnancy and labour, and then of the onset of a debilitating post-natal depression, itself augmented both by her inability to compose and by her partner's submission to alcoholism. After an epiphany on the Islay beach, Catherine returns to Glasgow, at which point she begins to write a work encapsulating many of the experiences broached throughout the earlier part of the text – sectarianism, familial strife, the joy and terror of motherhood, the apparently universal emotional economy of hope and despair. This two-part work, entitled *Vernicle*, is commissioned by BBC Scotland for a series celebrating folk themes or instruments. The instrument Catherine decides to feature is one of the icons of loyalist culture: the Lambeg drum. The last few pages of the book describe her nervous attendance at its first performance, as well as the work itself in extended detail. We may infer that shortly after the performance she receives word of her father's death, and returns home for the funeral which provides the focus for Part One.

Mac Laverty attempts to engage with music on a number of levels from the outset of the text. In the first two pages, Catherine hears cars going by in the rain, a man whistling, an engine idling, airport jingles and announcements, workmen hammering and sawing, a baby crying. It is immediately clear, in other words, that her apprehension of the world is dominated by sound – by the ear rather than the eye or any of the other senses. Life is noisy, the novel suggests, and when noise is formalised by human perception it becomes music.[7] Mac Laverty bypasses the notion of the Irish as an inherently musical race, however, by refusing to ally music with any particular tradition of national identity. Rather, music becomes the medium through which the individual subject and its others may commune. Thus, noting the seven syllables in the opening lines of the *Kyrie* (*Kyrie Eléison*) and the *Credo* (*Credo in unam Deum*), Catherine makes a connection between her own life and the mass she is trying to write:

> Seven in all. That was her. A mythic number. Seven little claps in all. Catherine Anne McKenna. Mysterious. The first voice like a precentor. Followed by others, each of whom is a precentor to the rest. Grace notes – notes which were neither one thing nor the other. A note between the notes. Notes that occurred outside time. Ornaments dictating the character of the music, the slur and slide of it. This is decoration becoming substance. Like a round in Granny Boyd's kitchen. Or Purcell's Songs of the Tavern. Soarings. Voices slipping. Joining folk music and art music. East and West. Male and Female.[8]

Although not stating so much at this point, this list of conjoined opposites will eventually also encompass Protestant and Catholic, loyalist and republican, nationalist and unionist. What these latter traditions cannot countenance, and what music precisely enables us to perceive, are, metaphorically speaking, the 'grace notes' that constitute life itself above and beyond the human ability to formalise. Our characteristic species inheritance is precisely this desire to formalise, it seems, to turn events into rituals, rituals into traditions, and traditions into markers of identity. What this process misses, however, is music's ineluctable *anti-formalism*. Musical discourse fetishises form (noise only becomes music, after all, when it is formalised) but this is paradoxical because what is ultimately valued about music is its mystery, its ability to present the unpresentable, to intimate to the listener things unapproachable through traditional forms. Thus, Catherine's use of the 'Protestant' drums in *Vernicle* functions for her as an affirmation of life in general rather than a celebration of one particular kind of life.

In this way, Mac Laverty brings a tradition of Irish musical fiction into creative dialogue with the tradition of Irish political fiction. More specifically, the cross-fertilisation of musical and political discourses is thematised throughout *Grace Notes* with reference to a phenomenon that performs a significant function in both aesthetic and political discourses: the phenomenon of repetition. Repetition is an important rhetorical resource in both literature and music; at the same time, it emerges as the predominant characteristic of nationalist and unionist discourses in Northern Ireland, fixated as they both are with preserving the past through practices and rituals of repetition. In *Grace Notes* Mac Laverty represents one medium of (musical) repetition by means of another (literary); he deploys both, furthermore, to reflect upon a sectarian society which has traditionally fetishised the ability to repeat the past without transformation.

In his book *Fiction and Repetition*, J. Hillis Miller describes two kinds of literary repetition; one, 'Platonic', based on *similarity* and 'grounded in a solid archetypal model which is untouched by the effects of repetition'; the other, 'Nietzschean', based on *difference* and giving rise to 'ungrounded doublings which arise from differential interrelations among elements which are all on the same plane'.[9] In his essay 'On Repetition', Edward W. Said pointed to a similar discursive economy. Making a connection between the use of repetition in Vico and Bach, Said (renowned as a critic both of music and literature) noted that in a composition such as the *Goldberg Variations* 'a ground motif [the *cantus firmus*] anchors the ornamental variations taking place above it. Despite the proliferation of changing rhythms, patterns, and harmonies, the ground motif recurs throughout, as if to demonstrate its staying power and its capacity for endless elaboration' (1991: 114). Said opposed this form of repetition (obviously of the 'Platonic' variety described by Hillis Miller) to one in which a repeated figure 'degrades' rather than 'enhances' the prior enunciation.[10]

Although Said did not make the connection, the musical equivalent of this 'Nietzschean' or 'degraded' repetition would be serialism, a system of musical composition in which, as Daniel Albright (in the context of an interesting essay on music in Beckett) puts it:

> you must sound each of the twelve notes of the chromatic scale, the scale that counts every semitone in the octave, before you repeat a note; and you must sound the twelve notes in the same order every time, though they may be gathered into chords at pleasure. This procedure ensures a kind of unity, in that certain melodic shapes are likely to recur, but it also ensures that unity will not derive from the persistence of a tonic note, since no note has greater prestige or frequency than any other note (1997/1998: 34–5).

On one level, *Grace Notes* implicitly supports a kind of signifying practice in which repetition 'degrades' rather than 'enhances' any notion of 'a solid archetypal model', an 'original' against which repeated forms might be measured. Repetition in this sense does not copy (repeat) the 'original' but changes – contrary to received notions of temporal linearity (and the political systems relying thereon) – its meaning.[11] Like Joyce in *Ulysses*, Mac Laverty wishes to show how '[a] repeated sign always refers back and illuminates a play of identity and difference which cannot entirely be appropriated by a reading directed towards a totalized meaning' (Kumar 1991: 48). Thus, it is only when she distances herself from Northern Ireland that Catherine can articulate the emotion she felt on first hearing the Lambeg drum during a childhood walk with her father. Because of her father's relation to the drum's sectarian heritage, the emotion could not be expressed without in some way denying him, and in some respects denying herself. The novel may thus be understood as Catherine's search for a means to express the sounds which have impacted upon her identity, but in such a way as to avoid repeating the relationships which set the limits on her father's life.

Grace Notes thus functions as a plea for political tolerance based on the notion of a form of repetition which does not reproduce an 'original'. Repetition is thematised in the text as part of the process – simultaneously artistic and socio-political – whereby Catherine refuses to be used by the past (either her father or the sectarian context into which she was born) but instead finds the strength and courage to use it as part of her own ongoing project of creative self-identity. By incorporating the 'Protestant' drums into her work, she metaphorically kills her father; at the same time, however, she salvages him as a positive, creative influence on her own life, the independent life she must lead if she is not to remain the sum of the influences to which she has been exposed.

The themes of repetition and tension between generations are ones which obviously recall modernism in general, and Joyce in particular. But the thematisation of repetition in this novel is also linked with Joyce's attempt to install musical discourse at a formal level within 'Sirens'. The text works continually to point up the differences which occur when themes, emotions and situations are repeated in different contexts, or when they are remembered from alternative perspectives, what the narrator refers to as 'the ability unique to music to say one or more things at once' (275), or (focalised by Catherine) the ability both to appreciate and to articulate 'the same sound but with a different meaning' (275). This is signalled throughout the text by a series of linguistic puns and homophones: 'linseed oil' and 'Lynn C. Doyle' (24); 'Bartók' and 'bar talk' (25), 'pressing' (ironing) and 'pressing' (urgent) (49), 'stand' (arise) and 'stand' (tolerate) (108), and so on.

As with Joyce, this theme is also borne out at a formal level. Thus, the bells Catherine hears early in the text (50) remind her of the bells on a strap used for childhood chastisement. The taped bells which sound as her father's remains are being removed to church (56) excite in her emotions of loss and guilt, while also making intertextual reference to all the other Catholic funerals that have taken place in this sectarian society. However, these generally negative connotations are mitigated by the bells she hears (123–4) when visiting the composer Melnichuck in Kiev, bells which create in Catherine an infectious 'excitement and joy', and whose description – 'Tin-tinn-ab-you-la-ish-on' – recall the seven syllables which will in time re-spark her own creativity. Because of the form of the text, however, there exists no straightforwardly linear relationship between these moments. The plot – *first* childhood, *then* Kiev, *then* funeral – is belied by the narrative – *first* childhood, *then* funeral, *then* Kiev. We may assume that Catherine's negative response to the taped bells at her father's funeral (56) relates to her negative experience of bells in childhood (50), but we will eventually learn that it is also a response to the positive experience of bells in Kiev (123–4). We may also assume that the 'excitement and joy' Catherine felt on hearing the bells of Kiev was in itself a response to the negative connotations carried from childhood. All these moments are then positively reclaimed and formalised in the final appearance of the bells (274) as part of the second movement of *Vernicle*, the orchestral composition which closes the novel.

It is in respect of this musical work, and more importantly its place within the text's double structure, that the issue of repetition is presented most forcefully. In the first movement, the Lambeg drums are male, minatory and hostile, in conflict with the main orchestra:

> Insistent, cacophonous rhythm. Disintegration. The tormented orchestra tries to keep its head above the din of these strangers. The black blood of hatred stains every ear ... Their aggression, their swagger put her in mind of Fascism ... A brutalising of the body, the spirit, humanity. Thundering and thundering and thundering and thundering. When the drums stopped on a signal from Randal the only thing that remained was a feeling of depression and darkness. Utter despair (272–3).

These are the connotations which set the limits on her father's understanding of the drums, while the depression and darkness recall Catherine's own emotional state after the birth of her baby and the breakdown of her relationship. After despair comes joy, however:

> The second movement is the other side of the arch ... At the moment when the music comes to its climax, a carillon of bells and brass, the Lambegs make another entry at maximum volume. The effect this time is not one of terror or depression but the opposite ... The Lambegs have been stripped of their bigotry and have become pure sound ... On this accumulating wave the drumming has a fierce joy about it. Exhilaration comes from nowhere. The bell-beat, the slabs of brass, the whooping of the horns, the battering of the drums. Sheer fucking unadulterated joy (273–6).

Repetition thus preserves the original while also transforming it; in a different context, the same drums (signifying aggression and despair) have created a different effect (exhilaration and joy). Catherine has repeated her father's engagement with the drums, but created her own meaning from them. This transformative aesthetic, moreover, is borne out in a more general sense by the form of the text. The artistic triumph comes at the end of the narrative (277), but the form of the text then sends us back to the beginning (3) – Catherine arriving back in Northern Ireland for her father's funeral – at which point her doubts and fears re-emerge. The musical joy she experiences at the end of Part Two is then repeated by the personal joy she experiences on holding her baby again upon her return to Glasgow (138).[12] While the plot shows us Catherine slowly healing herself in artistic and personal terms, the narrative reveals the extent to which impressions of linearity are belied by a series of overlapping internal temporalities in which joy and despair co-exist, and in which the past subsists within, even as it is transformed by, its repetition in the present. This insight in itself depends in large part upon a second reading, one which repeats the first (the same pages are read) but this time with a knowledge of the significance – indeed, the existence – of key themes and structures.[13]

The overall effect is to reveal the illusion consequent upon the conventional perception of time as linear, *and everything that rests upon that erroneous perception*. What I mean by this is that the possibility of a repetition which both retains and transforms the original is obviously intended by Mac Laverty to resonate in the political context of the 'Troubles'. We may be doomed to repeat the past, but aesthetic experience (Mac Laverty's, Catherine's, the reader's) also helps us to move towards a realisation that every repetition represents, despite itself, a transformation, and that this contributes to a liberation from the notion that effective identity resides only in the ritualised repetition of originary essences. We can (indeed, we must) acknowledge the past, but we do not need to be enslaved by it. Music, the novel suggests, is the principal modern cultural practice affording this insight, because it remains unencumbered by the necessity for narrative progression, and because it uses repetition to point up possibilities for transformation rather than replication.

A series of repetitions thus infuses *Grace Notes*: the two parts of the text, the two parts of *Vernicle*, Catherine's emotional oscillation between despair and joy, Northern Irish society's paradoxical fetishisation of the past through rituals of originality; the text's demand for a second reading. The novel is *about* music – which is to say, it uses musical discourse to dramatise the overlapping tensions between the personal, the professional and the political. Catherine's artistic crisis simultaneously mirrors and is caused by a wider social crisis into which, as a late twentieth-century Irish woman, she has been born. The insight she gains as an artist – that the same sounds can mean different things in different contexts, and that this process is ultimately inscrutable – resonates in socio-political terms also, registering as a plea for tolerance and respect for difference. At the same time, *Grace Notes* does not try merely to *present* these things, but to *encode* them in the form of an organic text that is itself doubled, with incidents, motifs and insights repeated so as to reveal their different impact in different contexts. Mac Laverty's book, in other words, clearly aspires to be musical, attempting (like 'Sirens') to actuate musical forms and effects rather than just represent them.

Although *Grace Notes* implicitly opposes the notion of repetition as the sign of originality, a question mark remains over the extent to which it actually supports a form of 'Nietzschean' repetition for which, as we have seen, the musical equivalent would be serialism. Music (generically considered) is celebrated by Mac Laverty as that which 'unhomes' us by virtue of its ability to transform through repetition; yet the musical imagination validated in and by the text is resolutely 'homed', nostalgically wedded to a narrative of unalienated identity. That same imagination in fact falls well short of a full-blooded serialism in which music would be entirely 'unhomed', in which sounds repeat systematically but without reference to a home key. The text's guiding aesthetic could legitimately be described as neo-romantic; the composers valued by Catherine belong to (or at least are routinely claimed by) the tradition of European expressionist art music – the music of Bach, Mozart and Beethoven; at a lesser level, of Purcell, Vivaldi, Janácek and a host of other composers name-checked throughout the text. Even the fictional character of Melnichuck (who seems to be a composite of Arvo Pärt and Einojuhani Rautavaara) writes music into which '[thousands] of years were compressed', music that expresses for Catherine recognisable emotions of 'pain and love, joy and loss' (226). As with *An Equal Music*, however, the tradition of twentieth-century anti-expressionism gets very short shrift indeed, as when Catherine characterises a piece by Stockhausen as ugly, ineffectual, totally abstract, a theoretical conspiracy of lies (260).[14]

In Lyotard's terms, then, *Grace Notes* is resolutely 'modern', ultimately offering 'the reader ... matter for solace and pleasure' by virtue of the 'recognizable consistency' of its form. No rational person would wish to experience pain and loss, but at the same time we are assured by our ability to recognise them, and more importantly by the possibility (around which so much bourgeois culture is organised) that we can modify our behaviour and our circumstances so as to realise their opposites: love and joy. *Vernicle* repeats and reflects *Grace Notes* in so far as both attempt to present the unpresentable, sustained by the conviction that, in art as in life, form is everything. This in turn is directly linked to Mac Laverty's political vision, which might be described as typically liberal-humanist, registering as a plea for tolerance in the face of otherness, or simply a recognition of the otherness that informs identity. *Grace Notes* seeks to accommodate identitarian discourse, rather than (as with serialism or Lyotard's 'postmodern') to question the signifying framework within which identitarian discourse functions as 'reality'. And just as the limits of musical expression are set by the (invariably bourgeois) context in which the artist works, so liberal humanism is entirely enmeshed with the (nationalist-colonialist) values and practices it seeks to modify.

'Sing your melody, I'll sing along': Mimetic and Diegetic Uses of Music in Once

The film *Once* (2007) was shot on a relatively tiny budget of 130,000 Euros in and around Dublin over seventeen days in January 2006. Written and directed by John Carney, it tells the story of an unnamed Irish busker (played by Glen Hansard) who meets an unnamed Czech immigrant (Markéta Irglová) on Grafton Street in the city centre. As they become friends they reveal to each other a little about their troubled lives. They write and record some songs together, after which the Irishman leaves to join his estranged girlfriend in London, while she remains in Dublin where she is joined by her husband.

Once was a commercial success far beyond the expectations of its backers or makers. Having been spotted at the Galway Film Festival, it was invited to screen at the prestigious Sundance Film Festival where it won the Audience Award. On the strength of that exposure, one of the film's featured songs, 'Falling Slowly', was nominated for, and subsequently won, the 2007 Academy Award for 'Best Original Song'. It went on to win the Independent Spirit Award for 'Best Foreign Film', while both the soundtrack and 'Falling Slowly' were also nominated for Grammies.

Clearly, Carney's film is approachable from any number of theoretical, methodological or political perspectives. In terms of Film Studies, *Once* offers a fascinating example of low-budget, semi-independent movie-making, with many of the characteristics of such an undertaking: amateur actors, skeleton crew, a minimum of equipment, improvised script, and so on. In terms of Cultural Studies, the narrative incorporates a number of salient elements from contemporary Irish life, most notably the presence of a growing immigrant population – many of whom are (like the female lead) of east European origin – against the background of uneven economic development. The emergence of such a population remains an important issue in modern Irish life, and its function in relation to established Irish cultural discourses has yet to be assessed. *Once* would be an important reference point within such as assessment.

My emphasis here, however, is on the music, in which terms this film is an especially fascinating text. Before going on to look at the use and representation of music in *Once*, and in order to provide a context within which to offer some comments, I want briefly to consider some of the ways in which film-makers have used music over the century or so since the inception of the medium.

MUSIC AND/IN FILM

Music has enjoyed a ubiquitous presence within film discourse since the development of the fiction film towards the end of the nineteenth century. From the use of improvised accompaniment for silent films to the most sophisticated modern soundtrack, however, the relationship can be organised into two main categories: on the one hand, the music of the soundtrack which emanates, apparently, from nowhere to accompany the unfolding visual narrative; and on the other, the use of various kinds of musical text (such as songs) within the narrative itself. Such a relationship, moreover, may be conceptualised with reference to one of the oldest aesthetic theories to which we have access: the Platonic distinction between mimesis and diegesis.[1]

The classic Hollywood soundtrack was by and large a product of the late-nineteenth-century Romantic imagination in western art music, in as much as it tended to be highly melodic, densely orchestrated and invariably programmatic (Paulin 2000). Hollywood composers also exploited to the full the Wagnerian development of the leitmotif – a short, recurring phrase which 'represents' a particular feature of the unfolding narrative – a character, relationship, place, emotion or such like (London 2000). At the same time (and ironically in the light of the preceding point) the role of film music was, as Wendy Everett describes it, to 'remain entirely "inaudible" or at least inconspicuous ... its fundamental role is to support and protect the narrative without drawing attention to itself' (2000: 103). No-one could doubt that music was a crucial element in the construction of 'meaning' within a film; it created particular atmospheric conditions, directed the audience towards particular emotional responses, cued them for particular narrative developments, and so on. Such blatant manipulation could not afford to be foregrounded, however, as it would detract from the audience's emotional investment in the narrative, and thus threaten to undo the mimetic contract between spectacle and spectator. In an important sense, then, the audience should not 'hear' the music which is so managing their emotional engagement with the filmic text.

In such a dispensation, as Everett goes on to point out, 'familiar music (into which category popular songs must be placed) should be avoided because it runs the risk of drawing attention to itself as music, and again, in so doing, of distancing the spectator from the film's narrative' (2000: 103). At a certain point, however, Hollywood was obliged to acknowledge the power (economic as well as emotional) of popular song. The enormous success of the classic Hollywood musical is one indication of that power, although it should be noted that such texts realised an enormously complex set of musical relations (Altman 1987). Many musicals existed in other forms before their adaptation for the screen, and selected aspects (individual songs, for example) could enjoy a significant extra-cinematic career. Each filmic text was also obliged to negotiate a relationship between its properly incidental music and that moment when the quasi-realistic action is suspended and the dynamics of the individual song take over. Altman calls this moment the 'audio dissolve' – a technique which

> involves a passage from the diegetic track (e.g. conversation) to the music track (e.g. orchestral accompaniment) through the intermediary of diegetic music. This simple expedient, perhaps more characteristic of the musical than any other stylistic trait, has long been sensed as a typical – and somewhat unrealistic – musical technique (1987: 63).

The 1950s represents the period of the classic Hollywood musical. Interestingly, Jeff Smith (2003) has described the advent of film industry/record industry 'synergy' during that same decade as part of a response to various demographic and social changes in the post-war western world. That synergetic revolution was only partly successful according to Smith, but one of its lasting contributions has been the film studio-sponsored soundtrack album. These recordings became a vital part of the musical's marketing strategy, often achieving remarkable commercial success in their own right (as in the case of *The Sound of Music* [1965] for example). From this phenomenon was born the soundtrack album featuring a compilation of music drawn from the diegetic narrative level. Unlike the musical (whose songs were embedded within the narrative), films began to feature soundtrack material which, although perhaps chosen to illustrate a particular narrative point or to indicate a particular socio-cultural context, was at the same time possessed of its own extra-narrative significance. In such cases the spectator's emotional response would oscillate between their appreciation of the music's aptness in the context of the film narrative and their relationship (all points between ignorance and full identification) with the song's non-filmic status.

Of special significance is the film genre in which music features as a significant thematic element within the narrative, in which respect it is worth noting that *The Jazz Singer* (1927) – generally regarded as the first successful 'talkie' – was a film about competing musical traditions. Although music as an overt topic was already well established (in biographies of famous musicians or composers, for example), it was really with the advent of the rock 'n' roll era that the film-about-music came into its own. In such instances, as Kay Dickinson suggests,

> music is neither something tacked-on in post-production not a wilfully coherent pre-existing unit inserted into a cinematic cavity. Instead it is a prominent bearer of far-reaching cultural propositions, acting beyond the limitations of any more internal concept of musical grammar (2003: 7).

There is a sort of circular ideology at work in many of these films, in which the representation of music *within* the narrative functions as an analogue of the *extra-textual* role of music – that is, the relationship between music and film in the real world where decisions are taken about what kinds of film will and will not be made. The British 'pop movie' of the late 1950s and early 1960s provides a good example of this ideological movement in action: the entertainment industry (of which cinema formed a significant part) controlled the initial anarchic thrust of rock 'n' roll by making movies in which rock 'n' roll was reconciled with the entertainment establishment, becoming in the process a different discourse: pop (Medhurst 1995).

Some of the issues raised by film music (or more specifically, by the inclusion of popular song in film) may be addressed by a consideration of selected moments from the cinematic engagement with the music of Bob Dylan. Introducing a song by that artist onto the soundtrack of a film (such as Dennis Hopper's *Easy Rider* [1969], for example) encourages in the spectator a range of interpretative and emotional responses derived in part from its narrative pertinence, and in part from that particular artist's popular musical (which is to say, non-filmic, extra-textual) profile, which is itself constantly changing and contested.[2] Dylan's 'Knockin' On Heaven's Door' featured in Sam Peckinpah's *Pat Garrett and Billy the Kid* (1973), in which it functioned (in lyrical terms) as a commentary upon the experience of various characters (including the eponymous outlaw), and at the same time as a recurring musical leitmotif. Any 'meaning' imputed to this music is rendered more problematic by Dylan's presence within the film as the character 'Alias'. The song itself remains one of his best-known compositions, its 'classic' status confirmed by a number of high-profile cover versions, of which the one by Los Angeles rock band Guns 'n' Roses (1991) is perhaps the most successful.

In Todd Haynes's celebrated *I'm Not There* (2007), the film soundtrack is comprised of various original Dylan recordings plus a number of his songs as performed by a range of modern musicians. Some of these latter performances are mimed during the course of the film by the six different actors who have been cast to 'play' various aspects of Dylan's life and musical career, while some (such as the version of 'Knockin' On Heaven's Door' by Antony and the Johnsons, which plays over the closing credits) have no imitative pretension, but are quite clearly 'by' the performing artist. The result is a dauntingly complex series of semiotic significations, as spectator focus switches between the original compositions, their re-interpretations by contemporary musicians (who may or may not be familiar), and the 'performance' of these songs by actors (such as Cate Blanchett and Christian Bale) who are themselves possessed of specific iconographical resonances. Haynes's film is an example of what Dickinson refers to as 'a cinema where music is not subservient to film narrative's "melody", and does not merely run alongside it holding up cue cards in a desperate attempt to heighten an audience's response to the story-line's main current' (2003: 11).

A version of Dylan's 'You Ain't Goin' Nowhere' (a song with an extremely complex recording history) as performed by Glen Hansard and Markéta Irglová appears on the soundtrack album for *I'm Not There* (2007). Before turning towards a consideration of *Once*, however, it is necessary to take note of some of the ways in which Ireland and Irishness have been represented in film music over the last century.

THE SOUND OF IRISHNESS

An authentic indigenous film industry has been slow to develop in Ireland. For much of the twentieth century, the story was one of impositions from without, interspersed with occasional initiatives which pointed to the possibility of a viable domestic practice (Pettitt 2000: 28–48). That possibility seemed bound always to be undone by a lack of imagination, ambition and/or economic support, however. The result was a cinematic vision of Irish identity which was dominated by the highly active film industries to the east (in Britain) and west (in the US).

The representation of Ireland in film was derived from discourses active within the wider cultural representation of the country. The cinematic versions of 'Irishness' (different in detail but similar in essentials) produced by Britain and the US were developments of ideologies refined during the nineteenth century, and each spoke to specific features of the relationship between a small, economically unsuccessful country and the two large, successful states with which it was so closely connected. The British cinematic representation of Ireland was by and large a product of Celticism: a nineteenth-century strategy for 'containing' Irishness within a flexible discursive array ranging from childish ineptitude to calculated aggression (Donnelly 2007, 56–68; Smyth 1996; see Chapter 6). The American case was more complex, containing Celticist elements alongside an impulse that was both more inclusivist and more sentimental (Pettitt 2000: 64–7). The point remains, however, that the cinematic representation of Ireland throughout the twentieth century was dominated by non-indigenous agencies in pursuit of their own ideological (and economic) agendas.

In terms of our concerns here, we note that '[the] strategies evident in films set in Ireland,' as K.J. Donnelly puts it, 'are designed to furnish a sense of Irishness through their music as much as, if not more so, than the visual aspects of the film' (2005: 67). In fact, the representation of Irishness operated along a continuum running between two ideal states or personalities that elsewhere in this volume I have described as 'Paddy Sad' and Paddy Mad' (see Chapter 4). Each was attached to a set of musical conventions which, upon their introduction (either on the 'inaudible' soundtrack or within the story itself), signified a narrative development associated with, or determined by, that state or personality. The conventions are complex and under constant negotiation, although in broad terms we can say (with the understanding that all the following descriptive phrases are in imaginary scare quotes) that Paddy Sad is invoked by slow tempo, quasi-modal melody, pure timbre and expressive phrasing, whereas Paddy Mad may be referenced by higher tempos, driving rhythms, often featuring ensemble performance of complex melodies played in unison.

A few brief examples from well-known films illustrate the tendency. The music playing over the opening credits of John Ford's *The Quiet Man* (1952) includes a lush, densely orchestrated version of 'The Isle of Innisfree', a song written in the 1940s by a policeman from Kells named Dick Farrelly. The lyric (very loosely based on the celebrated poem by W.B. Yeats) tells the story of an exile who dreams of returning from a great modern city to his idyllic home in rural Ireland. The song was well known in the country when Ford came to spot locations for his forthcoming movie. He suggested to the composer Victor Young that it be adapted (although unacknowledged) in *The Quiet Man*, where it initially signifies the attitude of the returning emigrant Seán Thornton (John Wayne) towards his ancestral home, before becoming a theme for the love story between Seán and Mary-Kate Danaher (Maureen O'Hara).[3]

The soundtrack to *The Quiet Man* also features a number of up-tempo tunes, including jigs and hornpipes, which have been scored for orchestra by Young. This kind of music is heard during moments of heightened emotion, such as the protracted fight sequence between Seán Thornton and his brother-in-law Red Will Danaher (Victor McLaglen). The music accompanying such scenes may be described as 'ideological' in as much as it appears to articulate an ineluctable excitability within the Irish psyche – a perennial state, the 'truth' of which subsists, first of all, in the very existence of the music (it must be the cultural product of an excitable race); and secondly, in its repetition in contexts which appear to confirm the 'truth' (see the fight, hear the music).[4] It is important to note, moreover, that the 'Irish' elements featured on the soundtrack exist alongside a range of 'neutral' musical conventions, at which point the soundtrack reverts to its classic role as 'inaudible' guide to audience response.

Perhaps the most notorious example of musical Irishness from modern cinematic history is provided by James Cameron's *Titanic* (1997), in which the aristocratic Rose DeWitt Bukater (Kate Winslett) is taken to 'a real party' by the impoverished Jack Dawson (Leonardo DiCaprio) in the hold of the ship where an Irish traditional dance band is in full, if somewhat anachronistic, swing.[5] Removed from the refined, sedate music upstairs, Rose indulges the 'mad' dimension of her own personality which she had been forced to suppress due to a combination of family obligation and convention. The doomed romantic affair between the two leads became closely associated with the song 'My Heart Will Go On', written by the composer James Horner (who was also responsible for the film soundtrack), and an international hit in the lung-bursting rendition by Celine Dion. The song features on the closing credits, although it is referenced at various points throughout the film, most notably in the celebrated 'flying' section during Rose and Jack's windy embrace at the Titanic's prow. Featuring a recognisably 'Irish' tune played on a reverb-laden whistle, 'My Heart Will Go On' also draws on the accumulated iconographical associations of the melancholic Celt; and like 'Falling Slowly' ten years later, it also won an Academy Award for Best Original Song.

As Donnelly points out, many 'Irish' films are co-productions with international partners (frequently British or American), and there is as a consequence a degree of pressure for such films to announce their credentials in a clearly recognisable sonic register (2005: 67). Certain kinds of music (jigs, reels and airs played in a 'traditional' style, for example) thus function as a kind of brand, signifying Ireland for international audiences and thus helping to locate the film in a recognisable (and more comfortable) context. These musical discourses include the stereotypes of 'Paddy Sad' and 'Paddy Mad' mentioned above, and more recently the refinement of the former within the modern category known as 'Celtic music'.

Not unexpectedly, many modern Irish film-makers have attempted to distance themselves from such branding. In fact, films such as *Intermission* (2003), *Adam and Paul* (2004) and *Garage* (2007) deliberately avoid conventional sonic signifiers of Ireland or Irishness. The first of these examples begins with some recognisably Irish music, with U2's 'Out of Control' (1980) offering a diegetic comment on the character played by Colin Farrell: Lehiff, a 'Paddy Mad' for the Celtic Tiger era. Thereafter the composer John Murphy reverts to a less manipulative (and certainly less ethnic) soundtrack: strummed acoustic guitar for general exposition, an urgent conga rhythm during a moment of tension, and so on.[6] Indeed, if such films share a distinguishing characteristic at all, it is a certain minimalist approach to the use of diegetic music. *Adam and Paul* features a soundtrack composed by the conceptualist sound artist Stephen Rennicks, part of which is comprised of variations (including whistling) on what sounds like an eastern European melody played in waltz time. Rennicks' score for *Garage* continues this non-directive aesthetic, with long sections of the film lacking in any form of musical diegesis. The general rule seems to be: the more independent the film, the less 'Irish' the soundtrack. It was in the context of this rule, and of the debates and issues introduced above, that *Once* was produced.

Once

Unlike the minimalist approach of the modern Irish films noted above, *Once* is dominated by music from beginning to end. The music, moreover, is embedded within both the diegetic and the mimetic levels of narration, and functions by means of a constant exchange between each. This is apparent from the outset: Carney's film opens with the sound of a man singing with accompaniment from acoustic guitar. But is this part of the soundtrack (that is, belonging to the diegetic level of narration) or does it belong to the world of the story that is just about to unfold? With the onset of the visuals we observe that the latter is in fact the case: the song is being performed, apparently live, by a man standing on a street. That initial question recurs throughout, however, because the film consistently blurs the boundaries between music as a key element within the unfolding story and music as an essential component of the film's emotional narrative. The ambiguity thus created, moreover, soon becomes a naturalised element of the viewing/listening process, determining in large part both the kind and the extent of the audience's developing relationship with the film.

The situation is complicated further by the casting of Glen Hansard – lead singer and mainstay of The Frames, a band with a significant profile in Ireland – and further still by the fact that the director John Carney played bass guitar with that band for a number of years in the early 1990s. In *Once*, Hansard plays the part of a musician who writes, arranges and performs songs that are to all intents and purposes indistinguishable from the ones with which he is associated in 'real life'. The music of The Frames is characterised by lyrical intensity, emotional commitment and dynamic arrangements (Campbell and Smyth 2005: 136–9). A song such as 'What Happens When the Heart Just Stops' (from the album *For The Birds*, 2001) offers a typical example in so far as the listener is taken on a sonic journey which attempts to replicate – in some aspects and to some degree – the emotional journey described in the lyric. At the outset, the protagonist quietly addresses his erstwhile love, accompanied by music that is barely audible; the listener appears to inhabit a particular kind of musical environment – low-key, reflective, restrained – one that is, moreover, directly expressive of analogous emotions: sadness, defeat, confusion. The music begins to change in response to the different emotions which emerge with the passing of time 'within' the narrative of the song, however. It grows in volume and intensity until the song reaches a powerful climax in which lyric, voice and music unite to express the protagonist's disappointment and his attempt to retrieve something positive from a failed relationship. This radically different sonic environment is followed by a short coda which re-establishes the original mood before the song ends.

Over the course of his career, Glen Hansard has become identified with the personae of songs such as 'What Happens When the Heart Just Stops'. This process of identification appears to be deeply encoded within one strand of popular music discourse: authenticity is determined by the degree to which a musician 'represents' (in the sense of 'embodies') the subjects they 'represent' (in the sense of 'depict'). And so, like the protagonists he creates, Hansard has come to be regarded as emotional, intense, committed; and both the musician and the music have been criticised and lauded in precisely those terms. By casting his friend and former band mate as the male lead, Carney has recruited Hansard's wider profile as part of the discursive fabric of the film.

With *Once*, it is as if Carney has written a screenplay to dramatise (or more accurately, to 'cinematise') one of Hansard's emotionally charged songs. The story – concerning a short, intense friendship which just about fails to blossom into love because of complex circumstances

– represents classic Frames territory. The song which best 'illustrates' or 'represents' that on-screen relationship is likewise a typical Hansard composition. The 'I' persona of 'Falling Slowly' (a composite of Hansard and the film's unnamed male lead) addresses a 'you' persona (the Irglová character) in terms which move ambiguously between romantic attraction and platonic support. Both are in search of redemption after periods of suffering; both suspect that the idea of a relationship is a convenient game which will probably play itself out. The man offers the woman support to make the 'choice' with which she is faced, even if that means losing her. The lyric ends with a musical image – 'Falling slowly, sing your melody, I'll sing along' – which skirts the border between independence (a single melodic line) and liaison (the harmony of singing along).

In typical Frames style, the music of 'Falling Slowly' reflects the intense, ambiguous relationship broached in the lyric. The opening twenty-eight seconds – in which Hansard's voice quietly doubles a melody introduced on acoustic guitar – connotes the simplicity and vulnerability of an initial attraction. Voice and guitar are joined by Irglová singing harmony, while the piano which had hovered uncertainly around the opening section begins to grow in emphasis. The female voice then drops out, signalling the uncertain nature of the woman's role within the unfolding musical narrative. Hansard sings close to the bottom of his range during the modulation to A-minor, which makes the melodic leap during the chorus (nearly two octaves above the initial note of the song) all the more striking. The acoustic guitar, which had been sensitively picked during the opening sections, is now strummed with full arm movements as the music grows in intensity and volume. The song reaches a climax with guitar and piano vigorously improvising around a single chord for twenty-six seconds (a relatively long time considered in relation to the song's overall duration of four minutes and four seconds), before subsiding once again and reprising the opening section with lightly picked guitar and barely audible piano.

To the extent that 'Falling Slowly' is a musical rendering of the film's central relationship, *Once* clearly draws on Glen Hansard's public profile as the writer and performer of certain kinds of songs. Carney asked his friend to play a character who dresses, talks, looks, sings, and indeed acts exactly like the persona of a Glen Hansard song – the authenticity of which, we recall, is directly linked to its identification with the 'real' Glen Hansard. This makes for an extremely complex viewing experience, in which different levels of reality – filmic, musical, so-called 'real-life' – constantly overlap and modify each other.

This uncertainty with regard to the level of reality engaged by the audience is reflected in the use of music throughout the film. The initial performance of 'Falling Slowly', for example, clearly derives from the mimetic level of narrative. The spectator observes the man teaching the song to the woman in a deserted music shop – naming chords, describing the structure, singing the melody, providing cues, and so on. The ensuing performance represents an important development within the world of the narrative: the musical compatibility of the two musicians broaches the possibility of a romantic liaison (the duet as a kind of intercourse) and the spectator's attitude is modified accordingly. At a certain point (19.27), however, diegesis overtakes mimesis: the duet continues on the soundtrack but the shot shifts from the music shop to an arcade through which we observe the characters walking.[7]

This version of 'Falling Slowly' ends with the two characters sitting at the back of a bus, at which point the woman questions the man about 'the special girl you write this song for'. The implication is that the song they have recently performed pre–dates their acquaintance – that it was in fact written with a previous relationship in mind – in which case there must be a question mark over its subsequent association with the failed relationship between the two leads. By the time 'Falling Slowly' is repeated towards the end of the film (beginning at 1.17.42), however, that association is revisited and fully established: the song plays over images of the man travelling to the airport and checking in, and of his gift of a piano arriving at the woman's flat. The strings which are introduced as the song approaches its climax (1.20.00) differentiate it from the earlier version; although recalling that first performance in the empty music shop, we are clearly hearing a different version of the same song. The strings introduce a new perspective which, in keeping with the ambivalent nature of the film's central relationship, appears caught between hope and pity – hope for the new start each has embraced, and pity for the relationship they have denied each other.

The man's response to the woman's question is an apparently extempore performance of 'Broken-Hearted Hoover-Fixer Sucker Guy' – a song that appears to provide a light-hearted, almost trivial, moment amid all the charged emotions on view. In fact, the song provides important narrative information, filling in much of the back story necessary for the emotional development of the story; and it is entirely in keeping with the ethos of the film that such background should be communicated in musical form. As in a 'proper' musical film, it emerges as an element within the mimetic level of narration; 'reality' is temporarily suspended with the introduction of a discursive mode (a song) that, in terms of both its formal and its conceptual discourses (in broad terms, what it sounds like and what it is about), modifies the audience's relationship with the narrative. *Once* plays with the convention of the 'audio dissolve' – that moment in the classical musical when speaking ends and singing begins. We may come to understand that 'Broken-Hearted Hoover-Fixer Sucker Guy' is an on-the-spot creation, but not before an allusion is made to a different kind of film in which different narrative modes are employed.

Hansard's supposedly improvised performance during this sequence does more than just inform the audience about his character's current situation. The film works hard to locate its fictional music within an actual, and more of less familiar, Irish musical landscape peopled by the likes of Van Morrison, Aslan and Thin Lizzy (all referenced over the course of the film). At the same time, the deeply serious songs of love and loss written and performed by the two leads come to function as a form of musical reality within the film; songs such as 'Falling Slowly', that is to say, establish the formal and lyrical parameters within which the film functions, and within which a preferred meaning is available. It is in relation to these parameters that the audience is invited to respond to 'Broken-Hearted Hoover-Fixer Sucker Guy' as a comic, quasi-country music version (complete with fake southern US accent) of 'real' songs such as 'Lies', 'Leave' and 'All The Way Down'. And yet, one could argue that what such a performance really achieves is an exposure of the conventionality of all musical meaning – that the impact of a song such as 'Falling Slowly' is *achieved* rather than *revealed*, and that emotional expression in music, no matter how 'committed' or how 'real', is always a function of musical genre.

Of the many sequences throughout *Once* when mimesis and diegesis overlap, one of the most effective occurs when the woman (who has agreed to write lyrics for a melody provided by the man) walks home from a shop where she has gone to buy batteries for a portable CD player. We observe the woman fitting a set of earphones as she leaves the shop, at which point she commences to sing, presumably to the musical accompaniment which is also audible on the soundtrack. Both the song and the walk home take approximately three minutes, during which time she is continuously in shot. The performance thus retains mimetic plausibility, even as it makes intertextual reference to a genre of popular music video in which a singer performs while walking towards camera through a quasi-realistic environment.[8] Again, the suspicion arises that the film has been adapted to suit the music, the effect of which is to blur the boundaries between different narrative modes: those in which the characters reveal something of themselves from *within* the world of the narrative, and those in which the internal 'reality' of the film is revealed through the use of some kind of framing device (in this case, the aesthetics of popular music video).

As Kay Dickinson suggests, film music is

> simultaneously a vast store of resources for provoking emotional response; a shared but debated means of communication; an instrument for smoothing over the ruptures caused by film editing ... a lifestyle choice through which we delineate our social identities; a commodity which is fed through huge international networks; and much more besides (2003: 11).

All of these factors bear upon an understanding of the use of music in *Once*. The focus here, however, has been on the effect of the film's constant shift between diegetic and mimetic modes of narration. Like many similar projects, *Once* was obliged to make a virtue of necessity, and to try to find ways to overcome its budgetary restrictions through imagination and creativity. The use of filming techniques drawn from documentary and *cinéma vérité* help to create the illusion of realism which is all the more effective for its understatement. At the same time, Carney's decision to employ musicians as actors enabled him to develop a narrative in which music was at the centre of both the story *and* the storytelling process, and in which, as a consequence, mimesis and diegesis are in constant conversation with each other. While this makes for a range of logical inconsistencies, most commentators are agreed that the resulting film did succeed in meeting two of the most important criteria for any form of artistic endeavour: effectiveness and pleasure.

Notes

INTRODUCTION

1. I have since discovered that Magical Strings is a family band from the American north-west which specialises in 'intertwining Celtic roots with classical/world music influences'. The featured instruments are the harp and the hammered dulcimer. See www.magicalstrings.com/Bio-Short.html.

CHAPTER 1

1. In the introduction to a special number on the subject of music in April 2004, I noted that the *Irish Studies Review* (the leading Irish Studies journal in Great Britain) had published only three main articles (two of which were written by the present author) and fewer than ten reviews on the subject of music since its inception in 1992. Since that edition, there have been no articles and only one review (of my book *Noisy Island: A Short History of Irish Popular Music*) of the subject. On the ideological configuration of Irish Studies, see Connolly (2004).
2. Martin Stokes suggests that 'music is socially meaningful not entirely but largely because it provides means by which people recognise identities and places, and the boundaries which separate them (1994: 5). He goes on to discuss the way in which certain instruments (such as the bouzouki) have been welcomed within Irish traditional music circles, while others (such as the guitar) are still regarded with suspicion. See also O'Shea (2008).
3. See O'Flynn (2009: 1–24) for an overview of the modern institutional contexts within which contemporary Irish music is situated.
4. In a speech at the formal launch of the Irish Music Rights Organisation in March 1998, then taoiseach Bertie Ahern said: 'Music and writing have always played a central role in the social and cultural life of Ireland. Not alone as a source of entertainment, but also as an effective way of recording Irish history and communicating its stories widely throughout the country and the world. In addition to the historical function of music and song, they also play an important role in defining the identity of a nation and its people. They help to tell us who we are, to express our hopes and aspirations, our trials and tribulations, in a way that makes us uniquely Irish. Internationally, the Irish nation is perceived very much through the medium of its music' (quoted in Smyth 2005: 2).

CHAPTER 2

1. Ogle was also the composer of a famous drinking song entitled 'Banish Sorrow', and a member of a Dublin society known as the Monks of the Screw which espoused the 'Patriot' cause in the 1780s, and which included many famous figures from contemporary Irish life, including John Philpot Curran and Temple Emmet (elder brother of Robert).

2. The version of 'On Music' recorded as 'When Through Life Unblest We Rove' by Ailish Tynan (soprano) and Iain Burnside (piano) corresponds with the air entitled 'The Banks of Banna' included in O'Neil's *Music of Ireland: Airs and Songs*. Bunting eventually got around to publishing a version of the tune under the title 'Down Beside Me', which he annotated 'Very ancient, author and date unknown' (1840: 30). This was a version of an air entitled 'Sín Síos agus Suas Liom' ('Lie Up With Me and Lie Down With Me' – although it had other titles) that appeared throughout the eighteenth century. The folklorist Breandán Breathnach traced it back at least as far as 1714, and pointed out that it was probably 'the first Irish air with associated words to have appeared in print' (quoted in O'Sullivan 1983: 60). The significance of this association between music and language will emerge over the course of the chapter.
3. At least eight of the twelve tunes in the first volume, and four in the second, were derived from Bunting (Ní Chinnéide 1959: 118–21).
4. Consider the fate of the lotus-eaters in Tennyson's eponymous poem of 1832, who desire 'slumber's holy balm' (1979: 1105, l. 66) in an ominous oriental environment not unlike that described in the second verse of 'On Music'. The imagery used by Moore to describe that environment, incidentally, might be regarded as an early instance of the orientalism so influentially broached in *Lallah Rookh* (1817; 1910: 340–452).
5. The essay is reproduced in a volume published in London to celebrate the centenary of Moore's birth; the quote is from p. xii.
6. Bunting had to deploy some particularly creative thinking to explain this aspect of his practice, the burden of his argument (in the 1797 preface) being that the ancient harpers had been so skilled that they had composed their music *as if* aware of a later harmonic system.
7. 'Translation' and 'treason' are etymologically linked, as for example in the Italian words *traduttore* and *tradittore* (Cronin 2000: 101). The duality implicit in 'treason' (a denial of or turning away from one side in favour of another – see next note) is echoed in the figurative definition of 'translation' as connoting a sense of movement 'across, through, over, to or on the other side of, beyond, outside of, from one place, person, thing or state to another' (*OED*, 1989 XVIII: 409).
8. The *OED* defines 'treason' as 'the action of betraying: betrayal of the trust undertaken by or reposed in any one: breach of faith, treacherous action, treachery (1989 XVIII: 458)'. A legal distinction is made between high and petty treason: the first refers to the violation by a subject of his allegiance to his sovereign or to the state; the second refers to a similar offence against a subject – for example, murder of one's master or husband. The same source defines 'betray' as 'to give up to, or place in the power of, an enemy, by treachery or disloyalty ... To be or prove false to (a trust or him who trusts one) ... To cheat, disappoint ... To disclose or reveal with breach of faith (a secret, or that which should be kept secret)' (1983 II: 150).
9. The French critic Thérère Tessier (as paraphrased by Terry Eagleton) '[found] it little short of a miracle that Moore was not arrested for slander or sedition, given that the composers of Irish political ballads could be imprisoned for much less offensive stuff' (1998: 142).
10. One of the most notorious of these informers was the lawyer Leonard MacNally (1752–1820), who regularly betrayed his clients (including Emmet) to the government. In his youth in London, MacNally had written successfully for the musical stage. His most famous composition was 'Sweet Lass of Richmond Hill'. See William J. Fitzpatrick's *The Sham Squire and the Informers of '98* (1866, Other Sources) for a colourful depiction of the culture of betrayal which characterised the period.
11. 'When First I Met Thee' is one of three lyrics from the series (along with 'On Music' and 'Oh! Blame Not the Bard' – the latter in a slightly different formulation) which features the phrase 'pleasure's dream'.
12. Besides those mentioned in the main body of the chapter, music features as a theme within the following songs: 'Go Where Glory Waits Thee' (180); 'Tho the Last Glimpse of Erin with Sorrow I See' (183); 'The Legacy' (185); 'Drink to Her' (190); 'The Origin of the Harp' (195); 'Love's Young Dream' (195); 'By that Lake, whose Gloomy Shore' (198); 'At the Mid Hour of Night' (201); 'Farewell! But Whenever You Welcome the Hour' (204); 'Oh! Doubt Me Not' (204); 'No, Not More Welcome' (206); 'My Gentle Harp' (211); 'Echo' (220); 'Shall the Harp, Then, Be Silent' (220); 'Twas One of those Dreams' (222); 'Quick! We Have But a

Second' (223); 'Sing, Sweet Harp' (228); 'The Wandering Bard' (229); 'The Night Dance' (230); 'There are Sounds of Mirth' (231); 'The Wine-Cup is Circling' (233); 'Silence is in our Festal Halls' (234). On the ubiquity of harp imagery among the United Irishmen see Thuente (1994).
13. Describing a dinner party attended by himself and his elder contemporary, Moore (in a journal entry for 25 October 1820) wrote: 'Wordsworth rather dull – I see he is a man to *hold forth*, one who does not understand the *give & take* of conversation' (Dowden 1988: 355, original emphases).
14. Human language, particularly the question as to its origins, was the subject of intense debate in the latter half of the eighteenth century. James Burnet, author of a six-part study of the subject, attributes to his contemporary Thomas Blacklock the notion that language evolved originally in imitation of birdsong, and that the first systematic verbal communication was therefore musical in nature (1773: 313–14). This idea does not feature in Blacklock's *Essay on Universal Etymology* (1756).
15. Blacklock wrote: 'The *interjection*, Nature's genuine voice, / Discovers when we suffer, when rejoice, / Here all the feelings of the soul were found / First mark'd by inarticulate sound' (1756: 5).

CHAPTER 3

1. Another useful way to consider the ballad (also drawn from natural science) might be in terms of the 'rhizome' – an audacious rhetorical concept developed by the French philosophers Gilles Deleuze and Felix Guattari (1987) to describe any non-hierarchical network in which established practices of logic, causation, filiation, and so on, cannot function. See Chapter 6.
2. See Würzbach and Salz (1995: 116–17) for an index of the motifs invoked in 'The Lass of Roch Royal'.
3. See Friedman (1956: 78–9) on the influence of this ballad in the United States. With its archetypal tale of love betrayed, 'The Lass of Aughrim' also points us back towards Chapter 2, in which context we should also note that it was a lyric by Moore ('Oh Ye Dead!') which inspired Joyce's title and some of the imagery deployed in his short story.
4. Herd 1973: 149–53. Lochroyan (or Loch Ryan) lies in Galloway in south-west Scotland, near Stranraer, a port with strong Irish connections. A patriotic editor pointed out that 'Several islands, such as Ailsa and Big Scaur, containing the remains of towers, any of which might have been that of Lord Gregory, stand in the neighbouring seas' (Eyre-Todd n.d: 100). Herd's version influenced Robert Burns – who composed a typically melodramatic version entitled 'Lord Gregory' in 1793 (1968: 678–9) – as well as the thirty-nine stanza version included by Walter Scott in the third volume of his *Minstrelsy of the Scottish Border* of 1802 (1902: 255–63). A broadside version, entitled 'The Lass of Ocram', published in London around 1790 (although possibly as early as 1765 according to Scott's editor, 1902: 254) was the basis for a version by the English 'peasant poet' John Clare. Intriguingly, Hugh Shields (1990: 71–2) notes a French translation from 1901 of a variant (claimed as Irish but Scottish in fact) by Joyce's future friend and translator Valéry Larbaud.
5. See Duffin (2004) for an analysis of the 'false mother' convention in Scottish balladry, and how it functioned in relation to the evolution of 'The Lass of Roch Royal'.
6. This is the meaning referenced by Ellmann (1983: 296) and (following him) Jeri Johnson (2000: 277). Terence Brown refers to 'seduction [and] betrayal' (1998: 38), presumably *of* the lass *by* the lord. In Burns, the virgin is betrayed by an aristocrat whose heartlessness is signalled by his silence in the face of her pleas. Despite the retention of the cruel mother motif in Scott's version, there is residual evidence of a fairy enchantment as the cause of Lord Gregory's reticence.
7. The concluding verse of Child D (derived from a Scottish MS ca. 1783), which includes the mother's role, is: 'O he has mournd oer Fair Anny / Till the sun was gaing down, / Then wi a sigh his heart it brast, / An his soul to heaven has flown' (Child 164, 677). Again, it is not possible to know if the echoes discernible in the concluding paragraph of Joyce's story are the result of direct knowledge or his ironic reference to stock imagery.

8. Joyce 2000: 156. In a note to this passage, Jeri Johnson points out that 'in Christmas 1903, the Gaiety pantomime was *Babes in the Wood*; the part of the "Chocolate Coloured Coon" was played by "Negro impersonator" G.H. Elliott, not himself black' (2000: 274).
9. Richard Ellmann explains that Bartell D'Arcy is a conflation of two people: 'Barton M'Guckin, the leading tenor in the Carl Rosa Opera Company' and 'P.J. D'Arcy, an overseer at the General Post Office [who sang] sometimes under the name of Bartholomew D'Arcy' (1983: 246). On D'Arcy's role in 'The Dead' and *Ulysses* see Ingersoll (1993).
10. Helen O'Shea (2008: 154, n. 67) makes a similar point in relation to a recording of the song 'Eileanóir a Rúin' by the *sean-nós* singer Joe Heaney, and Thomas Moore's adaptation of the air for his song 'Erin, the Tear and the Smile in Thine Eyes', sung in the *bel canto* style by Irish tenor John O'Sullivan. On the notion of vocal 'grain' see Barthes 1977: 179–89. On Irish singing styles, and *sean-nós* in particular, see Hast and Scott (2004), 100–3.
11. One might speculate that D'Arcy was trying to impress Miss O'Callaghan by the espousal of values to which he was not aesthetically or politically inclined.
12. Ellmann discusses the role of Moore's song in the evolution of Joyce's story. He suggests that Joyce perhaps considered using 'Oh, Ye Dead', but 'he must have seen that "The Lass of Aughrim" would connect more subtly with the West and with Michael Furey's visit in the rain to Gretta. But the notion of using a song at all may well have come to him as the result of the excitement generated in him by Moore's song' (1983: 248).
13. Joyce's scene is an echo of the one in which the young English nobleman Horatio comes upon Glorvina, the 'Wild Irish Girl', playing the harp (Owenson 1999: 52–3). This scene is also reprised in Sir Walter Scott's *Waverley* (1969 191ff). In both descriptions there is a strong 'painterly' aesthetic at work. The relationship between the 'civilized' heroes and the 'wild' Celtic women offers another analogue of the Gabriel/Gretta relationship.
14. Paraphrasing Lacan in her book *Sexuality in the Field of Vision*, Jacqueline Rose writes: 'The voyeur is not ... in a position of pure manipulation of an object, albeit distant, but is always threatened by the potential exteriorisation of his own function ... the subject is depossessed of its object, the subject posits a full equivalence between itself and another subject, the subject is led to realise that this apparent reciprocity is grounded on the impossibility of complete return' (1986: 194).
15. The parallels with Schopenhauer's representation of music as temporary respite from the otherwise relentless action of Will are suggestive.

CHAPTER 4

1. I should explain straightaway that I am not concerned (at least in the first instance) with the question of 'style' in Irish music – with, for example, 'the lonesome touch' (O'Shea 2008: 70–4) that has come to represent one strand of contemporary traditional music (that associated with east Clare). The focus is not so much on the music, as on what certain people have made of the music – the ideological work to which it has been (and continues to be) put.
2. See Frye (1957), especially the first essay: 'Historical Criticism: Theory of Modes' (33–67), in which he discusses the generic and stylistic provenance of tragedy and comedy as cultural energies.
3. Sachs is also interested in music's function in relation to brain damage. He describes how one of his patients, who seemed 'incapable of feeling', would become animated when he sang: 'He had a fine tenor voice and loved Irish songs. When he sang, he showed every emotion appropriate to the music – the jovial, the wistful, the tragic, the sublime ... It was if music, its intentionality and feeling, could 'unlock' him or serve as a sort of substitute or prosthesis for his frontal lobes and provide the emotional mechanisms he seemingly lacked. He seemed to be transformed while he sang, but when the song was over he would relapse within seconds, becoming vacant, indifferent, and inert once again (2008: 334).
4. The degree of correspondence between the ancient modes and the modern stereotypes remains a matter for conjecture, however. In *A History of Irish Music* (1905), William H. Grattan Flood quoted the late eighteenth-century antiquarian Joseph Cooper Walker to the effect that the three ancient modes equated to the Dorian (sorrowful), Phrygian (joyful) and

Lydian (sleep) modes of medieval western music. To modern ears, however, it is the Ionian and Aeolian modes which correspond most closely to the major and minor scales of the western tonal tradition, and which therefore are more likely to suggest the emotional states of joy and sorrow.
5. Interestingly, the music historian and harpist Máire Ní Chathasaigh understands the distinctiveness of traditional music as tending in itself towards the sad end of the emotional scale: 'The use of these modes, together with the practice common in dance music of switching between one mode and another in the course of a tune, help to give Irish music its characteristically *plaintive* undercurrent, even in such a rapid musical form as the reel' (Vallely 1999: 243, added emphasis). Nearly a century earlier, William H. Grattan Flood noted 'an undercurrent of tenderness, even in the sprightliest tunes' (1905, www.libraryireland.com/ Irish Music/Contents.php); for Moore, likewise, the dominant mood of Irish music, despite the manifest presence of polar emotional states, was melancholy.
6. These terms are associated with (respectively) Marxism, the *Annales* school, Michel Foucault, and Raymond Williams.
7. In *Noise* Attali writes: 'Music is prophesy. Its styles and economic organization are ahead of the rest of society because it explores, much faster than material reality can, the entire range of possibilities in a given code' (1985: 12).

CHAPTER 5

1. For representative analyses of *The Commitments* in these terms see Booker (1997), Donnelly (2000), McGonigle (2005) and Taylor (1998).
2. On the function of authenticity within the discourse of contemporary popular music, and the role of technology in the conversion of 'noise' to 'music', see Gracyk (1996).
3. Hence the old rock joke: What do you call someone who hangs out with a band? A drummer.
4. The embargo on 'rednecks and southsiders' (Doyle 1987: 15) has an obvious comic resonance, but it is also indicative of the way in which local music-makers tend to cluster around particular geographical locations and socio-cultural practices.
5. The provision of rehearsal rooms for new bands in the Temple Bar Music Centre was an attempt to formalise an activity that had been unofficially (often illegally) practised in and around Dublin since the 1960s. Access to this space remains strictly regulated, however, and for many people this and similar initiatives (such as popular music courses and new band showcases) should be seen not (or not only) as the sudden response on the part of a semi-state organisation to a perennial need, but as part of the Irish music industry's drive for even greater success in the international market. Of course, there is nothing *wrong* with such a policy, but questions surround the extent to which popular music can be directed – hothoused, to all intents and purposes – in this fashion.
6. See the chapter 'I'll Be Your Mirror: Recording and Representing' in Gracyk (1996: 37–67) for an analysis of the function of performance and recording in rock music.
7. For many traditionalists within the popular music industry, this is the point at which attempts to formalise the discourse through official or semi-official institutions fail: how do you teach a young musician to be 'up for it'?; what combination of alcohol and drugs will work for them? How, even with talent and the best will in the world, do you manufacture something so nebulous as 'atmosphere'?
8. Smyth 1997: 104. This suspicion is shared by Jimmy, who at one point thinks that 'Imelda might have been holding The Commitments together' (Doyle 1987: 124).
9. In this context, the significance of The Commitmentettes may be traced through a lineage of black singers (both individual divas and 'girl groups') such as The Three Degrees, The Supremes, Dionne Warwick, Tina Turner, Diana Ross, Chaka Khan, Donna Summer and Whitney Houston, rather than through the parallel 'rock chick' genealogy which runs through white female rock musicians such as Grace Slick, Janis Joplin, Debbie Harry, Chrissie Hynde, Siouxsie Sioux and Courtney Love. And over all these popular female performers hovers the highly charged presence of Madonna.
10. On the evolution of Irish rock see Prendergast (1987) and Smyth (2005). For a re-assessment of the showband legacy see Power (1990) and Waters (1994).

11. Dublin-based bands such as The Inmates and RootsGroup (both featuring the young Paul Brady on guitar) played a mixture of soul and rhythm 'n' blues during the mid-1960s, gradually increasing the amount of original material they performed.

CHAPTER 6

1. It passes for common knowledge that the only modern, fully established 'Celtic' country is the Republic of Ireland. See Bohlman (2002), Melhuish (1998) and Stokes and Bohlman (2003).
2. 1988: 57. For Renan's theories on the emotional configuration of the Celt see Chapter 4.
3. The spatial underpinning of structuralism is not very frequently remarked, although it does tend to emerge implicitly in overviews and comparative analyses of the movement. See for example James Schmidt's study of Maurice Merleau-Ponty (1985).
4. It should be clear that I am referring not to the geopolitical organisation of space within the capitalist world view, but to a form of discursive spatiality which enables both the emergence of capitalism and the hegemony of its sense-making procedures.
5. Again, I refer not to the organisation of space which is a consequence of unequal gender relations, but to the forms of thought which enable those relations to be adapted as 'reality'.
6. The literature on traditional music is substantial, but see Hast (2004) and O'Shea (2008) for analyses informed by contemporary theory. On the wider fate of music in Irish history see White (1998, 2008).
7. As Ian Buchanan writes in the introduction to *Deleuze and Music*: 'The rhizome is the kind of matrix ... one forms if one is able to proceed by way of connections; the arborescent is the kind of matrix one forms if one is only able to proceed by way of conjugations. Reality, though ... is generally an unstable admixture of the two' (2004: 12).

CHAPTER 7

1. Bakhtin in Morris 1994: 90. Morris suggests that '[it] is helpful to recognize a figurative terminology of seeing, hearing and spatiality underlying Bakhtin's sense of aesthetic activity' (1994: 88). Michael Chanan (1994: 37–51) interestingly discusses various aspects of music history and aesthetics in the light of Bakhtin's theories without, however, emphasising the derivation of 'polyphony' as a specifically musical term.
2. The literature is enormous, but besides the sources already referenced in this section see in particular Aronson 1980; Bauerle 1993; Bucknell 2001; Grim 1999; Kumar 1991; Smith 1981; Weaver 1998; White 1998, 2008; Wilson 1931.
3. 'As opposed to the official feast, one might say that carnival celebrated temporary liberation from the prevailing truth and from the established order; it marked the suspension of all hierarchical rank, privileges, norms, and prohibitions. It was hostile to all that was immortalized and completed' (Bakhtin, quoted in Morris 1994: 199).

CHAPTER 8

1. The text of the amendment, as well as extracts from the debates in the Irish parliament and Senate leading up to its enactment, may be found at www.johnpghall.pwp.blueyonder.co.uk/constit.htm#amending.
2. See www.christymoore.com/discography.php for a list of Moore's recorded repertoire.
3. The comment may be found in the 'More Info' section of the notes on *Voyage* at www.christymoore.com/discography.php.
4. *Voyage* was produced by Donal Lunny, and was recorded at three Dublin studios in the early months of 1989. Notable musicians who contributed to the album include Mícheál Ó Súilleabháin (future head of the Irish World Music Centre at the University of Limerick), singer Mary Black, Paddy Moloney of The Chieftains, and Elvis Costello.
5. Duhan was a member of seminal Irish progressive beat group Granny's Intentions, whose sole album *Honest Injun* was released by Deram in 1969. His memoir *There Is a Time* (2001) describes the Irish music scene during the 1960s.

6. This tendency (frequently coupled with an environmentalist discourse) is most clear on *Burning Times* (2005), an album containing a number of songs in which the plight of women is dramatised: 'Motherland' by Natalie Merchant, 'The Lonesome Death of Hattie Carroll' by Bob Dylan, 'Beeswing' by Richard Thompson and 'Magdalene Laundries' by Joni Mitchell. While bemoaning the early modern witch hunts, the title track (by Charlie Murphy) also describes an unbroken tradition of female power throughout history.
7. See Chapter V, 'Bells, Mourning' at www.sacred-texts.com/etc/fcod/fcod08.htm. A striking example of the use of the 'passing bell' for mimetic purposes may be heard in the fifth movement of Hector Berlioz's *Symphonie Fantastique*.
8. O'Connor played a minor character named Sinéad. The case of Ann Lovett is in fact referenced at a key moment during the film.
9. In a country in which Mariology was traditionally engrained, the location of Ann Lovett's death next to a grotto of the Virgin Mary was regarded as particularly poignant. The 'moving statues' phenomenon, during which thousands of people throughout the island claimed to have witnessed statues of Mary levitating, occurred during the summer of 1985.

CHAPTER 9

1. Musicological analysis proper is the task of musicologists – individuals trained to elucidate the formal and historical aspects of the musical text. Such a discourse might be incorporated into the novel as part of a Bakhtinian carnival of voices; as such, however, it would possess no disciplinary force, and no sensible person would expect to consult a novel as an authority for understanding counterpoint in Bach, Mozart's melodic imagination, or Beethoven's structural genius.
2. Rushdie, especially, has exploited the elisions within narrative fiction as a means of exposing the partiality of that particular model of Western subjectivity which the novel was in part responsible for developing. It was perhaps inevitable that sooner or later he would turn to the mode of expression – music – through which Western novelists have traditionally expressed their scepticism towards the validity of received narratives and their autonomous, self-present subjects.
3. See David Lloyd's essay 'Adulteration and the nation' in his book *Anomalous States: Irish Writing and the Post-Colonial Moment* (1993: 88–124), in which he discusses 'the dislocation of the colonized culture' (100) alongside the postcolonial critic's 'nostalgia for the universal position occupied by the intellectual in the narrative of representation' (124). One could argue that 'dislocation' and 'nostalgia' have been the principal impulses of Irish critical discourse since the Famine.
4. Of the enormous critical literature focused on the emergence of Irish modernism, Deane (1997), Gibbons (1996) and Kiberd (1995) have been particularly influential.
5. Musical ability was the one redeeming native feature noted by Giraldus Cambrensis in his *History and Topography of Ireland*. On the Celtic revival of the eighteenth century see Smyth 1998: 54–64.
6. Umberto Eco has discussed the possibility of considering the entire text of *Ulysses* in musical terms, specifically the three-part sonata form (1989: 47).
7. On the relationship between music and noise, and the implication of this relationship in questions of social power, see Attali (1985). This revolutionary study is based on the dual premise that '[for] twenty-five centuries, Western knowledge has tried to look upon the world. It has failed to understand that the world is not for beholding. It is for hearing. It is not legible, it is audible' (3), and that '[listening] to music is listening to all noise, realizing that its appropriation and control is a reflection of power, that it is essentially political' (6).
8. MacLaverty 1997: 133. Although grace notes are an established aspect of Western art music (representing the composer's desire to accommodate various 'timeless', 'hidden' or 'leaning' sounds), they are also the distinguishing characteristic of the Irish singing style known as *sean-nós* (meaning 'old style'), one important element of which is the singer's ability to improvise vocal ornamentation.
9. Hillis Miller 1982: 6. The dichotomy upon which Hillis Miller bases his study is derived from Gilles Deleuze's *Difference and Repetition* (1968), and from various Derridean sources. On Joyce's use of repetition see Kumar (1991).

10. Although lying beyond the scope of this chapter, there is yet another aspect of repetition which bears upon musical discourse: the repetition consequent upon late capitalist economics and its peculiar semiotic regime, founded as it is upon mass production and the ubiquity of simulacra. See the chapter on 'Repeating' in Attali (1985), 87–132.
11. Repetition is thus linked to expressionism – the idea of a correspondence between emotion and meaning – which has itself been the central issue of music aesthetics since Eduard Hanslick rejected it in his study *On the Beautiful in Music* (1854). In recent years the debate has evolved into a stand-off between neo-Platonists (who maintain that composers express – and thus repeat – pre-existing meanings) and nominalists (who reject the notion of art as expressive of abstract phenomena, emphasising instead its performative – and thus transformative – character). For representative discussions of each proposition see Kivy (1980) and Goodman (1968).
12. In another twist on the repetition theme, MacLaverty seems to comprehend the joy of creativity as an essentially female emotion, closely connected with the joy of birth. Although dominated by men, in other words, music is indelibly linked to the feminine, constituting as it does a polyvocal alternative to language and its relentless drive towards monoglossic meaning. Hence, the description of the emotional / aesthetic context within which Catherine composes: 'She feels she is carrying this rhythm within her, she is pregnant with it – the way she sometimes carries her creativity with such care – like a brimming beaker, determined not to spill a drop' (134).
13. The effect is similar to that engineered in *The Magic Mountain*, whose author Thomas Mann explained that it was only during a second reading that the reader is able to 'really penetrate and enjoy its musical associations of ideas. The first time the reader learns the thematic material; he is then in a position to read the symbolic and allusive formulas both forwards and backwards' (quoted in Aronson 1980: 32).
14. One reviewer referred to *An Equal Music*'s 'gleeful philistinism' in matters of modern and postmodern music (Adam Mars-Jones, cited in Porlock 1999, 2). Despite his well-documented antipathy towards modern music, Joyce is the modern writer whose technique (especially in *Finnegans Wake*) functions most obviously as a response to serialism, and who in turn influences what Timothy S. Murphy calls 'the post-serial avant-garde', including John Cage, Pierre Boulez and Luciano Berio (http://hjs.ff.cuni.cz/archives/v2/murphy/index.html).

CHAPTER 10

1. In Book III of The Republic, Plato writes: 'Of poetry and tale-telling, one kind proceeds wholly by *imitation* ... another, by the poet's own *report* ... and still another by both – this is found in epic poetry and *many other places*, too' (1968: 72, added emphasis). One of these 'many other places' is the film in which music oscillates between *imitation* (inside the narrative) and *reportage* (the soundtrack).
2. The situation is complicated still further by the fact that the version of Dylan's song 'It's Alright, Ma (I'm Only Bleeding)' featured on the soundtrack was in fact performed by Roger McGuinn of The Byrds.
3. Bing Crosby had a hit with his version of 'The Isle of Innisfree' in 1952 on the back of the film's success. Yeats's poem (1981: 44) was originally published in 1893.
4. The film also includes a range of 'real' music (that is, performed by characters within the story) which replicates the sad/mad dichotomy, including songs such as 'The Wild Colonial Boy', 'The Humour is on Me Now', and a particularly maudlin version of 'Galway Bay'. On the use of traditional ballads in Irish-related film see Barton (2005).
5. Cameron's screenplay at this point includes the line: 'The tune ends in a *mad* rush' (emphasis added; quoted in O'Shea 2008: 5). In her reading of the movie, O'Shea emphasises the gender implications of Ireland's dual musical aesthetic.
6. Music features at a mimetic level within the film, as with the 'Celtic music' favoured by certain characters. *Intermission* also features a version of the song 'I Fought the Law' sung by Colin Farrell over the end credits; while this performance relates to the Lehiff persona, it also draws on Farrell's extra-narrative reputation as one of the 'wild men' of Hollywood.

7. Subsequent revelations of a romantic involvement between the two leads contributed further to the overlap between on-screen and 'real-life' meanings.
8. See for example the videos for 'Bittersweet Symphony' by The Verve and 'Yellow' by Coldplay, each of which features a charismatic individual (Richard Ashcroft and Chris Martin) walking towards the camera through a landscape (an urban street and a beach, respectively) which 'reflects' the song they are singing.

References

(All titles published in London unless otherwise stated)

M.H. Abrams (ed.), *The Norton Anthology of English Literature*, 4th ed. (W.W. Norton, 1979)
Theodor W. Adorno, *Philosophy of Modern Music*, trans. A.G. Mitchell and W.V. Blomster, (New York: Seabury, 1973)
Daniel Albright, 'Beckett as Marsyas: music and modernism in Beckett', *Bullán: An Irish Studies Journal*, 3, 2 (Winter 1997/Spring 1998), pp.34–5
John Allen, 'Italian opera in Dublin', in Pine (1998), pp.56–64
William Allingham (ed.), *The Ballad Book: A Selection of the Choicest British Ballads* (London and Cambridge: Macmillan and Co., 1864)
Rick Altman, *The American Film Musical* (Bloomington, IN: Indiana University Press, 1987)
Matthew Arnold, *On The Study of Celtic Literature* (1867; Smith, Elder & Co., 1900)
Matthew Arnold, *Irish Essays and Others* (Smith, Elder & Co., 1891)
Alex Aronson, *Music and the Novel: A Study of Twentieth-Century Fiction* (New Jersey: Rowman and Littlefield, 1980)
Jacques Attali, *Noise: The Political Economy of Music* (1977), trans. B. Massumi (Manchester: Manchester University Press, 1985)
Mikhail Bakhtin, *Rabelais and his World* (1965), trans. H. Iswolsky (Bloomington, IN: Indiana University Press, 1984)
Kevin Barry, *Language, Music and the Sign: A Study of Aesthetics, Poetics and Poetic Practice from Collins to Cambridge* (Cambridge: Cambridge University Press, 1987)
Roland Barthes, *Image – Music – Text*, trans. S. Heath (Fontana, 1977)
Ruth Barton, 'The potency of cheap music: ballads and performance in Irish cinema', in Harte, Whelan and Crotty (2005), pp.199–207
Ruth H. Bauerle (ed.), *Picking up Airs: Hearing the Music in Joyce's Text* (Champaign, IL: University of Illinois Press, 1993)
Philip E. Bennett and Richard Firth Green (eds), *The Singer and the Scribe: European Ballad Traditions and European Ballad Cultures* (Amsterdam: Rodopi, 2004)
H. Stith Bennett, *On Becoming a Rock Musician* (Amherst, MA: University of Massachusetts Press, 1980)
Stephen Benson, *Literary Music: Writing Music in Contemporary Fiction* (Aldershot: Ashgate, 2006)
Walter Bernhart, Steven Scher and Werner Wolf (eds), *Word and Music Studies: Defining the Field* (Amsterdam: Rodopi, 1999)
Thomas Blacklock, *An Essay On Universal Etymology* (1756; Menston: Scolar Press, 1971)
Alan Bloom (trans.), *The Republic of Plato* (New York: Basic Books, 1968)
Philip V. Bohlman, *World Music: A Very Short Introduction* (Oxford: Oxford University Press, 2002)
Dermot Bolger, *Father's Music* (Flamingo, 1998)
M. Keith Booker, 'Late capitalism comes to Dublin: "American" popular culture in the novels of Roddy Doyle', *Ariel: A Review of International English Literature*, 28, 3 (July 1997), pp.27–45
Georgina Born and David Hesmondhalgh (eds), *Western Music and its Others: Difference, Representation and Appropriation in Music* (Berkeley, CA: University of California Press, 2000)

Pierre Bourdieu, *Distinction: A Social Critique of the Judgement of Taste* (1979), trans. R. Nice (Routledge, 1984)
Andrew Bowie, *Music, Philosophy, and Modernity* (Cambridge: Cambridge University Press, 2007)
Calvin S. Brown, *Music and Literature: A Comparison of the Arts* (Athens, GA: University of Georgia Press, 1948)
Terence Brown, 'Music: The cultural issue', in Pine (1998), pp.37–45
Ian Buchanan and Marcel Swiboda (eds), *Deleuze and Music* (Edinburgh: Edinburgh University Press, 2004)
Brad Bucknell, *Literary Modernism and Musical Aesthetics: Pater, Pound, Joyce, and Stein* (Cambridge: Cambridge University Press, 2001)
James Buhler, Caryl Flinn and David Neumeyer (eds), *Music and Cinema* (Hanover and London: Wesleyan University Press, 2000)
Edward Bunting, *A General Collection of the Ancient Irish Music of Ireland* (Dublin: William Power, 1797)
Edward Bunting, *The Ancient Music of Ireland Arranged for the Pianoforte* (Dublin: Hodges and Smith, 1840)
James Burnet, *On the Origin and Progress of Language* (1773), vol. 1 (Menston: Scolar Press, 1967)
Robert Burns, *The Poems and Songs of Robert Burns*, ed. J. Kinsley, vol. II (Oxford: Clarendon Press, 1968)
Giraldus Cambrensis, *History and Topography of Ireland*, ed. and trans. J.J. O'Meara (Harmondsworth: Penguin, 1982)
Seán Campbell and Gerry Smyth, *Beautiful Day: Forty Years of Irish Rock* (Cork: Atrium, 2005)
Ciarán Carson, *Last Night's Fun: A Book about Music, Food and Time* (1996; Pimlico, 1997)
Michael Chanan, *Musica Practica: The Social Practice of Western Music from Gregorian Chant to Postmodernism* (Verso, 1994)
Francis James Child (ed.), *The English and Scottish Popular Ballads*, vol. II (Boston and New York: Houghton, Mufflin and Company, 1885)
Mary Clark and Clement Crisp, *The History of Dance* (Orbis, 1981)
Eric F. Clarke, *Ways of Listening: An Ecological Approach to the Perception of Musical Meaning* (Oxford: Oxford University Press, 2005)
Martin Clayton, Trevor Herbert and Richard Middleton (eds), *The Cultural Study of Music: A Critical Introduction* (Routledge, 2003)
Tony Clayton-Lea and Roger Taylor, *Irish Rock: Where It's Come From, Where It's At, Where It's Going* (Dublin: Gill & Macmillan, 1992)
Nancy Anne Cluck (ed.), *Literature and Music: Essays on Form* (Provo, UT: Brigham Young University Press, 1981)
Jonathan Coe, *The Rotters' Club* (2001; Penguin, 2002)
Ronald D. Cohen, *Rainbow Quest: The Folk Music Revival and American Society, 1940–1970* (Amherst, MA: University of Massachusetts Press, 2002)
Sara Cohen, *Rock Culture in Liverpool: Popular Music in the Making* (Oxford: Clarendon, 1991)
Linda Connolly, 'The limits of "Irish Studies": historicism, culturalism, paternalism', *Irish Studies Review*, 12, 2 (August 2004), pp.139–62
Carol Coulter, *The Hidden Tradition: Feminism, Women and Nationalism in Ireland* (Cork: Cork University Press, 1993)
David Couzens Hoy (ed.), *Foucault: A Critical Reader* (Oxford: Blackwell, 1986)
Michael Cronin, *Across the Lines: Travel, Language, Translation* (Cork: Cork University Press, 2000)
Seán Crosson, *'The Given Note': Traditional Music and Modern Irish Poetry* (Newcastle: Cambridge Scholars Press, 2008)
C.P. Curran, *James Joyce Remembered* (Oxford: Oxford University Press, 1968)
Carl Dahlhaus, *The Idea of Absolute Music*, trans. R. Lustig (1978; Chicago: University of Chicago Press, 1991)
Mary E. Daly, *Women and Work in Ireland* (Dublin: Economic & Social History Society of Ireland, 1997)
Séamus Deane, *Celtic Revivals: Essays in Modern Irish Literature* (Faber and Faber, 1985)

Séamus Deane, *Strange Country: Modernity and Nationhood in Irish Writing Since 1790* (Oxford: Clarendon Press, 1997)
Louis de Bernières, *Captain Corelli's Mandolin* (1994; Vintage, 1998)
Michel de Certeau, *The Practice of Everyday Life* (1974), trans. S. Randall (Berkeley, CA: University of California Press, 1988)
Gilles Deleuze, *Difference and Repetition* (1968), trans. P. Patton (New York: Columbia University Press, 1994)
Gilles Deleuze and Felix Guattari, *A Thousand Plateaus: Capitalism and Schizophrenia* (1980), trans. B. Massumi (Minneapolis, MN: University of Minnesota Press, 1987)
Jacques Derrida, *Of Grammatology* (1974), trans. G.C. Spivak (Baltimore, MD: Johns Hopkins University Press, 1976)
Kay Dickinson (ed.), *Movie Music: The Film Reader* (Routledge, 2003)
Brian Donnelly, 'Roddy Doyle: from Barrytown to the GPO', *Irish University Review: A Journal of Irish Studies*, 30, 1 (Spring 2000), pp.17–31
K.J. Donnelly, *The Spectre of Sound: Music in Film and Television* (British Film Institute, 2005)
K.J. Donnelly, *British Film Music and Film Musicals* (Basingstoke: Palgrave, 2007)
W.S. Dowden (ed.), *The Journal of Thomas Moore: Volume 5 1836–1842* (Associated University Presses, 1988)
Roddy Doyle, *The Commitments* (1987), vol. I of *The Barrytown Trilogy* (Minerva, 1992)
Roddy Doyle, *Paddy Clarke Ha Ha Ha* (Secker & Warburg, 1993)
Roddy Doyle, *The Woman Who Walked Into Doors* (Jonathan Cape, 1996)
Roddy Doyle, *Oh, Play That Thing* (Jonathan Cape, 2004)
Charles Duffin, 'Echoes of authority: audience and formula in the Scots ballad text', in Bennett and Green (2004), pp.135–51
Johnny Duhan, *There Is a Time* (Dingle: Brandon, 2001)
Éamon Dunphy, *Unforgettable Fire: The Story of U2* (Penguin, 1988)
Terry Eagleton, *Crazy John and the Bishop and Other Essays on Irish Culture* (Cork: Cork University Press, 1998)
Umberto Eco, *The Middle Ages of James Joyce* (1962), trans. E. Esrock (Hutchinson Radius, 1989)
Richard Ellmann, *James Joyce* (1959; New York: Oxford University Press, 1983)
Wendy Everett, 'Songlines: alternative journeys in contemporary European cinema', in Buhler, Flinn and Neumeyer (2000), pp.99–117
George Eyre-Todd (ed.), *Scottish Ballad Poetry* (London and Edinburgh: Sands and Co., n.d.)
Michel Faber, *The Courage Consort* (Edinburgh: Canongate, 2002)
Samuel Ferguson, 'Hardiman's Irish minstrelsy', *Dublin University Magazine*: Part One (3, 16, April 1834), pp.465–77; Part Two (4, 20, August 1834), pp.152–67; Part Three (4, 22, October 1834), pp.447–67; Part Four (4, 23, November 1834), pp.514–42
Ruth Finnegan, *The Hidden Musicians: Music-making in an English Town* (Cambridge: Cambridge University Press, 1989)
Leo Flynn, 'The missing body of Mary McGhee: the constitution of women in Irish constitutional adjudication', *Journal of Gender Studies*, 2, 2 (November 1993), pp.238–52
R.F. Foster, *Luck and the Irish: A Brief History of Change 1970–2000* (Allen Lane, 2007)
William Freedman, *Laurence Sterne and the Origins of the Musical Novel* (Athens, GA: University of Georgia Press, 1978)
Albert B. Friedman, *The Viking Book of Folk Ballads of the English-Speaking World* (New York: Viking Press, 1956)
Simon Frith, 'The cultural study of popular music', in Grossberg, Nelson and Treichler (1992), pp.174–86
Simon Frith and Angela McRobbie, 'Rock and sexuality', in Frith and Goodwin (1990), pp.371–90
Simon Frith and Andrew Goodwin (eds), *On Record: Rock, Pop, and the Written Word* (Routledge, 1990)
Northrop Frye, *Anatomy of Criticism: Four Essays* (Princeton, NJ: Princeton University Press, 1957)
Janice Galloway, *Clara* (2002; Vintage, 2003)
George L. Geckle, 'The dead lass of Aughrim', *Éire-Ireland: A Journal of Irish Studies*, vol. 9 (1974), pp.86–96

Luke Gibbons, *Transformations in Irish Culture* (Cork: Cork University Press, 1996)
Jeremy Gilbert, 'The rhizomatic moment of improvisation', in Buchanan and Swiboda (2004), pp.118–39
Stuart Gilbert, *James Joyce's 'Ulysses': A Study* (1930; 2nd edn, Faber & Faber, 1952)
Gerard Gillen and Harry White (eds), *Irish Musical Studies: Musicology in Ireland* (Dublin: Irish Academic Press, 1990)
Nelson Goodman, *Languages of Art* (Indianapolis and New York: Bobbs-Merrill, 1968)
Theodore Gracyk, *Rhythm and Noise: An Aesthetics of Rock* (I.B. Tauris & Co, 1996)
Brian Graham (ed.), *In Search of Ireland: A Cultural Geography* (Routledge, 1997)
Colin Graham, '"… maybe that's just Blarney": Irish culture and the persistence of authenticity', in Graham and Kirkland (1999), pp.7–28
Colin Graham, *Deconstructing Ireland: Identity, Theory, Culture* (Edinburgh: Edinburgh University Press, 2001)
Colin Graham and Richard Kirkland (eds), *Ireland and Cultural Theory: The Mechanics of Authenticity* (Basingstoke: Macmillan, 1999)
Elizabeth A. Gray (ed.), *Cath Maige Tuired: The Second Battle of Mag Tuired* (Naas: Irish Texts Society, 1982)
William E. Grim, 'Musical form as a problem in literary criticism', in Bernhart, Scher and Wolf (1999), pp.237–48
Lawrence Grossberg, Cary Nelson and Paula Treichler (eds), *Cultural Studies* (Routledge, 1992)
Peter Guralnick, *Sweet Soul Music: Rhythm and Blues and the Southern Dream of Freedom* (Edinburgh: Canongate, 2002)
Stephen Handel, *Listening: An Introduction to the Perception of Auditory Events* (Cambridge, MA: MIT Press, 1989)
Eduard Hanslick, *The Beautiful in Music: A Contribution to the Revisal of Musical Aesthetics* (7th ed. 1885, trans. G. Cohen; New York: Da Capo Press, 1974)
Judith Harford, *The Opening of University Education to Women in Ireland* (Dublin: Irish Academic Press, 2008)
Maurice Harmon (ed.), *The Celtic Master: Contributions to the First James Joyce Symposium in Dublin* (Dublin: Dolmen Press, 1969)
Liam Harte, Yvonne Whelan and Patrick Crotty (eds), *Ireland: Space, Text and Time* (Dublin: The Liffey Press, 2005)
David Harvey, *The Condition of Postmodernity: An Enquiry into the Origins of Cultural Change* (Oxford: Basil Blackwell, 1989)
Dorothea E. Hast, *Music in Ireland: Experiencing Music, Expressing Culture* (Oxford: Oxford University Press, 2004)
David Herd, *Ancient and Modern Scottish Songs, Heroic Ballads, Etc.* (1776), 2 vols (Edinburgh: Scottish Academic Press, 1973)
Tom Hesketh, *The Second Partitioning of Ireland: The Abortion Referendum of 1983* (Dublin: Brandsma Books, 1990)
J. Hillis Miller, *Fiction and Repetition: Seven English Novels* (Oxford: Basil Blackwell, 1982)
Russell Hoban, *My Tango with Barbara Strozzi* (Bloomsbury, 2007)
John Hope Mason, *The Indispensable Rousseau* (Quartet Books, 1979)
Nick Hornby, *High Fidelity* (Penguin, 1995)
Bruce Horner and Thomas Swiss (eds), *Key Terms in Popular Music and Culture* (Oxford: Basil Blackwell, 1999)
Earl G. Ingersoll, 'Who is Bartell D'Arcy and why does he sing in both 'The Dead' and *Ulysses*?', *Irish University Review*, 23, 2 (Autumn/Winter 1993), pp.250–7
Kazuo Ishiguro, *The Unconsoled* (Faber & Faber, 1995)
Frederic Jameson, *Postmodernism: Or, The Cultural Logic of Late Capitalism* (Verso, 1991)
Frederic Jameson, *Late Marxism: Adorno, or, The Persistence of the Dialectic* (Verso, 2000)
Martin Jay, 'In the empire of the gaze: Foucault and the denigration of vision in twentieth-century French thought', in Couzens Hoy (1986), pp.175–204
James Joyce, *Dubliners* (1914), ed. J. Johnson (Oxford: Oxford World's Classics, 2000)
James Joyce, *Ulysses* (1922), ed. J. Johnson (Oxford: Oxford World's Classics, 1993)

Jackie Kay, *Trumpet* (Picador, 1998)
John B. Keane, *The Bodhrán Makers* (Dingle: Brandon, 1986)
James Kelman, *How Late It Was, How Late* (1994; Minerva, 1995)
Kieran Keohane, 'Traditionalism and homelessness in contemporary Irish music', in MacLaughlin (1997), pp.274–303
Declan Kiberd, *Inventing Ireland* (Jonathan Cape, 1995)
Peter Kivy, *The Corded Shell: Reflections on Musical Expression* (Princeton, NJ: Princeton University Press, 1980)
Lawrence Kramer, *Music as Cultural Practice, 1800–1900* (Berkeley, CA: University of California Press, 1990)
Lawrence Kramer, *Classical Music and Postmodern Knowledge* (Berkeley, CA: University of California Press, 1995)
Lawrence Kramer, 'Subjectivity rampant! Music, hermeneutics, and history', in Clayton, Herbert and Middleton (2003), pp.124–35
Udaya Kumar, *The Joycean Labyrinth: Repetition, Time, and Tradition in Ulysses* (Oxford: Clarendon Press, 1991)
Hanif Kureishi, *The Black Album* (1995; Faber & Faber, 2000)
Hanif Kureishi and Jon Savage (eds), *The Faber Book of Pop* (Faber & Faber, 1995)
MacEdward Leach (ed.), *The Ballad Book* (Thomas Yoseloff, 1955)
Jerrold Levinson, *Music in the Moment* (Ithaca and London: Cornell University Press, 1997)
David Lloyd, *Anomalous States: Irish Writing and the Post-Colonial Moment* (Dublin: Lilliput, 1993)
Justin London, 'Leitmotifs and musical reference in the classical film score', in Buhler, Flinn and Neumeyer (2000), pp.85–96
Jean-François Lyotard, *The Postmodern Condition: A Report on Knowledge* (1979), trans. G. Bennington and B. Massumi (Manchester: Manchester University Press, 1997)
Patrick McCabe, *Winterwood* (Bloomsbury, 2006)
Marie McCarthy, *Passing it On: The Transmission of Music in Irish Culture* (Cork: Cork University Press, 1999)
Susan McClary, *Feminine Endings: Music, Gender, and Sexuality* (Minneapolis, MN: University of Minnesota Press 1991)
Donagh MacDonagh, 'The Lass of Aughrim and the betrayal of James Joyce', in Harmon (1969), pp.17–25
Ian McEwan, *Amsterdam* (1998; Vintage, 1999)
Lisa McGonigle, '"Rednecks and southsiders need not apply": subalternity and soul in Roddy Doyle's *The Commitments*', *Irish Studies Review*, 13, 2 (May 2005), pp.163–74
Jim MacLaughlin (ed.), *Location and Dislocation in Contemporary Irish Society: Emigration and Irish Identities* (Cork: Cork University Press, 1997)
Noel McLaughlin and Martin McLoone, 'Hybridity and national musics: the case of Irish rock music', *Popular Music*, 19, 2 (May 2000), pp.181–200
Bernard MacLaverty, *Grace Notes* (1997; Vintage, 1998)
Andy Medhurst, 'It sort of happened here: the strange, brief life of the British pop film', in Romney and Wootton (1995), pp.60–71
Martin Melhuish, *Celtic Tides: Traditional Music in a New Age* (Quarry Music, 1998)
Gillian Mitchell, *The North American Folk Music Revival: Nation and Identity in the United States and Canada, 1945–1980* (Aldershot: Ashgate, 2007)
George Moore, *The Lake* (Heinemann, 1905)
Thomas Moore, *Moore's Irish Melodies with the Celebrated and Unsurpassed Symphonies and Accompaniments of Sir John Stevenson and Sir Henry Bishop. Illustrated by Twenty Original Steel Engravings. With a Biography of Thomas Moore and an Essay on the Music of Ireland* (The London Printing and Publishing Company, n.d.)
Thomas Moore, *The Life and Death of Lord Edward Fitzgerald* (Paris: A. and W. Galignani, 1831)
Thomas Moore, *The Poetical Works of Thomas Moore* (ed. A.D. Godley; Oxford University Press, 1910)
Joe Moran, *Interdisciplinarity* (Routledge, 2001)
Pam Morris (ed.), *The Bakhtin Reader: Selected Writings of Bakhtin, Medvedev, Voloshinov* (Edward Arnold, 1994)

Toni Morrison, *Jazz* (Chatto & Windus, 1992)
Terry Moylan (ed.), *The Age of Revolution in the Irish Song Tradition 1776–1815* (Dublin: Lilliput Press, 2000)
Jean-Luc Nancy, *Listening* (2002), trans. C. Mandell (New York: Fordham University Press, 2007)
Catherine Nash, 'Reclaiming vision: looking at landscape and the body', *Gender, Place and Culture*, 3, 2 (1996), pp.149–69
Catherine Nash, 'Embodied Irishness: gender, sexuality and Irish identities', in Graham (1997), pp.108–27
Keith Negus, 'Sinéad O'Connor: miniature portrait of the artist as an angry young woman', in Straw et al. (1995), pp.221–3
Christopher Norris, *Derrida* (Fontana, 1987)
Veronica Ní Chinnéide, 'The sources of Moore's melodies', *Journal of the Royal Irish Society of Antiquaries in Ireland*, 89, 2 (1959), pp.109–34
Seán O'Boyle, *The Irish Song Tradition* (Dublin: Dalton, 1976)
Lucy O'Brien, *She Bop: The Definitive History of Women in Rock, Pop and Soul* (Penguin, 1995)
Joseph O'Connor, *Cowboys and Indians* (Flamingo, 1991)
Joseph O'Connor, *The Secret World of the Irish Male* (Dublin: New Island Books, 1994)
Joseph O'Connor, *Star of the Sea* (Secker & Warburg, 2002)
Joseph O'Connor, *Redemption Falls* (Vintage, 2007)
Nuala O'Connor, *Bringing It All Back Home: The Influence of Irish Music* (BBC Books, 1991)
John O'Flynn, *The Irishness of Irish Music* (Farnham: Ashgate, 2009)
Seán Ó Riada, *Our Musical Heritage* (1962; Portlaoise: The Dolmen Press, 1982)
Helen O'Shea, *The Making of Irish Traditional Music* (Cork: Cork University Press, 2008)
Mícheál Ó Súilleabháin, 'Irish music defined', *The Crane Bag* 5, 2 (1981), pp.83–7
Mícheál Ó Súilleabháin, '"Around the house and mind the cosmos": music, dance and identity in contemporary Ireland', in Pine (1998), pp.76–86
Donal O'Sullivan with Mícheál Ó Súilleabháin (eds), *Bunting's Ancient Music of Ireland: Edited From the Original Manuscripts* (Cork: Cork University Press, 1983)
Sydney Owenson (Lady Morgan), *The Wild Irish Girl: A National Tale* (1806), ed. K. Kirkpatrick (Oxford: Oxford World's Classics, 1999)
Walter Pater, 'The School of Giorgione' (1877), in *The Renaissance: Studies in Art and Poetry* (1873; Macmillan, 1910), pp.130–54
Scott Paulin, 'Richard Wagner and the fantasy of cinematic unity: the idea of the *gesamtkunstwerk* in the history and theory of film music', in Buhler, Flinn and Neumeyer (2000), pp.58–84
George Petrie, *The Complete Collection of Irish Music as Noted by George Petrie* (Parts 1–2), ed. C.V. Stanford (Bosey, 1902)
Lance Pettitt, *Screening Ireland: Film and Television Representation* (Manchester: Manchester University Press, 2000)
Richard Pine (ed.), *Music in Ireland 1848–1998* (Cork: Mercier Press, 1998)
Harvey Porlock, 'Critical List', *The Sunday Times: Books* (4 April 1999), p.2
Richard Pine (ed.), *Music in Ireland 1848–1998* (Cork: Mercier Press, 1998)
Mark J. Prendergast, *Irish Rock: Roots, Personalities, Directions* (Dublin: The O'Brien Press, 1987)
Vincent Power, *Send 'Em Home Sweatin': The Showbands' Story* (Dublin: Kildanore Press, 1990)
Ernest Renan, 'The poetry of the Celtic races' (1859), reproduced in Storey (1988), pp.54–60
Richard A. Reuss, *American Folk Music and Left-Wing Politics, 1927–1957* (Lanham, MD: Scarecrow Press, 2000)
Bill Rolston, '"This is not a rebel song": the Irish conflict and popular music', *Race and Class*, 42, 3 (2001), pp.49–67
Jonathan Romney and Adrian Wootton (eds), *Celluloid Jukebox: Popular Music and the Movies Since the 50s* (British Film Institute, 1995)
Jacqueline Rose, *Sexuality in the Field of Vision* (Verso, 1986)
Salman Rushdie, *The Ground Beneath Her Feet* (Jonathan Cape, 1999)
Oliver Sachs, *Musicophilia: Tales of Music and the Brain* (Picador, 2008)
Edward W. Said, *Orientalism* (1978; Peregrine, 1985)
Edward W. Said, *The World, The Text and The Critic* (1983; Vintage, 1991)

Edward W. Said, *Culture and Imperialism* (Chatto & Windus, 1993)
James Schmidt, *Maurice Merleau-Ponty: Between Phenomenology and Structuralism* (Basingstoke: Macmillan, 1985)
Walter Scott, *Minstrelsy of the Scottish Border* (1802), 4 volumes, ed. T.F. Henderson (Edinburgh and London: William Blackwood and Sons, 1902)
Walter Scott, *Waverley* (1814; Dent 1969)
Vikram Seth, *An Equal Music* (Phoenix House, 1999)
John Shepherd, 'Text', in Horner and Swiss (1999), pp.156-74
Hugh Shields, 'The history of *The Lass of Aughrim*', in Gillen and White (1990), pp.58-73
Hugh Shields, *Narrative Singing in Ireland: Lays, Ballads, Come-all-yes and Other Songs* (Dublin: Irish Academic Press, 1993)
J.A. Simpson and E.S.C. Weiner (eds), *The Oxford English Dictionary*, 2nd ed. (Oxford: Clarendon Press, 1989)
June Skinner Sawyers, *The Complete Guide to Celtic Music: From the Highland Bagpipe and Riverdance to U2 and Enya* (Aurum Press, 2000)
John Sloboda, *Exploring the Musical Mind: Cognition, Emotion, Ability, Function* (Oxford: Oxford University Press, 2005)
Dom Noel Smith, 'Musical form and principles in the scheme of *Ulysses*', in Cluck (1981), pp.213-24
Jeff Smith, 'Banking on film music: structural interactions of the film and record industries', in Dickinson (2003), pp.63-81
Thérèse Smith, 'The fragmentation of Irish musical thought and the marginalisation of traditional music', *Studies*, 89, 354 (2000), pp.153-4
Zadie Smith, *On Beauty* (2005; Penguin, 2006)
Gerry Smyth, 'Who's the greenest of them all? Irishness and popular music', *Irish Studies Review*, no. 2 (Winter 1992), pp.3-5
Gerry Smyth, 'Amateurs and textperts: studying Irish traditional music', *Irish Studies Review*, no. 12 (Autumn 1995), pp.2-10
Gerry Smyth, '"The natural course of things": Matthew Arnold, Celticism, and the English poetic tradition', *The Journal of Victorian Culture*, 1, 1 (March 1996), pp.35-53
Gerry Smyth, *The Novel and the Nation: Studies in the New Irish Fiction* (Pluto Press, 1997)
Gerry Smyth, *Decolonisation and Criticism: The Imagination of Irish Literature* (Pluto Press, 1998)
Gerry Smyth, (ed.) *Music in Contemporary Ireland: A Special Edition of the Irish Studies Review*, 12, 1 (April 2004)
Gerry Smyth, *Noisy Island: A Short History of Irish Popular Music* (Cork: Cork University Press, 2005)
Gerry Smyth, *Music in Contemporary British Fiction: Listening to the Novel* (Basingstoke: Palgrave, 2008)
E.D. Snyder, *The Celtic Revival in English Literature 1760-1800* (Cambridge: Harvard University Press, 1923)
Edward Soja, *Postmodern Geographies: The Reassertion of Space in Critical Social Theory* (Verso, 1989)
Nicholas Spice, 'Mooching: review of *An Equal Music* by Vikram Seth', *London Review of Books*, 21, 9 (29 April 1999), p.16
Lawrence Sterne, *Tristram Shandy* (1760-7; New York and London: Norton, 1980)
James Stephens, *The Crock of Gold* (1912; Dublin: Gill & Macmillan, 1995)
Martin Stokes (ed.), *Ethnicity, Identity and Music: The Musical Construction of Place* (Oxford: Berg, 1994)
Martin Stokes and Philip V. Bohlman (eds), *Celtic Modern: Music at the Global Fringe* (Lanham, MD: Scarecrow Press, 2003)
Mark Storey (ed.), *Poetry and Ireland since 1800: A Source Book* (Routledge, 1988)
Will Straw et al. (eds), *Popular Music: Style and Identity* (Montreal: Centre for Research on Canadian Cultural Industries and Institutions, 1995)
Timothy D. Taylor, 'Living in a postcolonial world: class and soul in *The Commitments*', *Irish Studies Review*, 6, 3 (December 1998), pp.291-302
Timothy D. Taylor, 'Afterword: Gaelicer than thou', in Stokes and Bohlman (2003), pp.275-84
Alfred Tennyson, 'The Lotus-Eaters', in Abrams (1979), pp.1104-8

Downing A. Thomas, *Music and the Origins of Language: Theories from the French Enlightenment* (Cambridge: Cambridge University Press, 1995)
Mary Helen Thuente, *The Harp Restrung: The United Irishmen and the Rise of Irish Literary Nationalism* (Syracuse, NY: Syracuse University Press, 1994)
Mary Trachsel, 'Oral and literate constructs of "authentic" Irish music', *Éire-Ireland: An Interdisciplinary Journal of Irish Studies*, 30, 3 (1995), pp.27–46
Rose Tremain, *Music and Silence* (1999; Vintage, 2000)
Fintan Vallely (ed.), *The Companion to Irish Traditional Music* (Cork: Cork University Press, 1999)
Robert K. Wallace, *Jane Austen and Mozart: Classical Equilibrium in Fiction and Music* (Athens, GA: The University of Georgia Press, 1983)
Michael Walsh, 'Emerald magic', *Time*, 47, 11 (11 March 1996), pp.78–80
Margaret Ward, *The Missing Sex: Putting Women into Irish History* (Dublin: Attic Press, 1991)
Alan Warner, *Morvern Callar* (1995; Vintage, 1996)
John Waters, *Race of Angels: Ireland and the Genesis of U2* (Belfast: Blackstaff Press, 1994)
Jack W. Weaver, *Joyce's Music and Noise: Theme and Variation in his Writings* (Gainesville, FL: University Press of Florida, 1998)
Phyllis Weliver, *The Musical Crowd in English Fiction, 1840–1910* (Basingstoke: Palgrave, 2006)
Harry White, *The Keeper's Recital: Music and Cultural History in Ireland, 1770–1970* (Cork: Cork University Press, 1998)
Harry White, *Music and the Irish Literary Imagination* (Oxford: Oxford University Press, 2008)
A.N. Wilson, *Winnie and Wolf* (Hutchinson, 2007)
Edmund Wilson, *Axel's Castle: A Study in the Imaginative Literature of 1870–1930* (1931; Fontana, 1961)
W.K. Wimsatt, Jr. and Monroe C. Beardsley, *The Verbal Icon: Studies in the Meaning of Poetry* (Lexington, KY: University of Kentucky Press, 1954)
Jeanette Winterson, *Art & Lies: A Piece for Three Voices and a Bawd* (1994; Vintage 1995)
Werner Wolf, *The Musicalization of Fiction: A Study in the Theory and History of Intermediality* (Amsterdam: Rodopi Press, 1999)
William Wordsworth, 'The Two-Part Prelude' (1799) in Abrams (1979), pp.232–55
William Wordsworth, 'Ode: Intimations of Immortality from Recollections of Early Childhood' (1807a) in Abrams (1979), pp.213–18
William Wordsworth, 'I Wandered Lonely as a Cloud' (1807b) in Abrams (1979), p.211
Natascha Würzbach and Simone M. Salz, *Motif Index of the Child Corpus: The English and Scottish Popular Ballad*, trans. G. Walls (Berlin: De Gruyter, 1995)
W.B. Yeats, *The Collected Poems of W.B. Yeats* (London and Basingstoke: Macmillan, 1981)
Slavojíek, *The Parallax View* (MIT Press, 2006)

OTHER SOURCES:

Bertie Ahern's speech at the formal launch of IMRO (Irish Music Rights Organisation), Conrad Hotel (Monday, 2 March 1998)
William J. Fitzpatrick, *The Sham Squire and the Informers of '98* (1866), www.chaptersofdublin.com/books/shamsquire/shamindex.htm
William H. Grattan Flood, *A History of Irish Music* (1905) www.libraryireland.com/IrishMusic/Contents.php
James Kelly, 'Ogle, George (1742–1814)', *Oxford Dictionary of National Biography*, Oxford University Press, Sept 2004; online edn, Jan 2008 www.oxforddnb.com/view/article/20609 www.johnpghall.pwp.blueyonder.co.uk/constit.htm#amending (July 2008)
Christy Moore website www.christymoore.com (July 2008)
Timothy S. Murphy, 'Music after Joyce: the post-serial avant-garde', *Hypermedia Joyce Studies*, http://hjs.ff.cuni.cz/archives/v2/murphy/index.html
Bruce Olson, www.csufresno.edu/folklore/Olson/MERMUSTN.TXT
O'Neil's Music of Ireland: Songs and Airs
www.oldmusicproject.com/OneilsAirsSongs.html
www.sacred-texts.com/etc/fcod/fcod08.htm

References

DISCOGRAPHY

Hector Berlioz, *Symphonie Fantastique* (1830; LSO Live, 2001)
Clannad, *Magical Ring* (RCA, 1983)
Clannad, *Celtic Themes: The Very Best of Clannad* (Sony 2008)
The Commitments, *The Commitments: Music from the Original Motion Picture Soundtrack* (Universal/Island, 1991)
Enya, *The Celts* (BBC, 1987)
Enya, *Watermark* (WEA, 1988)
Enya, *A Day Without Rain* (WEA, 2000)
The Frames, *For the Birds* (Plateau, 2001)
Guns 'n' Roses, *Use Your Illusion II* (Geffen, 1991)
Glen Hansard and Markéta Irglová, *Once: Songs from the Motion Picture* (Columbia, 2007)
Dorothea E. Hast and Stanley Scot, *Music in Ireland: Experiencing Music, Expressing Culture* (Oxford: Oxford University Press, 2004), with accompanying CD
Andy Irvine and Paul Brady, *Andy Irvine and Paul Brady* (Mulligan, 1976)
Horslips, *The Táin* (1973; Edsel, 2005)
Peter Kennedy and Alan Lomax (eds), *The Folk Songs of Britain*, volume. 4 (Caedmon Records, 1961)
Christy Moore, *Paddy on the Road* (Mercury, 1969)
Christy Moore, *Prosperous* (1970; Tara (CD) 2000)
Christy Moore, *Ride On* (1984, Platinum 1999)
Christy Moore, *Ordinary Man* (1985; Warners, 2007)
Christy Moore, *Voyage* (WEA, 1989)
Sinéad O'Connor, *I Do Not Want What I Haven't Got* (Ensign, 1990)
Seán Ó Riada and Ceoltóirí Cualann, *Ó Riada sa Gaiety* (1969; Gael Linn, 2005)
The Pogues, *Red Roses for Me* (WEA, 1984)
Ailish Tynan and Iain Burnside, *A Purse of Gold: Irish Songs by Herbert Hughes* (Signum Records, 2007)
U2, *Boy* (Island, 1980)
Various Artists, *Romantic Ireland* (Marco Polo, 1996)
Various Artists, *Titanic* (Sony, 1997)
Various Artists, *I'm Not There* (Columbia Records, 2007)

FILMOGRAPHY

Lenny Abrahamson (dir.), *Adam and Paul* (Porridge, 2004)
Lenny Abrahamson (dir.), *Garage* (Element, 2007)
James Cameron (dir.), *Titanic* (Paramount/Twentieth-Century Fox, 1997)
John Carney (dir.), *Once* (Summit/Irish Film Board/RTÉ, 2007)
Alan Crosland (dir.), *The Jazz Singer* (Warner Bros, 1927)
John Crowley (dir.), *Intermission* (Company of Wolves/Parallel Film/Portman Film, 2003)
John Ford (dir.), *The Quiet Man* (Republic, 1952)
Mel Gibson (dir.), *Braveheart* (Twentieth-Century Fox, 1995)
Margo Harkin (dir.), *Hush-a-Bye Baby* (Derry Film and Video Workshop, 1989)
Todd Haynes (dir.), *I'm Not There* (Paramount, 2007)
Dennis Hopper (dir.), *Easy Rider* (Columbia, 1969)
John Huston (dir.), *The Dead* (Liffey Films, 1987)
Peter Jackson (dir.), *Lord of the Rings* (New Line, 2004)
John McColgan (dir.), *The Best of Riverdance* (2 Entertain, 2005)
David Mallett (dir.), *Lord of the Dance* (Vision, 1998)

Index

A

Abortion Referendum (1983), 125–7
accent, 136
Adorno, Theodor, 98
Act of Union, the (1801), 23
Adam and Paul, 165–6
affective fallacy, the, 60, 62
African–American culture, 78, 82–3, 141
Ahern, Bertie, 172
Albright, Daniel, 152
aleatory music, 144
Allen, Lily, xiv
Allingham, William, 35
Althusser, Louis, 91
Anglo–Irish community, the, 3
Anglo–Irish Treaty, the (1922), 4, 125
anthropology, 92
anti–Semitism, 61
antiquarianism, 2, 20–1
Antony and the Johnstons, 162
Arnold, Matthew, 2–3, 60, 85–7, 89
Aronson, Alex, 143
'Arthur McBride' (anti–recruiting ballad), 11
art music (European, western, classical tradition), 4–5, 20–1, 38–9, 41, 43, 55–6, 58, 92–3, 141, 143–4, 159, 172, 178
Ashcroft, Richard, 179
Aslan, 170
Atlantic (record label), 78
atonality, 144
Attali, Jacques, 1, 11–13, 64, 113, 176, 178
audio book, 102
authenticity, 11, 20, 38, 40–1, 43, 66, 68, 82, 87–8, 167–8, 176

B

Bach, Johann Sebastian, 144, 151, 156, 178
Bakhtin, Mikhail, 106–7, 113, 123, 177–8
Baker, Don, 133
Bale, Christian, 162
ballad tradition, the, 10, 23–6, 33, 40–3, 92, 128–30, 133–4, 173–4, 179

Barnacle, Nora, 35, 37, 43
Barnacle, Mrs, 35–6, 42–3
Barry, Gerald, 12
Barton, Ruth, 179
beauty, 9, 19, 21, 62
Beckett, Samuel, 9–10, 143, 152
Beethoven, Ludwig van, 61, 105, 144, 156, 178
Behan, Brendan, 58
bel canto, 41, 175
Belfast Harp Festival (1792), 16, 20–2, 24
Bellini, Vincenzo, 40
Bennett, H. Stith, 66, 68–9, 71, 75, 79–80
Benson, Stephen, 106, 112
Berio, Luciano, 179
Berlioz, Hector, 178
betrayal, 15–31, 35–8, 113
Bhabha, Homi K., 91
binary thought, 25, 29, 90, 99, 138, 150
Black, Mary, 88, 177
Blacklock, Thomas, 174
Blanchett, Cate, 162
blues (style, tradition), 78
bodhrán, 114–16
Bolger, Dermot, 116–18, 121, 123
Bono (Paul Hewson), 95, 130
Boston, 4
Boulez, Pierre, 179
Bourdieu, Pierre, xvi
bouzouki, the, 131, 172
Boydell, Barra, 5
Boyle, 4
Brady, Paul, 11, 177
Brahms, Johannes, 61
Braveheart, 95
Breathnach, Brendán, 173
British Broadcasting Corporation, 95, 149
Britishness, 3
British 'pop movie', the, 161
Brittany, 84, 132
Brooke, Charlotte, 2
Brown, James, 67, 82–3
Brown, Terence, 34, 41–2, 174
Browne, Jackson, 130
Buchanan, Ian, 177

Index

Bunting, Edward, 2, 16–22, 30–1, 173
Burnet, James, 174
Burns, Robert, 36, 174
Burnside, Iain, 173
'buzz', the, 72–4, 76, 78
Byrds, The, 179

C

Caddick, Bill, 130
Cage, John, 179
Cambrensis, Giraldus, 2, 84, 178
Cameron, James, 165, 179
Campbell, Sean, xvii
capitalism, 12, 90, 96–8, 101, 177, 179
Carney, John, 158, 166–8
carnivalesque, the, 10, 58, 113, 177
Carson, Ciarán, 7, 121
Cartwright, Dave, 130
'Cath Maige Tuired: The Second Battle of Mag Tuired (Moytura)', 54
Catholicism (Church), 38–9, 41, 43, 114–15, 125–7, 129, 136, 140
Celticism, 2–3, 52, 60, 62–3, 84–7, 89, 96, 134, 163
Celtic Music, 58, 84–101, 131–2, 134–6, 165, 172, 179
Celtic Revival, the (1890s), 86
    First Celtic Revival (eighteenth century), 2, 92, 178
Ceoltóirí Cualann, 57–8
Chanan, Michael, 177
Chieftains, The, 177
Child, Francis James, 34–5, 42
childhood, xvi, 26–9, 117, 152–3
Christy Minstrels, 39
chromaticism, 144
cinéma vérité, 171
Clannad, 95, 131, 134
Clare, John, 174
class, xvi, 40–1, 43, 65, 69, 74, 78, 82, 90–1
classical music, see 'art music'
'cock rock', 76–7
Coe, Jonathan, 141
Cohen, Sara, 66, 71, 79, 81
Coldplay, xiv, 179
colonialism, 2–3
competence (musical), 47, 53, 67, 69, 70–1, 73, 78, 108
composition, xv, 4, 5, 10, 13, 28, 39, 58, 62, 81–2, 84, 93, 104, 112, 144, 149, 161, 173
Connaught, 17
Constitution, the (1937), 125–6
Costello, Elvis, 130, 133, 177
counterpoint, 29, 106, 108

The Crock of Gold (James Stephens), 112
Cronin, Mrs Elizabeth ('Bess'), 36, 41–3
Crosby, Bing, 179
Crosson, Seán, 7, 11
cultural history, xv, xvii, 7–8, 11, 14, 64, 103
cultural musicology, xv, 103–4
cultural nationalism, 4, 40–1, 147–8
Cultural Studies, xvii, 142, 158
Curran, John Philpot, 172

D

D'Arcy, P.J., 175
de Bernières, Louis, 141
de Certeau, Michel, 122
Deleuze, Gilles, 98–100, 174, 178
Dempsey, Damien, 130
Derrida, Jacques, 29, 178
diaspora, xiv, 4, 14, 87, 89, 93, 96, 135
DiCaprio, Leonardo, 165
Dickinson, Kay, 161–2, 171
diegesis, 137, 159–61, 166, 169–70
Dion, Celine, 165
disability, 2
dissonance, 144
documentary (film), 171
Doherty, Johnny, 118
Donnelly, K.J., 163, 165
Dostoyevsky, Fyodor Mikhailovich, 106
downloading, 134
Doyle, Roddy, 65–8, 75, 82, 145
drums (in popular music; see also 'Lambeg' and 'bodhrán'), 69, 71
Dublin, 16, 32, 57, 66, 68, 71, 74, 78, 82–3, 119, 133, 158, 172, 176–7
Duhan, Johnny, 132, 177
Dunphy, Eamon, 6
Dylan, Bob, 12, 129–30, 162, 178–9

E

Eagleton, Terry, 173
ear, the, 44, 48, 56, 105, 150
Easy Rider, 162
Eco, Umberto, 178
Ellmann, Richard, 33–4, 37, 174–5
elitism, 57, 88
emigration, 130, 133
Emmet, Robert, 17, 23–4, 172–3
Emmet, Temple, 172
England (see United Kingdom), 22, 31, 35, 85–6, 110, 117
Enlightenment, the, 96
Ennis, Seamus, 118
Enniskillen Bombing, the (1987), 130

Enya, 88, 95–6, 131
ethnicity, 40, 101, 147–8
ethnography, 66
ethnomusicology, xv, 6
European tradition, see 'art music'
Everett, Wendy, 159–60
expressionism, 138, 156–7, 179
eye, the, 44, 150

F

Faber, Michel, 141
Famine, the, 10, 92, 178
Farrell, Colin, 166, 179
Farrelly, Dick, 164
Fascism, 154
feminism, 44, 49, 91, 126–7
Ferguson, Samuel, 3
file-sharing, 13
Film Studies, 158
Finnegan, Ruth, 66, 71, 79–80
Fitzgerald, Lord Edward, 23–4
Fitzgerald, Ella, 78
Fitzpatrick, William J.,
folk (music, lore), 5, 10–11, 32–4, 36, 38, 40, 56–7, 92
folk movement (1960s), 11, 92, 129–30
Ford, John, 164
formalism, 61, 150–1
Forster, E.M., 143
Foucault, Michel, 176
Frames, The, 166–8
Franklin, Aretha, 78, 94
Freedman, William, 111
Friel, Brian, 9
friendship, 17, 22, 24–5, 30, 158, 167
Frith, Simon, xvi
Frye, Northrop, 52, 175

G

Gaelic civilization, 3, 135
Gaelic language, 95, 128
Gaiety Theatre, the, 39, 57–8, 175
Gallicia, 84, 132
Galloway, Janice, 141
Galway Film Festival, 158
Garage, 165–6
garage band, 71
Geckle, George L., 37
Geldof, Bob, 80
gender, xvi, 65, 75–9, 81–2, 90–1, 126, 147, 177
gig, the, 72–4, 76
Gilbert, Stuart, 110

golltraigi and *genntraigi*, 55, 135
gospel, 78
Gracyk, Theodore, 176
Grammies, the, 158
Gramsci, Antonio, 91
Granny's Intentions, 177
Grattan Flood, William H., 175–6
Grim, William E., 105–7
Guattari, Felix, 98–100, 174
guitar, the, 58, 67–9, 77, 80, 130–1, 134, 166–8, 172
guitar hero, 69
Guns 'n' Roses, xiv, 162
Guthrie, Woody, 129–30

H

Hansard, Glen, 158, 162–3, 166–9
Hanslick, Eduard, 61–3, 179
Hardiman, James, 3
harmony, 12, 19, 22, 29–30, 51, 56–7, 144, 151, 168, 173
harp, the, 20, 25, 54, 135, 174–5
Harry, Debbie, 176
Harvey, David, 98
Haydn, Franz Joseph, 61
Haynes, Todd, 162
Heaney, Seamus, 7, 9
Heaney, Joe, 118, 175
hearing, 1, 47–9, 62, 177
Hegel, Georg Wilhelm Friedrich, 89
Hendrix, Jimi, 12, 94
Herd, David, 34–5, 174
Hillis Miller, J., 151–2, 178
historiography, 2, 33, 52
Hoban, Russell, 141
Holiday, Billie, 78
Hollywood, 159–60, 179
Hopper, Dennis, 162
Hornby, Nick, 141
Horner, James, 165
Horslips, 57–8
Hot Press, 6, 69–70
Houston, Whitney, 176
Hush-a-Bye Baby (1989), 136
Husserl, Edmund, 48
Huston, John, 41
Huxley, Aldous, 143
Hynde, Chrissie, 176

I

immigration, 2, 130, 158
I'm Not There, 162
imperialism, 3, 85, 96, 126

incidental music, 160
inspiration, 105–07
instruments (instrumentation), 2, 4, 13, 51, 57, 67–70, 74–5, 78, 81, 94, 97, 113, 128, 132, 134–5, 149–50, 172,
intentional fallacy, the, 61
interdisciplinarity, xvii, 10, 142
Intermission, 165
Irglová, Markéta, 158, 162–3, 168
Irish Music Rights Organisation, the, 172
Irish Studies, 1–2, 5–6, 8, 10–11, 14, 64, 66, 172
Irish World Music Centre, the, 5, 177
Irvine, Andy, 11
Ishiguro, Kazuo, 141

J

Jackson, Peter, 95
Jameson, Fredric, 98
Janácek, Leos, 156
Jay, Martin, 44, 46
Jazz Singer, The, 161
Johnson, Jeri, 110, 174–5
Joplin, Janis, 12, 176
Joyce, James, 9–10, 32–3, 35–7, 41–3, 47, 103, 109–11, 143, 149, 153, 174, 178–9
'The Dead', 32–3, 35–6, 38–9, 109, 149, 175
Dubliners, 32, 38, 109
Ulysses, 110–12, 149, 152, 175, 178
Finnegans Wake, 108, 179

K

Kant, Immanuel, 89
Katoomba (Australia), xiv, 4
Kavanagh, Patrick, 9, 113
Kay, Jackie, 141
Keane, John B., 113–118, 121, 123
Kelman, James, 141
Kerry, 4, 113
Khan, Chaka, 176
Kíla, 12
Kramer, Lawrence, xvii, 103–4
Kureishi, Hanif, xvi, 141

L

Lacan, Jacques, 44, 175
The Lake (George Moore), 112
Lambeg drum, the, 150, 152, 154
language, 16–18, 28–9, 45–6, 88, 93, 104–7, 110–11, 143–5, 147, 174
Larbaud, Valéry, 174

'Lass of Aughrim, The', 32–6, 174–5
leitmotif, 108, 159, 162
Levitin, Daniel, 54
liberal humanism, 157
listening, xv, 4, 8, 12, 13, 33, 44, 46–50, 54, 60, 73, 94, 102, 105, 117–18, 122, 132, 136, 138–9, 151, 166–7, 178
literary criticism, 2, 9–10, 103, 106, 108–9
literary genre,
  drama, 8, 11
  fiction, 8, 11, 102–23, 141–57, 178
  poetry, 7–8, 11, 19, 26, 53, 63, 105–6, 121, 128, 143, 179
Literary Revival, the, 8
literary tradition, 8–9, 172
Liverpool, xv, 76
Lloyd, David, 178
Locke, John, 89
Lomax, Alan, 36
London, 10, 97, 117–18, 131, 158, 174
looking, 14, 46, 73, 75
Lord of the Dance, 95
Lord of the Rings, 95
Los Angeles, 97, 162
Love, Courtney, 176
Lovett, Ann, 124–40, 178
Lunny, Donal, 131, 134, 177
Lyotard, Jean-François, 146, 157

M

McCabe, Patrick, 119–21, 123
McCarthy, Jimmy, 133–4
McCarthy, Marie, xvi
McColl, Ewan, 133
McCormack, John, 41–2
MacDonagh, Donagh, 37
McEwan, Ian, 141
MacGowan, Shane, 58, 130
McGuinn, Roger, 179
McLaglen, Victor, 164
McLaughlin, Noel, 88, 148
Mac Laverty, Bernard, 141, 146, 149, 155–7
McLoone, Martin, 88, 148
MacNally, Leonard, 173
Mac Nessa, King Conchobar, 25
Madonna, 176
Magical Strings, xiv, 172
major and minor scales, 54–5, 176
male gaze, the, 44–6
Malone, Carroll, 24
Maloney, Paddy, 177
Mann, Thomas, 109, 143, 179
Mariology, 178
Martin, Chris, 179

Martyn, John, 119
Marx, Karl (Marxism), 89–90, 98, 176
masculinity, 75–6
media, 54, 97, 127–8
melancholy, 52, 58, 85, 165, 176
melody, 5, 17, 19–22, 28–31, 43, 47, 51, 56–8, 135, 139, 144, 152, 162, 164, 166, 168–9
memory, 15, 24, 26–7, 43, 47
Merchant, Natalie, 178
Merleau–Ponty, Maurice, 177
meta–art, 16
metaphor, 7, 91, 105–07, 110, 138
M'Guckin, Barton, 175
mimesis, 111, 136–7, 139, 159–60, 166, 169–71, 179
Mitchell, Joni, 77, 130, 178
Modernism, 10, 98, 109, 111, 142–4, 146–7, 157, 178
modernity, 33, 52, 84, 118, 125, 129, 133
Monarchs, The, 83
Monks of the Screw, the, 172
Moore, Christy, 88, 124, 129–33, 140, 177
Moore, Thomas, 2, 15–31, 55–6, 84, 93, 119, 173–6
    Irish Melodies, 15–16, 24–5, 36, 41, 43, 173
    Lallah Rookh, 173
Morris, Pam, 177
Morrison, Toni, 141
Morrison, Van, 83, 170
Mozart, Wolfgang Amadeus, 61, 144, 156, 178
Moving Hearts, 130
Morrissey, 130
Murphy, Charlie, 178
Murphy, John, 166
Murphy, Timothy S., 179
music (see also 'art music', 'popular music', 'programme music', 'traditional music'),
    for dancing, 39, 73, 75, 92, 109, 128
    and education, 5, 38–9, 110
    and emotion, xiv, xv, 29, 47, 51, 53–65, 68, 105, 121, 135, 154, 159–60, 166–7, 170–1
    and psychology, 47, 54
    religious music, 38
    modal music, 20–1, 54, 87, 135, 164, 176
    as an oral tradition, 21, 34
    tonal music, 20, 54
music novel, the, 141–3, 145, 149
musical film, 159–6, 170
musicology, xv, 6, 33, 47–9, 92, 103, 178

N

Nancy, Jean–Luc, 47–50

narrative, 10, 43, 46–7, 108–9, 111, 121–2, 139, 143–4, 146–7, 155, 159, 161–2, 167–71, 178
Nazi regime, 98
nationalism, 33, 40, 43, 57, 93, 103, 126, 150, 157
Nation, The, 24
Nature, 26–30, 52, 62, 112, 116, 148
Negus, Keith, 137
Neilson, Samuel, 24
Nelson, Willie, 130
new age (philosophy), xiv, 132
Newtonian science, 89
Ní Chathasaigh, Máire, 176
N Chinnéide, Veronica, 16
Nietzsche, Friedrich, 151–2, 156
9/11, 95
noise, 1, 11–14, 63, 88, 94, 102, 144, 148, 150–1, 176, 178
Norris, Christopher, 30
Northern Ireland, 96, 130, 142, 146, 149, 151–2, 155
nostalgia, 52, 146, 178

O

O'Carolan, Turlough, xiii, 21, 84
O'Connor, Joseph, 10–11
O'Connor, Sinéad, 80, 124, 130, 136–40, 178
O'Flynn, John, 7
Ogle, George, 16, 172
O'Hara, Maureen, 164
opera, 40, 175
Ó Riada, Seán, 56–8, 100
orientalism, 173
O'Shea, Helen, 7, 175, 179
Ó Silleabháin, Mícheál, 5, 21, 177
O'Sullivan, John, 175
Owenson, Sydney (Lady Morgan), 51, 55
    The Wild Irish Girl, 51, 55, 112

P

'Paddy Sad and Paddy Mad', 2–3, 51–3, 55–9, 61, 63, 164–6
Parker, Alan, 65, 82
parochialism, 113
Pärt, Arvo, 156
Pat Garrett and Billy the Kid, 162
Pater, Walter, 107, 111
Patterson, Frank, 41–2
Peace Process, the, 96
Peckinpaw, Sam, 162
performance, xv, 4–5, 28, 43, 72–4, 81, 84,

93, 100, 104, 122, 130–1, 150, 162, 166–7, 169, 171, 176
Petrie, George, 20, 22
phenomenology, 44, 48–9, 122, 142
philosophy, 47–50, 53, 89, 105
Planxty, 130
Plato (Platonism), 27, 44, 151–2, 159, 179
playback technology, 4, 94, 139
  CD, 145, 170–1
  MP3, xiii, 13
  Apple iPod, xiii,
  Walkman, 116
pleasure, 13, 18, 25–8, 52, 71–2, 82, 91, 133, 142, 146, 152, 157, 171, 173
Pogues, The, 58
polyphony, 106, 134, 177
popular music, 4–6, 11, 39, 56–8, 65, 72, 81–2, 87–8, 95, 97, 141, 145, 148, 160–2, 171, 176
  country and western (country), 70, 119, 170
  hip–hop, 88
  jazz, 78, 88, 95, 131, 141
  punk, 58, 88, 108
  rhythm 'n' blues, 78, 177
  rock, 6, 11, 69, 72, 75–81, 88, 93, 118, 141
  rock 'n' roll, 161
  soul music, 68–9, 71, 77–83, 176–7
  techno, 118
  world, 84, 97, 131
Popular Music Studies, 66
positivism, 89, 91, 96
postcolonialism (postcolonial theory), xv, 2, 65, 91, 96, 103, 147–8, 178
postmodernism, xiii–xvii, 65, 92, 98, 101, 146, 148, 157
post–structuralism, 61, 92
practice, 70
programme music, 56, 61, 136, 159
Proust, Marcel, 109, 143
provincialism, 113
Pride, Charley, 119
Prophet–5 synthesizer, 134–5
psychoanalysis, 44, 49
puns, 153
Purcell, Henry, 150, 156

Q

Quiet Man, The, 164

R

race, xvi, 65, 90, 147
racism, 3, 130
rationalism, 89, 91
Rautavaara, Einojuhani, 156
reading groups, 10

realism, 89, 122, 134, 136, 139, 146, 171
Renaissance, the, 96
Rebellion of 1798, 17, 23
recording, 4, 72, 75, 94, 97, 100, 176
rehearsal, 70–1, 73, 81
Renan, Ernest, 60, 62, 85–6, 89, 177
Rennicks, Stephen, 166
repetition, 12–13, 108, 110–11, 122, 142–3, 151–5, 164, 178–9
republicanism, 17, 23, 130, 150
revisionism, xv, 2, 127–8, 140
'rhizome', the, 99–101, 174, 177
rhyme, 143
rhythm, 51, 57, 63, 106, 108, 115, 135, 143, 151, 164
Riverdance, 95
Rolfe, Nigel, 124, 137, 140
Romanticism, 17, 56, 59–61, 92, 159
Rose, Jacqueline, 175
Ross, Diana, 176
Rousseau, Jean–Jacques, 9, 26, 28–
Royal Irish Academy of Music, the, 39
Rushdie, Salman, 141, 178

S

Sachs, Oliver, 53, 175
Said, Edward W., 91, 151
Schmidt, James, 177
Schopenhauer, Arthur, 175
Schubert, Franz, 61
Schumann, Robert, 61
science, 1, 89, 174
Scotland, 35, 83–5, 96, 132, 149, 174
Scott, Sir Walter, 174–5
sean–nós, 135–6, 175, 178
sectarianism, 12, 23–4, 149, 151, 153
serialism, 144, 152, 156–7, 179
Seth, Vikram, 141, 145
sexuality, 2, 76, 79
Shaw, G. Bernard, 9
Shepherd, John, 104
Shields, Hugh, 33–5, 174
showbands, 82, 176
silence, 1, 12, 14, 25, 102, 114–15, 140, 174
singer–songwriter (genre), 77
Sinnott, Declan, 131, 134
Sioux, Siouxie, 176
Skinner Sawyers, June, 86–8
Slick, Grace, 176
slow airs, 3, 92
Smith, Jeff, 160
Smith, Zadie, 141
sonata form, 39
Sound of Music, The, 161

soundtrack album, 160–1
spatial imagination, 89–92, 96, 98–100
speech, 28–30, 143
Spivak, Gayatri Chakravorty, 91
sport, 12, 30, 76, 93
stereotypes, 3, 51, 55, 58–64, 78, 121, 132, 175
Stevens, Wallace, 8
Stevenson, Sir John, 17, 19–20
Stivell, Alan, 132
Stockhausen, Karlheinz, 156
Stokes, Martin, xvi, 172
Stokes, Niall, 6
structuralism, 177
Sundance Film Festival, 158
Summer, Donna, 176
Supremes, The, 176
syncopation, 56, 144
Synge, J.M., 9
synthesiser, the, 68–9

T

taste, 39, 53, 108, 146
Taylor, Timothy D., 101
technology, xiii, 12, 54, 68, 72–3, 94–5, 134–5, 176
'teenybop', 76–7
Temple Bar Music Centre, 176
tempo (see also 'time'), 517
Tennyson, Alfred, Lord, 173
Tessier, Thérèse, 173
Thin Lizzy, 170
Thompson, Richard, 178
Thomson, George, 16
Three Degrees, The, 176
timbre, 57
time, 48–50, 90, 111, 150, 155
Titanic, 95, 165
Top of the Pops, 95
Trachsel, Mary, 21
traditional music (as folk), 7, 11, 38, 40, 43, 55–8, 88, 92–7, 114, 117–18, 121–2, 128–9, 131–2, 148, 172, 176–7
Tremain, Rose, 141
tribute bands, 82
Tristram Shandy (Lawrence Sterne), 112
'Troubles', the, 130, 142, 155
Turner, Tina, 176
Tynan, Ailish, 173

U

Ulster, 16, 25, 35
United Irishmen, the, 23–4, 31, 174

United Kingdom (UK, Great Britain), 10, 23, 39, 86–7, 93, 96, 129, 131, 133, 137, 141, 163, 165, 172
United States of America, the, 9, 96, 98, 129, 137, 163, 165, 170, 174
U2, xvi, 6, 12, 80, 95, 132, 134, 166

V

Verve, The, 179
Vico, Giambattisto, 151
video, 171, 180
violence, 12, 58, 71, 77, 116, 118, 121
Vivaldi, Antonio, 156
vocal 'grain', 41, 47, 175

W

Wagner, Richard, 61, 159
Wales, 84–5, 96, 132
Walker, Joseph Cooper, 2, 175
Warner, Alan, 141
'War of the Romantics', the, 61
Warwick, Dionne, 176
Washington, Dinah, 78
Waters, John, 6
Wayne, John, 164
WEA (label), 131, 134
western tradition, see 'art music'
White, Harry, 5, 8, 11, 17, 21–2, 34, 38
Wilde, Oscar, 9
Williams, Hank, 119
Williams, Raymond, 176
Wilson, A.N., 141
Winslett, Kate, 165
Winterson, Jeanette, 141
Wolf, Werner, 111
Wollstonecroft, Mary, 16
WOMAD (World of Music, Arts and Dance), 131
Woolf, Virginia, 143
Wordsworth, William, 26–9, 174

Y

Yeats, W.B., 9, 127, 164, 179
Young, Victor, 164

Z

Žižek, Slavoj, 98

Narrative Singing in Ireland

Lays, Ballads, Come-All-Yes and Other Songs

Hugh Shields

Narrative Singing in Ireland is a definitive account of Irish traditions of singing as a storytelling art. Of interest to scholars and general readers, this book examines the varied associations of song and story in Ireland and why people sing as they do. It ranges from ballads in English, through Irish Heroic songs – of Fionn mac Cumhaill, Deirdre, the Big Fool and others, sung from earliest times to the present – to ballads of European tradition with the lyric songs of Irish.

Written in a lively and entertaining style, it includes chapters on: Irish narrative singing in general, Lays, Ballads – old and new, the lyric songs of Irish and their stories, Singers and songmakers, Traditional singing and the media and Narrative singing today.

October 2009   304 pages
978 0 7165 2500 4   paper €24.95/£19.95/$34.95

Film, Media and Popular Culture in Ireland
Cityscapes, Landscapes, Soundscapes
Martin McLoone

A collection covering a wide variety of media in Ireland, including broadcasting, film, popular music, radio and popular culture. Together these essays map out the role the media have played in the process of 're-imagining Ireland' over the last fifteen years, touching on aspects of Irish cultural identity and the (re)construction of notions of Irishness. The book addresses the more contemporary implications of both the peace process in Northern Ireland and the 'Celtic Tiger' phenomenon in the South.

2007   224 pages   illus
978 0 7165 2935 4 cloth   €60.00/£45.00/$75.00
978 0 7165 2936 1 paper   €24.95/£19.95/$32.50

The Gaelic Athletic Association, 1884–2009

Mike Cronin, Paul Rouse, and William Murphy, (Eds)

Introduction by Diarmaid Ferriter

This book brings together some of the leading writers in the area of Irish history to assess the importance of the GAA in Irish society since its founding in 1884 and is the first key book to centre on the GAA and Irish history. While there has been much written about the GAA, the bulk of work has concentrated on the sporting aspects of the Association – the great games and famous players – rather than the role that the GAA has played in wider Irish history. The chapters cover a large chronological span dating back to the origins of hurling, through the foundation of the GAA, its role in the political life of the nation and ending with an assessment of some of the main issues facing the GAA into the twenty-first century. Importantly the book also offers original and insightful work on areas including the class make up of the GAA, the centrality of Amateurism in the Association, the role of the Irish language and the ways in which films have featured Gaelic games.

June 2009   304 pages   illus
978 0 7165 3028 2   cloth   €29.95/£25.00/$44.95

Early Irish Cinema 1895–1921
Denis Condon

This book examines early and silent cinema and its contexts in Ireland, 1895-1921. It explores the extent to which cinema fostered a new way of looking in and at Ireland and the extent to which the new technology inherited forms of looking from the image-producing cultural practices of the theatre, tourism, and such public events as state occasions, political protests, and sports meetings. It argues that before cinema emerged as an independent institution in the late 1910s, it was comprehensively intermedial, not only adapting to the presentational strategies of such forms as the fairground attraction, the melodrama, and the magic lantern lecture, but actually constituting these forms and altering them in the process.

In locating cinema in relation to popular and elite culture during a key period of Irish history, it draws in particular on surviving films and photographs; articles and illustrations in newspapers, magazines, and trade journals; contemporary accounts; and official documents. Working against approaches that see early cinema as a precursor to the so-called 'classical' cinema of the 1920s onwards, it provide its readers with a wealth of contemporary material that allows them to see early cinema in its own terms as an evolving (audio-)visual form.

2008   304 pages   illus
978 0 7165 2972 9   cloth   €60.00/£45.00/$69.95
978 0 7165 2973 6   paper €24.95

The Irish-American in Popular Culture 1945-2000
Stephanie Rains

The main theme of this book is the process by which late-twentieth century Irish-America engages with Irishness, especially focusing upon the ways in which the diaspora relates to aspects of Ireland and Irish culture in the formation of their cultural identity. The book focuses upon popular culture and cultural practices relevant to this process of diasporic identity formation, such as film and television, genealogy research, cultural tourism, and material culture such as souvenirs and 'luxury' Irish products. There is also a consideration of the economic and political connections between Irish-America and Ireland during the later-twentieth century. Organised thematically, the book provides a unique examination of a wide range of popular cultural forms and practices during the later-twentieth century.

2007 288 pages illus
978 0 7165 2830 2   cloth €65.00/£50.00/$75.00
978 0 7165 2831 9   paper €27.50/£19.95/$30.00